CRAZY ABOUT THE CATS

by

Jamie H. Vaught

McClanahan
Publishing House

All book correspondence should be addressed to:
McClanahan Publishing House, Incorporated
P.O. Box 100
Kuttawa, Kentucky 42055
(502) 388-9388
1-800-544-6959

ACKNOWLEDGMENTS

If you are either a Kentucky Wildcat basketball fan or a junkie who just loves basketball, this book should be an enjoyable one. It is basically a look at the University of Kentucky's high-profile roundball program through the eyes of many personalities who have ties or played or coached with the Wildcats. Material for the book came from taped interviews with various individuals plus notes from the 500 or so columns that I have written for various publications. Also, excerpts from other sources were obtained by permission. The book would not have been possible without the cooperation of many players and coaches who were interviewed.

When I first began this project, my plan was to interview various sports personalities in the state of Kentucky, primarily in basketball and football circles. But, as the book progressed, I realized I had enough material to write about Wildcat basketball. So, I decided to focus on UK and here you have "Crazy About The Cats: From Rupp to Pitino."

There were many other Wildcat personalities whom I did not talk with because of space limitations. They are, in no absolute way, less important or colorful than the ones featured in the book. If I did more interviews, the book would have become a massive encyclopedia.

Special thanks go to many trustworthy and dependable individuals who were very helpful in this book project. Brenda Irvine, Verna Howell, Shannon Stivers, Pat Bowling and Danielle Douglas all did an excellent job in transcribing the interviews. Others who contributed in one way or another were Pam Jarrett, Lois McWhorter, David Douglas and Diane Jones.

Also give special thanks to *Henderson Gleaner-Journal* sports editor Jim Kurk and Darrell Musick for proofreading or editing many of the chapters before the manuscript was sent to the publisher. The outstanding photographers whose work appears in the book were Nick Nicholas, Susie Bullock, Bruce Orwin and Alen Malott. Thanks also go to The Camera Shop in Somerset for printing some pictures. Gratitude also to UK's Chris Cameron, assistant athletic director in charge of the sports information office, for arranging a book interview with coach Rick Pitino. I thank Larry Donald of *Basketball Times*, Mark Conrad, formerly of Somerset's *Commonwealth-Journal*, Oscar Combs of *The Cats' Pause*, Michael Agin of *Kentucky Kernel* and Larry Razbadouski of Chicago's Bonus Books for allowing the use of some of the materials or articles, including my columns, which appeared in their publications.

Finally, I would like to thank my mother Betty, my sister Nancy and family for their support and advice. They probably would say that I was kind of hard to live with for awhile as I constantly asked questions about different aspects of the book. I am very grateful for their patience. And I hope I didn't leave out any deserving individuals who helped me with the book. If I did, special thanks go to them as well.

Enjoy the book. Go Big Blue!

— Jamie H. Vaught

TABLE OF CONTENTS

1 HERKY RUPP AND HIS DAD

"My father was an entirely different person than most of these articles have painted him to be."

"They didn't have ball boys in those days," said Herky Rupp, who as a teenager helped his legendary father in the 1950s by doing various chores at Wildcats' home games in Memorial Coliseum. Even though Herky did more, it kind of reminded you of coach Rick Pitino's young sons who now serve as ballboys at the University of Kentucky's home games in Rupp Arena.

Herky's dad, the late Adolph F. Rupp, is the NCAA's all-time winningest basketball coach. He was the head coach at Kentucky for 42 years, guiding the Wildcats to an 875-190 mark, four NCAA championships, one NIT title and 27 SEC championships from 1930 to '72. His "Fabulous Five" team participated in the 1948 Olympic Games in London along with the Phillips 66 Oilers squad as the United States' gold-medal winning entry.

In an interview at his Lexington home, Herky recalled his duties with the team as a youngster, "It was a combination water boy and so forth. If you've seen a picture from that era, I'm usually sitting on the end of the bench, next to coach (Harry) Lancaster, then my father and the players. I did that for three or four years from the time I was a freshman in high school until my senior year in 1958 when we were in the NCAA tournament down in Louisville and beat Elgin Baylor and Seattle (for the national championship)."

Some of the Wildcat standouts on that championship team, known as the "Fiddlin' Five," were Vernon Hatton, Johnny Cox, John Crigler, Ed Beck and Adrian Smith. One of UK's reserves was Lincoln Collinsworth, the father of former NFL and Florida Gator star Cris Collinsworth.

This 1957-58 Kentucky edition would be coach Rupp's last national championship squad.

Adolph F. Rupp Jr., whom most everyone calls Herky, is the only child of Adolph and Esther Rupp. He grew up in Lexington following his dad's remarkable career. Before Herky attended the old University High School, where he played on the varsity basketball team, he and his mother traveled with the Wildcats frequently, visiting different places in the United States and the world.

"My traveling started in 1948," Herky said, "and I remember going to New York because (on the way) we made stops in two or three communities in Kentucky. The players went to the rear of the train to the doors and waved. The fans clapped and kind of gave them a send off on their way to New York (for the NCAA tournament).

"Mother and I would make one or two trips with them each year to different places, but not every road trip or anything like that. The SEC Tournament was in Louisville and you just rode there. But we went on some early plane rides that were unique and different. We went to Puerto Rico in 1951 for (a six-game) exhibition series they had (in the summer)."

After capturing their third NCAA championship crown earlier in the season, defeating Kansas State 68-58 behind the outstanding play of 7-0 All-American junior center Bill Spivey, the Wildcats traveled to that Caribbean island in August. And they captured all six (or five and a half) games in the exhibition tour, competing against various all-star squads.

"If you ever read in the Kentucky media that Kentucky won so many and a half ballgames, that's where the half ballgame took place," said Herky. "We were playing one of the teams in Puerto Rico (the U.S. Navy) that year and they put the court on the infield of a baseball field. During the halftime, a tremendous thunderstorm came up and lasted for a long time. So they called the game off. Kentucky had about a 30-point lead (actually 29, with a score of 52-23) so Kentucky got a half win for that ballgame."

After graduating from high school, Herky followed his dad's footsteps at UK. Under his father's guidance, he donned the Wildcat varsity uniform for three years (1959-62). But he didn't see much action. He was a little-used skinny reserve.

Interestingly, in his first varsity game as a Wildcat, Herky had what would be the biggest moment of his UK career. He was a raw sophomore, and Kentucky was playing host to Colorado State in its season opener at Memorial Coliseum. "I got a tip-in that put us over the 100-point mark," he said. "And that got quite a response (a standing ovation) from the crowd. You know how they (the fans) like to see you go over 100 points. That was a very nice moment." For the record, the visitors were no match for the Wildcats as UK defeated Colorado State 106-73.

On his playing days at Kentucky, Herky said, "I guess if I had one criticism of myself, I didn't weigh enough (155 pounds) at the time to play. I put all my weight on after I graduated from college. I was an excellent shot, one of the better shooters on the team. I was an adequate defensive player. I played forward and I probably needed to be a little taller for that. But I couldn't play guard. I couldn't handle the ball that well and I didn't have the speed for a guard. I played hard and did contribute."

While at Kentucky, Herky and his teammates compiled 18-7, 19-9 and 23-3 records. During his senior year of 1961-62, the Wildcats were ranked third national-ly by two wire service polls, behind No. 1 Ohio State (with All-Americans and future pro stars Jerry Lucas and John Havlicek) and No. 2 Cincinnati. But the year before when Kentucky posted a 19-9 worksheet, it recorded the most losses ever by a Rupp-coached team at that time. Herky said the team received some criticism, although it was not as bad as it would have been today.

"I may perceive things differently since I have gotten older. The fans, as I remember, were very supportive even though we were 19-9," he commented. "You didn't have all this criticism you have now (with radio call-in shows and more media coverage). The fans were supportive and they said simply that a game here and a game there could have gone either way. They said perhaps we don't have as much talent on this team as we have had in the past but just wait 'till next year.

"I don't ever remember a really strong criticism of the team from the fans or sportswriters. Today you have the phone-in shows and you have kind of a funny atmosphere. Kentucky is still better than a lot of places and I'm not picking on any particular area. But when you get into northern Kentucky, for example, you get into a professional atmosphere from the standpoint of fans and the media, and they find they can criticize things a lot easier on a pro level than they do on an amateur level. I think that now, with television and radio call-in shows, these criticisms tend to spread across the country and you find more people being far more critical and vocal against amateurs than they were in those earlier days."

When Herky was 17, he met his future wife, Linda, and they steadily dated for several years. "We went to high school together," he said. "She was a couple of years behind me when we went to University High School. I was a senior and Linda was a sophomore. We started going together and went all the way through college and then got married after college." University High, which was operated by the University of Kentucky, closed in the mid-1960s due to fiscal problems.

The couple now has two grown children, Chip and Farren. Chip, whose given name is Adolph F. Rupp III, played basketball at Henry Clay High where he was a third-team All-State performer and a two-year starter. Chip, a 6-7 forward, later signed with the Vanderbilt Commodores in 1985 before transferring to West Virginia.

Contrary to the way many articles and books have portrayed the outspoken coach Rupp, who was a strong disciplinarian, Herky says his father "was a very kind-hearted and good father and a great grandfather to Chip and Farren, too. His image and demeanor on the floor were entirely different than they were at home. Anything that happened on the floor, at the Coliseum, he left it there. We had an excellent, close relationship."

Herky's mother, Esther, still makes her home in Lexington. Some people have said that she doesn't like basketball as she doesn't go to the games. Not true, says Herky.

"She's a big basketball fan," he said. "But I think she kind of got burned out because she attended so many games. She understands the game very well and is a very good critic. But she is kind of tired of fighting the crowds and being all wrapped up in the confusion about parking, getting in and getting out, and getting home. She watches games on television."

Besides coaching, farming and reading, coach Rupp loved to tell stories. He was colorful and had a good sense of humor. One of Herky's favorite stories about coach Rupp involved an incident, at a small general store which sold country hams, while he was on a scouting trip.

"I think my favorite story — I don't know why — is about the time he was purchasing the country ham down in some rural area in Kentucky," said the younger Rupp. "He wrote the man (store manager) a check. Daddy asked the man if it was alright to write a personal check and the man said sure. Daddy wrote the check and signed it.

"Daddy pointed to the name on the line and said, 'Do you know who that is?' And he (the manager) said, 'I'm hoping it's you.'

"He still didn't know who it was. Daddy was trying to see if the man knew who he was and the man was trying to make sure the check was good."

Being known as coach Rupp's son doesn't annoy Herky. He readily accepts the situation. He explains that if you don't, you'll encounter problems in the rest of your life. But Herky, 50, recently had some interesting experiences as far as his personal identification is concerned.

"A funny thing has happened here lately, a whole

new angle on this identity thing," he said. "I've been introduced to people in the last year or so and they think I am coach Rupp's grandson rather than his son. I have to explain that I am his son and Chip is his grandson. It (being Rupp's son) doesn't bother me and I don't think it bothers other people in this same situation.

"It is something that you grow up with and learn to handle. I think you have to be able to accept it, or you would have problems. You keep everything in perspective. It sounds cocky, and I don't mean it to sound that way, but I guess you are a unique individual. But it really doesn't matter if you're some famous baseball player's son or daughter, or actress or whoever you might be."

What kind of person was coach Rupp?

He was a man of many dimensions. He was not just the basketball coach. He was more than that, having a lot of other interests. One of the smartest individuals who ever lived in the state of Kentucky, he read books and kept up with current events by reading magazines such as the *U.S. News and World Report, Wall Street Journal, Forbes* and the *American Hereford Journal.* He was well-educated, obtaining his master's degree in educational administration from Columbia University in New York in 1930 before coming to Kentucky. A successful farmer himself, he was elected president of a well-known state cattle organization many times.

For the past several years, coach Rupp has been cast in a somewhat unfavorable light by some publications, including the controversial book, *Raw Recruits,* which hit the newsstands in early 1990. And the Rupp family is deeply disturbed by these reports. Herky says there is nothing wrong with talking about his father if the reports are accurate. But they aren't.

"This has been a sore point with us," said Herky of the way his father has been portrayed. "The media people have, in our opinion, totally misrepresented my father in most ways. The bad thing about it is that it's been perpetuated. Another thing, which our daughter (Farren) is quite upset about, is a series of articles and books that were published about eight or 10 years ago which were quite negative.

"At the time we wanted to take a positive approach toward reprimanding those articles or repudiating them. We were told (by friends) to forget about it, that we would only create an interest in those articles and cause people to buy the newspapers and magazines or books to find out what was really being said. Now I wish we had done what we originally wanted to do.

"As our daughter said, 'What you are going to run into is that several years down the road, students will be asked to do research papers and reports. They are going to have to use these (materials) for reference books and they are going to have the wrong impression of Pop (as coach Rupp was called in the family).' She was right. The bad thing is that people don't want to write the good things because that doesn't sell. That may be true, but you shouldn't perpetuate bad things to help somebody sell articles for their newspaper or whatever.

"At this particular point, we are very concerned about some of the articles, television shows — one TV show in particular — and a couple of other things that have come out in the last year or year and a half. We are considering what to do about that.

"My father was an entirely different person than most of these articles have painted him to be. The thing that's got us upset is that nobody has ever asked us our opinion or what our feelings are or what the man was really like. Nobody has really seemed to care.

"My father was a very brilliant man. You don't find many people walking around with a master's degree from Columbia University. Daddy read all the time. People say this, and I agree with them, and I'll say it — he could have been anything he wanted to be. I have no idea what his IQ was, but it had to be very high. When he left the Coliseum, he left basketball there. He came home in the evening and he did not particularly care to watch television. He thought it was a waste of time. He would read many things. He would read books. He was very big in cattle (farming). He was 16-consecutive term president of the Kentucky Hereford Association."

Off the court, coach Rupp actively participated in several charity projects. They required much of his time but he enjoyed them.

"He worked on his Shrine project because he was past potentate of the Shrine," Herky said. "He was the chair of (Shrine) Crippled Children's Hospital. He was involved in many, many things. You see, he wasn't a one-dimensional person. He was a 3, 4 or 5-dimensional person because he was able to take on all these things and not just do them, but do them well. He didn't do things as a figurehead. During the years when he worked on the American Cancer Society as crusade chair, he didn't just lend his name to them. If he said he was going to do something, he did it. You take all these things and wrap them up into a ball of wax and you find that basketball was just one part of a many-dimensional person."

Many writers and fans have accused coach Rupp of being a racist and treating blacks as second-class citizens. That description of Rupp is totally inaccurate, says Herky, who cited several examples of coach Rupp showing respect for another race. And he is getting tired of reading or hearing stories about his father not wanting any blacks around.

"The latest thing that has us really irritated is the racial issue," Herky said. "Daddy was not anti-anything. He did more to help black people than anyone. They try to say he was one of the last in the SEC to recruit black athletes."

In a meeting during the early 1960s, coach Rupp and school president John Oswald clashed over the issue of recruiting blacks for the basketball program. Rupp argued that he didn't want a "token" black player sitting on the bench. He wanted players — white or black — who could play. "They (the media) try to play up this issue where he and John Oswald had a disagreement on recruiting," Herky said. "It was a very simple thing, but again nobody wants to tell the truth. The whole point was that John Oswald wanted to integrate the team, which was fine. That was no problem.

"His (president's) approach was, 'I don't care if they can play or not. I want you to recruit a black player.' Daddy's approach was, 'Alright, I have 15 scholarships. I have to use them to the best of my advantage and I'm not going to recruit a person just because he is black, if he can't play. If I recruit a black player, I want him to be able to help the team and I'm not going to recruit him just to make him a token player on the team.'

"Because daddy did stand up for what he believed and because he told Oswald that this was the way he felt about it, this meeting has been blown out of proportion to where they've tried to make daddy look like he did not want to recruit any black athletes."

The SEC did not become integrated until 1965. Until that time, SEC schools did not actively recruit blacks in all sports. Perry Wallace, a prep All-Stater from Nashville, made SEC basketball history in 1966 when he signed with Vanderbilt, becoming the first black basketball player in the conference. Rupp recruited Wallace, but lost out to Vandy coach Roy Skinner.

During his varsity playing days from 1967 to '70 at Vanderbilt, Wallace was a 6-5 star forward, leading the team in rebounds for three straight seasons. Averaging nearly 18 points a game and serving as the team captain, he made the All-SEC team his senior year. He is a member of the school's 1,000-point club, having scored 1,010 points in his Commodore career.

Although Skinner — a native of Paducah, Ky. — received credit for signing the league's first black roundball performer, Rupp and Tennessee's Ray Mears had previously tried to recruit blacks. Their efforts, however, were unsuccessful. The sticky problem was that many black athletes feared playing in the troubled deep South.

In mid-1960s, Rupp sought the services of two of the state's top black players, future NBA stars in Wes Unseld of Louisville Seneca High and Butch Beard of Breckinridge County High. Unseld and Beard won Kentucky's Mr. Basketball honors in 1964 and 1965, respectively. Louisville won the recruiting battles as the youngsters inked with the Cardinals.

"My father tried to recruit Unseld," Herky recalled. "That was three or four years before the SEC was integrated and I was coaching at Louisville Atherton. He (coach Rupp) came and stayed in our apartment on his trips over to visit Westley Unseld. He also tried to recruit Butch Beard. The reason I know he tried to recruit Butch Beard was because my wife and I were among the people who entertained him. We thought we had him. It was very close. It went down to the last minute and he ended up signing with Louisville.

"There were many, many other (black) players who were recruited by Kentucky. Jim McDaniels (the 7-2 center from Scottsville, Ky., who later starred at Western Kentucky) was another one. And daddy wanted Ron Thomas — another kid who went to U of L — real bad."

If things had gone accordingly for UK, Thomas — not 7-footer Tom Payne of Louisville Shawnee High — would've made history by becoming the first black ever to wear a Wildcat basketball uniform. Somehow, in the recruiting process, things went awry during the 1967-68 season. A prep football and basketball star at Thomas Jefferson High in Louisville, the 6-5, 220-pound Thomas didn't sign with UK. He later went to a junior college before returning to his hometown to play for the Louisville Cardinals.

"Ron Thomas came up here (to Lexington) and worked an arrangement with (then-football) coach John Ray and my father to play both football and basketball," Herky explained. "Daddy sent one of his recruiters to sign Ron Thomas. The recruiter came back and said he (Thomas) doesn't want to come and he's going to U of L (even though he later went to a junior college)."

It would be about five years before coach Rupp knew why Thomas didn't come to Kentucky. It was after Rupp retired from coaching and was serving as the new president of the Memphis Tams of the old American Basketball Association during the 1972-73 season. Maverick owner Charles O. Finley, who also owned the Oakland A's major league baseball franchise at the time, had just purchased the financially-troubled ABA team and hired Rupp to run the club.

Just fresh out of college, Thomas tried out for Memphis but never did play for the Tams as he was cut from the squad. But he did meet Rupp.

"Why did you not go ahead and sign me to the scholarship?" Thomas asked coach Rupp. "I kept waiting for you to send somebody there."

Rupp was stunned.

Apparently there had been some communication foulups between the parties in the recruiting game. Consequently, Thomas never got the message. Herky said, "He would have probably been the first black player on (UK) basketball scholarship."

After Thomas was cut by Memphis, he later signed a free agent contract with ABA's Kentucky Colonels in the middle of the 1972-73 campaign. And the following season, Rupp, interestingly, joined Thomas in Louisville when the Colonels' majority owner Ellie Brown, then wife of millionaire John Y. Brown Jr., named the Baron vice chairman of the board of directors for the Colonels. Rupp held that post for three years.

Thomas played for the Colonels for four years until they folded in 1976 during a pro basketball merger. Nicknamed "Plumber" at U of L, he was also known as the guy who married Charmin Pride, niece of country music star Charley Pride, in Las Vegas following the Colonels' ABA championship in 1975.

As the 1971-72 season neared, after losing All-SEC center Tom Payne to the NBA and starting guard Kent Hollenbeck to a pre-season injury, coach Rupp was short of good players on his squad, which would be his last at Kentucky. This was the year the Wildcats had three walk-ons who dressed every contest. Also, early in the season, two black players from the Wildcat football team — Darryl Bishop and Elmore Stephens — joined Rupp's depleted squad.

"The basketball team came up short on players for one reason or another at the end of the first semester," Herky said. "They needed some players so daddy went out and recruited two from the football team. Elmore Stephens was actually working himself up to a starting position. Unfortunately, he missed a plane trip (for the LSU and Alabama games) and that ended his career on the basketball team. That (racial issue) had nothing to do with it — that was how the basketball team was run." (Bishop was also dropped from the team for the same reason.)

Of coach Rupp's alleged racial bias, Herky said, "The whole thing has been totally blown out of proportion and misrepresented. This is one of the things that has us upset. Nobody has bothered to refute them or to even check into it. In other words, they (writers) just take it for granted that someone said it so it must be the truth."

A couple of other incidents indicated that coach

Rupp was not a racist. The coach just gave people the wrong impression, perhaps because of his strong personality and sarcasm, and the media would blow the issues out of proportion. The egotistic coach was misunderstood by many folks.

In December of 1961, Temple had a game scheduled with Kentucky at Memorial Coliseum. But the Owls ran into trouble in downtown Lexington. It had nothing to do with basketball. A hotel manager refused to let a couple of black players eat with the whites in the dining room. So, Temple officials contacted coach Rupp for help.

"Temple came to Lexington back in the early 1960s to play a regular season game," recalled Herky, who was a UK senior at the time. "They stayed in the old Kentuckian Hotel. They called my father one evening."

"Coach, we have a problem down here with the restaurant people," Temple officials told coach Rupp. "This hotel manager won't let a couple of black players eat in the dining room with the rest of the people. They're making them eat in the kitchen."

The Wildcat mentor assured the visitors that he would take care of the problem. "That's not gonna work," he said. "I'm coming down there to get that straightened out."

When coach Rupp arrived at the hotel, he was disgusted and told the manager, "Look, we don't invite teams to play the University of Kentucky in Lexington and treat their black players like this. If they can't eat in the dining rooms with the rest of the fans, we're going to have to make some other arrangements. This isn't the way we do things around here."

The whole matter was solved, but the trip to the Bluegrass, nevertheless, left a sour taste with the Temple basketball family. And the Owls were soundly beaten by Kentucky 78-55. Since that ugly incident, they have not visited Lexington. Kentucky faced the Owls on the road the next season and it marked the last meeting between the schools.

In the early 1970s, coach Rupp was honored at halftime of a Sugar Bowl football game during the New Year's festivities. The bowl officials praised the Baron for practically saving the Sugar Bowl Basketball Tournament in New Orleans many years earlier. Because of racial problems, the tourney almost folded. But coach Rupp wouldn't let it happen.

"The game (Sugar Bowl) was more or less dedicated to him," Herky said. "The reason he was the honored guest was because he literally saved the Sugar Bowl Basketball Tournament from being wiped out. One of the Sugar Bowl tournaments back in the 1960s had Kentucky and a couple of SEC teams, or at least one other SEC team and one other Southern team. And the (fourth) team was from outside the South and had black players on it.

"When these two teams realized that the fourth team had black players on it, they said they were not playing in the tournament. The Sugar Bowl people had no way to go except to cancel the tournament."

However, coach Rupp went on a rescue mission. He told the tournament officials to relax. "Don't worry," he said, "I'll get two teams and we'll play the tournament." The tourney was saved. "That put the Sugar Bowl back on an every-year basis from then on," Herky said.

During his glorious career at Kentucky, coach Rupp once considered leaving the school for a coaching post in the professional basketball ranks in the late 1950s. He was offered a job by the Cincinnati Royals of the National Basketball Association with an ownership interest in the club. Several of his former Wildcat stars were in the NBA and they included Cliff Hagan (of the St. Louis Hawks) and, Frank Ramsey and Lou Tsioropoulos (both of the famed Boston Celtics), among others.

"This came up about 1958," Herky said, "when the Cincinnati Royals wanted daddy to coach and were going to give him a large percentage of the ball team if he came up there. He considered it only briefly."

Coach Rupp was never really interested in pro basketball. He remained at Kentucky because he enjoyed being around the college kids.

"He had no desire to coach the pros," said his son. "He loved the college atmosphere and the kids you work with. He didn't consider it long."

After his forced retirement from UK in 1972, coach Rupp had another opportunity to be a pro basketball coach.

He turned down a coaching offer by Charles O. Finley, the owner of the Memphis club in the ABA, but he agreed to a three-year contract as a high-ranking executive with the Tams. The league featured several ex-Wildcats whom Rupp had coached. They were Dan Issel, Mike Pratt, Louie Dampier and Adrian Smith (a former NBA star who played only one season in the ABA for the Virginia Squires before retiring).

"Charlie Finley called and told daddy that he could be president, coach or general manager," Herky said. "All three or any combination he could choose. Daddy took the idea of being president/general manager and he turned the coaching over to somebody else (Bob Bass).

"He had the chance to coach. All he had to say was, 'I'll do it.' And he didn't."

At that time, coach Rupp was still bitter about the way Kentucky had coerced him to retire at 70. Staying active in basketball with Memphis eased his pain. Yet, his new job did not make him completely happy or satisfied. He had wanted to remain as the coach of the Kentucky Wildcats. As far as he was concerned, his old UK post was the best one in the world.

"He was very bitter and certainly unhappy," Herky said. "Dr. Otis Singletary (UK president) told daddy on two occasions that he would not ask him to retire and yet all of this turned out to be wrong, because he did (later). He waited (to make the announcement) until he (coach Rupp) was in Alabama speaking at a basketball banquet. Daddy loved to coach."

The sensitive issue of Rupp's retirement had put Singletary and the school's athletics board in an extremely difficult position. The well-respected school president was in a no-win situation and he was just trying to follow the university's mandatory retirement rule. The board felt that no one, including Rupp, should be exempted from the retirement rule.

Coach Rupp had told Singletary, "I'll coach for nothing if you'll just let me coach. I'm not coaching for the money. I'm coaching because I enjoy it."

Herky said, "He would have coached for the pure pleasure of it, if they would have let him, but they didn't."

As it turned out, coach Rupp eventually became involved in the ABA. It was certainly better than his sitting around the house doing nothing. And, when he came to the Colonels a year later, life was more bearable.

"He enjoyed that (his years with the Colonels) because that was back home," Herky commented. "He had Dan Issel, Mike Pratt, Louie Dampier and Ron Thomas. It was easier than going to Memphis. He was living in Memphis in a Howard Johnson motel five days out of the week and that got to be pretty tough."

Approximately a year after his retirement from UK, coach Rupp almost became the head coach at Duke University. Duke president Terry Sanford, the former North Carolina governor who is now U.S. Senator (D-N.C.), and other school officials seriously considered the 72-year-old Baron to revive their struggling roundball program, just days before the start of practice for the 1973-74 campaign. Duke mentor Bucky Waters, who is now a television sportscaster, had resigned after four mediocre years at the Blue Devil helm, avoiding a probable lame duck status as he had one year remaining on his contract.

Coach Rupp was very interested. For the Baron, it would be a great opportunity to show the world that the old man could still coach. In fact, there was even some discussion that Herky was going to be his father's chief assistant at Duke. Although the younger Rupp had never coached in college, he had seven years of head coaching experience in high school (two years at Louisville Atherton, three at Lexington Lafayette and two at Shelby County) with two appearances in the state tournament.

"Daddy got a phone call from the president of Duke University," Herky explained. "He said, 'Coach, we need a coach. We've dismissed (Waters) and we want you to coach.'"

In amazement, coach Rupp said, "Are you sure? These people around here in Kentucky thought I was too old to coach. And here you are wanting me to coach."

"Age makes no difference to us," replied Sanford. "We want a person we know can coach. We want a person of your stature and you are the one for the job."

Coach Rupp continued the phone conversations with Sanford for a couple of days about the Duke post. But then his farm manager died and he had no one to operate his 500-acre cattle farm in Bourbon County. The possibility of his returning to the coaching profession didn't appear too promising.

"What happened was that the man on our farm died October 13 and basketball practice was to start on Oct. 15," Herky said. "Daddy called the chancellor at Duke University and told him we had a difficult situation because we had the farm and didn't have anyone to take care of it. We had a large investment there. He was afraid he was going to have to turn the job down."

However, the officials at Duke refused to accept the notion that coach Rupp couldn't take the job, saying, "We'll let the assistant coaches carry on until you can come here."

Coach Rupp was skeptical. "Well, I don't think that's the way to go," he said.

The Atlantic Coast Conference school, nevertheless, gave coach Rupp one week to straighten out his business affairs. He agreed, saying, "If I can't get it straightened out by then and I don't feel comfortable with them, I'm going to let you name another person to coach."

Herky recalled, "We tried to solve the problem over the weekend. In fact, I was going to be his chief assistant because he was going to work with three assistant coaches who didn't know our system at all. He had to have someone teach them as well as teach the players.

"But we couldn't resolve the problem on the farm. Daddy said in order to be fair with Duke and the basketball program, there was no way to delay this any longer. He told the gentleman he certainly appreciated the offer and he felt terrible about it, but there was nothing we could do. He said go on and name somebody else to coach. The man sure didn't want to."

The "somebody else" whom Duke named as its new coach was Neill McGeachy, who had been the top assistant under Waters. He lasted only one year at Duke.

"It was awfully, awfully close," said Herky of his daddy's interest in taking the Blue Devil position.

Coach Rupp, who in 1969 was inducted to the Basketball Hall of Fame in Springfield, Mass., had his share of problems in his long career.

Back in the summer of 1951, it was learned that some of his former and current Wildcat stars were involved in a shocking point-shaving scandal. They had been "fixing" certain games since 1948. According to published reports, Rupp apparently had no knowledge about his players being involved in the gambling scandal. UK president Herman Donovan cleared Rupp of any major wrongdoing, calling him "an honorable man," and the coach stayed on at the school. But Rupp was hurt by the highly-publicized mess.

Consequently, some of the players who were charged received suspended sentences from New York judge Saul S. Streit, who wrote a blistering 63-page summary about coach Rupp and the Kentucky scandal. And both the NCAA and the SEC later penalized Kentucky for various violations. Kentucky did not play a regular season schedule in 1952-53. During that time, the Wildcats, by the way, were not the only collegiate athletic program troubled by the "fix" scandal. Several schools such as 1950 NCAA and NIT champion City College of New York (CCNY) and Long Island University had players involved in the scandal.

"All of the things that happened with the players involved in the scandal were strictly one-on-one between them and the people that were doing whatever it was," Herky said. "It was outside influence on individuals and had absolutely nothing to do with the university, coaches or the NCAA. People have tried to say Kentucky has been known for this situation down through the years. They haven't been known for this type situation.

"The coaches were totally unaware of anything going on with their players and the only time they became aware of it was after it happened — after the players had been arrested and the whole thing was brought to light."

Not surprisingly, the scandal made coach Rupp mad. Like a hungry bear, he was very determined to "beat up" the world in the 1953-54 season. He wanted the opponents to pay the price for the scandal that he really had no control over.

And he did just that. After sitting out the previous season, the Wildcats came roaring back and finished with a No. 1 ranking and a glittering 25-0 mark behind All-Americans Cliff Hagan and Frank Ramsey. Even though

Kentucky had won a playoff game with LSU in Nashville, determining the league's representative to the NCAA tournament, it declined a trip to the NCAA since its top three players — Hagan, Ramsey and Lou Tsioropoulos — would not be eligible for the tournament because they were graduate students. The schools had tied for SEC crown due to a schedule disagreement.

In an 1989 interview with the author which appeared in *The Cats' Pause*, one of coach Rupp's former players said the Baron was not a difficult person to deal with, despite his "mean" reputation.

"Coach Rupp was a very easy coach to play for," said Terry Mills, who was on UK's 1969-70 top-ranked club as a starting guard. " When I was there, he was sick a lot and missed some practices and some games. I wasn't intimidated by him, even though we respected him a great deal. Before I went to UK, I heard lots of tales about how mean he was, but it didn't turn out to be that way. I enjoyed playing for coach Rupp. He was a comedian so he kept us laughing all the time. We really enjoyed being around him.

"Also, at that time, coach Harry Lancaster was his assistant and he was very strict and a real disciplinarian. We really had to walk the line around him. Of course, Joe Hall was there too, as the head recruiter and became the assistant in my senior year in college."

As far as the team rules were concerned, coach Rupp was very strict. "The best thing I can remember is that when he told us to be at some place at 5:00 (p.m.), he really meant 15 minutes before that," Mills said. "If we were late, he would go without us. For instance, we were flying on a trip down South and one of the players was late. He was pulling into the parking lot while we were on the plane. And coach Rupp told the pilot, 'Go ahead and leave,' because the player was 30 seconds or a minute late and he wouldn't wait on him."

Like many former Wildcat players, Mills still follows Kentucky, as he attends many of its home games. In another newspaper interview, former Wildcat star Larry Conley couldn't come up with some of coach Rupp's funny stories or comments. "Gosh, it's been so long I doubt if I could come up with something. But those that I could, you could not print," he said, laughing. Conley is currently a television sportscaster.

Members of the Rupp family were delighted when UK retired a jersey in honor of Adolph Rupp in a 1990 pre-game ceremony held at Rupp Arena, which of course is named after the legendary coach. His retired "jersey" is now hung from the Rupp Arena rafters, along with those of 18 other Wildcat greats, including former coach Joe B. Hall.

"When they called and said they were going to retire his jersey, I wondered what they were going to retire because he never played for Kentucky," Herky said. "I was curious. I thought, maybe, they would have something that looked like a brown suit coat up there.

"But we were naturally very pleased and thrilled that they did retire his jersey — I don't know what else to call it. It was quite humbling."

Coach Rupp never encountered a losing season at UK. His worst record was 13-13 in 1966-67, the season after the Rupp's Runts nearly captured the NCAA championship.

By the time his father retired, Herky was practically maintaining a low profile in the public eye as he got out of coaching. During the 1970s, he worked in a Lexington bank and then taught at Millersburg Military Institute (MMI) near Paris, Ky. Previously, he had coached basketball at three Kentucky high schools after graduating from UK. While at Shelby County High, Herky posted a glittering 55-9 mark, including a couple of trips to the Sweet Sixteen.

In 1985, after teaching at MMI for seven years, Herky left the private school to run the family farm in Bourbon County. And today, in addition to his farm work, he works for the state government in the agricultural department where he is principal assistant to the commissioner.

Herky has fond memories of his coaching days. "We had some real good teams and we really had a lot of fun and enjoyment," he said. "I see a lot of young men that I coached in those days. I have real nice memories of those days."

On Dec. 10, 1977, only minutes after No. 1 Kentucky defeated host Kansas — coach Rupp's alma mater and his home state — by seven points before a capacity crowd of 15,620 in Lawrence, it was learned that the coach had died of cancer, among other complications.

He was 76.

And Kentucky Wildcat basketball has never been the same.

2 WAH WAH

"I never did even know
what scholarship I was
playing on at Kentucky."

Although it's been well over 40 years since he played basketball as a member of coach Rupp's 1947-48 Fabulous Five squad, Wallace Jones remains a legendary figure.

And he is perhaps the best athlete UK has ever produced. Yes, Kentucky has produced some basketball players who were also baseball stars in Frank Ramsey, C.M. Newton, Dick Parsons, Cotton Nash, Randy Embry, Allen Feldhaus, to name a few. But Jones' exploits on the field stand out the most. Besides playing All-American basketball, Jones excelled in football as well as baseball, earning an unbelievable total of 11 letters during his Wildcat days.

In football, playing for coach Paul "Bear" Bryant, Jones was a two-time All-SEC end. He played in the school's first bowl game, the Great Lakes, which took place in Cleveland in 1947. On the diamond, Jones was a pitching standout for the Bat Cats.

Before coming to Lexington in 1945 as a freshman, Jones was already a very popular basketball figure. After all, he had set a national prep record in scoring 2,398 career points while at Harlan High School out in the Eastern Kentucky mountains. His Harlan teams went to the state tournament four times (one championship, one runner-up finish, and third-place). And his prep teammates included his older brother, Hugh, and future Wildcat student manager Humzey Yessin.

Since Jones also played football and baseball, many colleges, including SEC schools, took notice of his wide-ranging skills. Before he signed with Kentucky, he toured the Big Orange Country and nearly signed with the Tennessee Vols. Harlan County is located on the Kentucky-Tennessee border and the area shared a lot of UK and Tennessee fans.

"I don't think I really was that close (to signing with the Vols), but I went down to Tennessee to visit and they were putting on a lot of pressure to sign," Jones recalled. "Actually, at that time in athletics, you didn't sign. If you played a game, you became their property. They (the Vols) wanted me to stay over and send after my clothes. I was using all kinds of excuses to get back (to Harlan) and think about things.

"In my heart I always thought about going to UK. It was a case of going (to Tennessee) and talking to them to fulfill a promise. I had told some friends of Tennessee that I would come and talk. So, they painted a real good picture (about the Vols). I made a lot of friends in Tennessee and still have a lot of friends there.

"I came back and the University of Kentucky sent somebody down to pick me up and bring me here (to Lexington) and we got out of that."

His girlfriend from Middlesboro, Ky., Edna Ball, who was attending UK at that time, also influenced Jones' college decision. Miss Ball couldn't stand the Vols. And, when Jones enrolled at UK, he and Miss Ball saw each other quite often and eventually married in August of 1947.

Today the couple have one son and two daughters, all of whom still live in Kentucky. They are also the proud grandparents of four children.

Coach Adolph Rupp didn't want to see Jones getting married. Or any of his players. He thought married players took away some of his "power" over them. "He didn't really like it because he didn't feel like he had charge of the program," Jones explained. "He thought maybe somebody at home had charge." And Rupp had to put up with Jones' married life for two seasons (junior and senior years).

At that time, Rupp had several players who were older and mature. Players like Cliff Barker, Alex Groza and Ken Rollins had returned from service in World War II. And some were married. So, Rupp reluctantly understood the situation and accepted married players. "He didn't say anything about it or try to stop it," Jones said. "He went along with the program."

Jones has been on everybody's All-Nickname team. He is popularly called "Wah Wah."

Why the nickname?

"My younger sister couldn't pronounce the name of Wallace so she got the words 'Wah Wah' out and the local sportswriter picked that up when I was in grade school and used it in the newspaper, the *Harlan Daily Enterprise*," explained Jones. "So they got that started and it just kept on going. It has been with me all the time and we kind of got it shortened to a little bit. Now everybody calls me 'Wah.'

"My wife calls me Wallace. Coach Bryant called me Wallace. Those are the only two people I know that I can remember who call me Wallace."

Rupp didn't call the player 'Wah Wah,' either. What did the Baron call him?

"Jones," replied the ex-Wildcat star.

In the Eastern Kentucky mountains, Jones grew up in a middle-class family. The family was in the restaurant business, but paying the bills wasn't easy. They struggled as his parents split. His mother, Fay, practically ran the restaurant and supported the family, which included five children.

"As we were growing up, she more or less had to run the restaurant," said Jones. "My parents separated and divorced early. We moved all the restaurant equipment up to our home and she started a boarding house. She fed most of the people in Harlan.

"While we were going to school, my brother, my sister and I would run back at lunchtime and wait tables, bus dishes and wash dishes. Then we would rush back to school and I would have football or basketball practice after that.

"My mother worked very hard. She fed a lot of the miners who were getting ready to go to work. She would have fried pies and stuff baked and take them to the different restaurants. The miners bought them for their lunch pails.

"During the war (World War II), my mother took on the big project of taking care of a lot of the people who were going to the electronics school there. She had sometimes six or eight to a room and fed them all. We used to feed the juries. She kept us working as much as we had time for. She knew what we wanted to do. My older brother was in athletics and kind of pushed us the way to the basketball and football sports arena. My sister waited tables most of the time at home at our boarding house."

Since he was a high school star, playing different sports, Jones strangely never knew what Kentucky or other colleges recruited him for. Were they recruiting him for football? basketball? Or perhaps both?

"Well, I never did know," Jones smiled. "I never did even know what scholarship I was playing on at Kentucky. (Tennessee football coach) General Robert Neyland talked to me and had other people talk to me about coming to Tennessee. He was a friend of my (would-be) father-in-law.

"(Tennessee's) Johnny Mauer was a coach in basketball and he came to see me play in Pineville. He was very much interested. They were recruiting on both sides wanting me to come to Tennessee and Kentucky was doing the same thing."

Speaking of UT's Mauer, he had been a successful coach at Kentucky. He guided the basketball Wildcats for three years from 1927 to '30, winning a total of 40 out of 54 games (.740), before Rupp took over the UK helm in 1930.

Miami (Ohio) lured Mauer away from Kentucky with a better offer. And he eventually returned to the SEC where he was head coach at Tennessee (eight years) and Florida (nine years). While at Tennessee from 1939 to 1947 (no team in 1943-44 due to war), Mauer posted a 127-41 overall record for a winning percentage of .756, which is even higher than the .713 mark compiled by the Vols' Ray Mears, the school's all-time winningest basketball coach with 278 victories.

Jones said coach Rupp wasn't too thrilled about him getting involved in other sports at Kentucky. "I always felt like Rupp didn't want me to play football," he said. "But he couldn't say anything about it. The people knew we needed some more football players and they knew I could play football so the people kind of kept him from demanding that I just play one sport.

"Coach Bryant liked to have me out there and he didn't mind me playing basketball. Coach Bryant also went so far as to let me play baseball. A lot of football coaches want you to have spring training. But we had one of the assistant football coaches who was the baseball coach and Bryant was trying to help him in getting enough players to have a baseball team. So, he was very good to me and I got along really well with Bryant. It didn't bother me playing all three sports."

Rupp and Bryant were similar as far as their coaching personalities were concerned. "There wasn't a whole lot of difference (between them)," Jones commented. "They were both demanding that you do it the right way and give all you've got 100 percent. I always did that so I got along real well with both of them.

"With coach Rupp being the legend he is and coach Bryant the legend he is and being named All-American (actually All-SEC) under two legends, I'm the only guy who could ever say that. It's a real good feeling."

Once, when Kentucky visited Cincinnati in a rugged football game, Jones saw himself with a bloody mouth when he chased the Cincy quarterback. "I had been sacking the quarterback and they put in a substitute who was a little quicker than the other one. He caught me in the mouth with his elbow and kindly knocked my tooth loose," recalled Jones. "I was bleeding. So I went over to the sidelines and was standing there by coach Bryant. Then something happened on the play and he wanted me to go back in and I said something about my teeth in my mouth and bleeding."

Like a tough Marine drill sergeant, Bryant ignored the player's excuse and said, "Well, go in there, you don't run on your teeth."

While playing basketball, Jones had many interesting encounters with Rupp. And he remembers one of them particularly well when the Wildcats were staying in New York on a road trip. Some of the players, including Jones and Kenny Rollins, decided to seek some entertainment. They went to see the Perry Como show at the Radio City Music Hall.

When the show ended, they returned to the hotel where the players were staying. And they ran into Rupp. "Coach Rupp was sitting on the couch there at the hotel as we walked in the door," Jones remembered.

"Where have you all been?" said a curious Rupp.

"We've been to see Perry Como," said one of the players.

"Who does he play for?" Rupp questioned.

Looking back, Jones said the coach "didn't know Perry Como from anything, but he knew if we were going to see somebody, we ought to be seeing somebody who plays basketball. He was always thinking about the game and basketball was his program and he wanted you to know that."

Like most other coaches, Rupp had team rules in regard to smoking. He didn't tolerate smoking by his players. "They weren't supposed to (smoke), but we had some people that did," Jones said. "They did it back away from anybody. They were older people like Barker and Rollins — some of them who had been in the service and came back. (Ralph) Beard and I were freshmen so we didn't do any of that anyway.

"I'm sure that Rupp knew about it and he didn't do anything about it. I had to room with Barker sometimes and he would get up in the middle of the night and light a cigarette. It didn't bother me but it would wake me up sometimes."

Another story about Rupp. Once during the 1947-48 season, after Kentucky had raced to a commanding 34-point halftime lead, Rupp was mad as heck in the locker room. "We were beating the team real bad and he was trying to get us to keep on going and keep our attention," Jones said. "I think the other team only had about six or eight points at halftime. So, coach Rupp gets in there and he gets his scorebook. He asks us who is guarding the player (who had four points)."

One of the Wildcat players raised his hand and said, "I am, coach."

Rupp shouted back, "You are going to have to get on him. He's running wild."

The coach was sometimes hard to figure out. "He would come out with some pretty good language every now and then," Jones said. "You would always wonder what he was going to say when he got in the dressing room. And here we're winning real easy. He was a great motivator and he wanted you to get the job done."

In a Wildcat basketball uniform, the 6-4 Jones played 140 games and won 130 of them. In other words, he only lost 10 games in his entire UK career. During his four-year tenure, the Wildcats won the SEC championship every year. And they were national champions twice. Like forward Jack Tingle who was a couple of years ahead of them, Jones and Beard made All-SEC team four straight seasons. The trio are the only UK players in history to have been chosen All-SEC four different times in their careers.

UK's 1947-48 team, with a record of 36-3, had the starting unit which became known as the Fabulous Five, consisting of Groza at center, Jones and Barker at forward, and Beard and Rollins at guard. After winning the NCAA championship, the Fabulous Five, along with five members of the Phillips Oilers' AAU championship team, helped the United States capture a gold medal in the 1948 London Olympics. And Rupp served as assistant coach for the U.S. team.

"We had a lot of good times together," Jones said. "We were winning. Every year we would maybe lose two, three or four games. We only lost 10. We all got along together well. We knew what it took to get the job done and we tried to play the game like it was supposed to be played and help each other out. I think that's the secret of it. We didn't mind getting the ball to the guy who was open, the guy who was going to do the job so that we could win. Some teams get carried away with one player who has to do it all and when he has a hard time they don't win.

"Playing on the Olympic team and getting a gold medal probably is the highlight of anybody's career. When we stood there at the (Wembley) Stadium, they played our national anthem and we were given gold medals. I've had a lot of things to happen in sports but I guess the Olympic Games probably would be the top notch."

Before going to England, the Fabulous Five and Phillips Oilers played a series of three exhibition games in the summer to raise funds for the Olympics. They played in Tulsa (Oklahoma), Kansas City and Lexington. Playing outdoors under the lights, the Lexington matchup drew a crowd of over 14,000 at UK's Stoll Field, home of the football Wildcats. It marked the largest crowd at the time to see a basketball contest in the South. Until Rupp Arena opened in 1976, it was also a Lexington attendance record for a basketball game. The Olympic officials were stunned as the game drew $15,000 profit. By comparison, the other two exhibition games only produced a total net income of $12,000.

On the Lexington game, Jones said, "They brought the floor out of the Louisville Armory and put it down on the football field at Stoll Field." Since Kentucky's Alumni Gym with its estimated 4,000 seats was too small to accommodate an expected large crowd, Rupp had decided to move the game to the football stadium.

Another highlight in Jones' playing career includes a 1949 all-star game in Chicago in which he participated after finishing his senior year at UK. Playing for the College All-Star squad against the NBA champion Minneapolis Lakers, he was named the game's MVP. "We played the best in the pros with the college all-stars and they only beat us four points," Jones said. "I got 22 points which was a lot of points at that time. I was voted the Star of Stars award and received a trophy for that game. That was one of the big awards." Rupp also served as a coach in that game.

After the 1948-49 campaign ended with their second consecutive NCAA title, UK seniors went on a barnstorming tour around the state. And, later they were contacted by a group of prominent businessmen from Indianapolis about the possibility of playing together in the National Basketball League (NBL), which shortly changed its name to National Basketball Association after NBL and rival Basketball Association of America (BAA) decided to join forces. Some of the NBL owners plus the Indianapolis group felt the Kentucky players would give the league instant drawing power at the gate. The players liked the idea and subsequently were given the majority ownership shares of a new team called the Indianapolis Olympians. In a situation which was something unheard of, former Wildcats — Jones, Groza, Beard, Barker and Joe Holland — became player-owners. In addition to owning the club, Jones said, "We agreed to accept a salary of $5,000 each." (At the time, another member of UK's Fabulous Five, Kenny Rollins, was playing for the Chicago Stags.)

Holland, who was named All-SEC in 1947 as a 6-4 senior forward, was persuaded to join the group in Indianapolis. "Joe Holland took leave from his business and joined us and was part-owner of the team," Jones explained. "Babe Kimbrough was a former newspaper reporter. He was sports editor of the (Lexington) *Herald*. So he left the *Herald* and went with us as business manager of the club. We had the five players who owned the stock in the company. And we sold other stock to people in Indianapolis."

With Barker serving as head coach, the 1949-50 Olympians won the league's Western Division championship with a 39-25 mark in their first year of pro competition. Indianapolis, however, was knocked out of playoffs when it lost to the Anderson (Ind.) Packers two games to one in the best-of-three series. In becoming a rising pro star, Groza was NBA's second-leading scorer with 23.4 points, just behind Minneapolis' 6-10 George Mikan who averaged over 27 points. Beard averaged 14.9 points, 12th best in the league. Jones wasn't far back as he gunned in 12.5 points.

All five ex-Wildcats continued to play together in

the NBA the following season. But, as a group, it would be their last year. With Groza and Beard doing most of the scoring, the Olympians finished the 1950-51 campaign with a 31-37 worksheet. They were eliminated from the playoff picture in the first round. Groza again finished second to Mikan in NBA scoring. Groza and Beard both made All-NBA teams for the second year in a row.

After Barker stepped down as head coach after 56 games into the second season, Jones took over the helm. "I was injured one year and I stepped in to be the coach because I couldn't play and it wasn't that great of a deal," said Jones who finished with an 8-7 career coaching mark. "We knew what we had to do and it was just making the substitutions and all that stuff." During that season, Jones had seen action in only 22 games.

Then came along the infamous gambling scandal which rocked college basketball, including Kentucky. Groza and Beard, along with a few other former UK players, pleaded guilty to their involvement in the scandal. And both were forced out of the NBA. They lost their ownership shares in the Indianapolis club. Jones, Barker and Holland, however, stayed on with Indianapolis for the 1951-52 season. But things weren't the same without Groza and Beard.

"We tried to play without those two," said Jones, who finished his three-year NBA career with an average of 10.2 points, "but it went downhill from there. We got out of the pro business and I came back to Lexington. We had people coming to the games but when we lost players like Groza and Beard, and start losing, then you lose the crowd."

By the way, coach Rupp wasn't too happy with what Jones and other players had done shortly after their playing days at UK ended. "When we left the last of the year, we didn't have much conversation with coach Rupp," Jones said. "He got a little bit mad because we went out on our own and did the barnstorming trip and later owned our team (in Indianapolis) and all that. He was a little bit miffed at us and it took him awhile to kind of get over that. But when he did get over that, he was okay. He treated us real nice and we were more or less like one of his that he tried to keep us in the right lane."

Because he was an outstanding college football player, Jones nearly became a National Football League performer. But Jones interestingly gave up a better contract offer from an NFL team to play pro basketball. "I was offered $8,500 to play pro football with the Chicago Bears," he said. Jones added that the Indianapolis package deal which "looking down the road was the right deal because you may be cut from football the first month or first year. This (deal) could have worked into a bigger thing except for the unfortunate situation that happened. We lost whatever we had. More or less our time is what we lost because we didn't put up that much (money)."

Asked if he regretted not having the opportunity to play in the NFL, Jones replied, "I had thought about it. I guess you always wonder how you would have come out."

His football teammate at Kentucky, quarterback George Blanda, was also given a contract at the same time by Chicago Bears' owner/coach George Halas to play for his club. "They offered George $7,500 to play," Jones said. Blanda and Jones come close in continuing their football careers as teammates in the NFL. But things didn't work out. "He stayed with the Bears and I came back to Indianapolis," Jones explained.

Blanda went on to become a legendary star in the NFL and the old American Football League.

When Jones returned to Lexington, after quitting his brief pro basketball career, he launched a new magazine called *TV in the Bluegrass* He came up with his venture idea after seeing a similar publication in Indianapolis, which listed different television programs. Back then, in the early 1950s, there were no TV stations in Lexington. But, with TV antenna, Kentuckians could obtain the picture from five nearby stations in Louisville and Cincinnati. Jones eventually built up a sizeable subscription list for his magazine.

As the magazine grew, he became involved in politics. The local Republicans asked Jones to run for the Office of Fayette County Sheriff. Like his basketball career, Jones made history after he barely won the election in a Democratic-controlled county. "At that time I was the first Republican Sheriff (in Fayette County) since the Civil War," he said.

While Jones served as sheriff for four years (1954-58), he campaigned for another office. During the 1956 election, Jones ran against John C. Watts for a seat in the U.S. Congress. But the former UK player lost the congressional race. "He only beat me close to 6,000 votes in 20 counties," Jones commented. "(During the race), I had an opportunity to go to the White House and visit Eisenhower and take pictures in the Oval Office which was a great experience. Then he came here and made a speech at Memorial Coliseum."

Later Jones went back to work full time in his successful business ventures. But he also did some color commentary at UK games for the Ashland Oil Basketball Network which included Lexington radio station WLAP. "At that time, three or four stations were broadcasting Kentucky basketball and they all had their own announcers and own color people," Jones said. "J. B. Faulconer did the games and I did the color for Kentucky's games for quite a few years."

Jones currently attends UK games at Rupp Arena on a regular basis. He has had season tickets since the days of Memorial Coliseum. With today's three-point field goals, Jones jokingly said, "They ought to go back and give me a point for every field goal I made because all of mine were from the three-point range."

Asked if he has any favorite Wildcat team as a spectator, Jones replied, "I don't know. I guess maybe I got hooked up with Johnny Cox's (1958 national championship) team during that time because Johnny being from Hazard and playing real tough basketball. But I followed and enjoyed all of them. We've had some good players and the Cotton Nash group was good. I didn't get to see the 1951 and '52 (teams) play as much but the (Frank) Ramsey group was a great group. We were playing (in the NBA) at the same time and didn't get to see them as much as I wanted to. Louie Dampier and his group, and (Kyle) Macy. We had so many good groups. It's hard to pick one out. But I've enjoyed the game."

3 THE MAN WHO GOT AWAY

"I just felt lost. I was
immature and that was
basically the reason
I went back to Western."

When Wayne Chapman signed his first professional
basketball contract to play for the Kentucky Colonels of
the American Basketball Association in 1968, his rookie
salary was $25,000 a year.

That's approximately $650,000 less than his son,
Rex Chapman, reportedly earned — 20 years later —
during his 1988-89 rookie season with NBA's Charlotte
Hornets. Rex's first-year salary was estimated to be
$675,000.

But, back in the late 1960s, Wayne certainly thought
$25,000 was a lot of money. Indeed, it was at the time. So,
what was the first item he did after inking the contract?

"The first thing I did was go on vacation for a week
and take my wife down to Florida," recalled the elder
Chapman, who married the former Laura Little of London,
Ky., during their college days. "Then we moved to Louisville
and bought a house out in Middletown (a Louisville suburb).
That was one of the wisest things we did. We got that
advice, I'm sure, from Laura's aunt or someone who told us
to buy a house instead of renting an apartment. It was a
good investment for us."

Just fresh out of college, having graduated from
Western Kentucky University where he was a basketball
star, Chapman was very happy with the bucks he was

getting from his first "real" job.

"That was a lot of money back then," he said. "I would have never thought in my lifetime that I would have made that much money. Of course, now, what the players make is unbelievable. What we made back then was good money, but you couldn't retire on it. They can sign one contract now and retire after they get through playing. So, things have a way of changing but I'll tell you the biggest thing that changed it was cable television. It changed the entire market."

Taking a break from a 1990 summer basketball camp that bore his famous son's name at Southern High School in Louisville, Wayne Chapman fondly remembers his childhood, growing up in Owensboro, Ky., in the 1950s. In his backyard where he had a basketball goal, Chapman pretended he was a "real" Kentucky Wildcat hero, playing for coach Adolph Rupp.

"We'd always argue about who was going to be Frank Ramsey and who was going to be Cliff Hagan when we'd play sandlot basketball," said Chapman, the former head coach who guided Kentucky Wesleyan College to two NCAA Division II national championships in 1987 and '90. "I guess Cliff Hagan and Frank Ramsey were my heroes growing up. When I was a real young kid, I wanted to be a professional football player, for some reason. I don't know why. But when I found out you had to hit people on purpose, I decided to play basketball."

Like Chapman, Hagan hailed from Owensboro where he led Owensboro High to the Sweet Sixteen championship in 1949, scoring a then-state tournament record of 41 points in final contest.

During the days of the John F. Kennedy presidency in the early 1960s, Chapman attended Daviess County High School in Owensboro. He was a basketball star, making all-state teams his junior and senior years. He played for the Kentucky All-Star squad in the annual Kentucky-Indiana series in 1963.

He was good enough to get a lot of letters from many colleges. But actually only three schools recruited him hard. They were Kentucky Wesleyan, Western Kentucky and Kentucky. Yes, the Man in the Brown Suit from Lexington was very interested in obtaining the services of this 6-6 player.

Unlike today's crazed recruiting world of college basketball which is filled with recruiting newsletters and high-profile summer camps, there wasn't a lot of importance placed on recruiting at that time. Recruiting just wasn't that big of a deal.

"Back then, recruiting was a completely different story," said Chapman. "There were people (players) in your own state sometimes that you didn't know of and that's, of course, unheard of now. So, if you can play basketball now, there are a lot of schools out there that know about it. Back then, very few schools knew about the good athletes. Of course, recruiting was changing about that time. The black athlete was starting to go to the predominantly-white schools. I guess we were just on the verge of breaking into what we call modern-day recruiting. But there wasn't a whole lot of emphasis placed on it."

When it came time to sign high school players, Rupp drove to Owensboro and inked Chapman to a basketball scholarship. "A guy named Neil Reed recruited me and Adolph came down. We had a brand new restaurant in Owensboro and he signed me there," Chapman recalled. "That was actually the only contact I ever had with him other than my visit (earlier) when I went to the University of Kentucky. But Adolph was already a legend by the time I came along so just to have him in Owensboro and to be able to meet him was something of an experience in itself."

Chapman said he signed with Kentucky because he had read and heard a lot about the Wildcats all of his life and idolized their players, such as Hagan and Ramsey.

"Why did I pick Kentucky?" he said, repeating the question. "(It) was because if you could play basketball, there was only one school at that time and that was Kentucky. The only thing I heard about growing up was the University of Kentucky. So, naturally, when they offered me a scholarship, I jumped at it."

So, Chapman became a Wildcat in 1963. He was a happy kid. On cloud nine. But, would his happiness continue in Lexington in the fall when school began? He would be about 175 miles away from home.

During his first season at UK, Chapman played for coach Harry Lancaster on the freshman team. Lancaster was Rupp's right-hand man for many years. Some of his teammates include Louie Dampier, Pat Riley, Brad Bounds and Gene Stewart. The Kittens had a superb season, winning 13 out of 16 games, scoring 1,600 points for an average of exactly 100 points a game.

"Harry was our coach and three of us averaged over 20 points a game," said Chapman of Dampier, Riley and himself. This turned out to be Chapman's last year at Kentucky. After staying one year in Lexington, he transferred to Western Kentucky in Bowling Green.

"What was ironic about it was that two years later in the (NCAA) Mideast Regional in Iowa City, Iowa, all three of us made the NCAA All-Mideast Regional (tournament) team," he said. "So, all three of us were freshmen on the same team and we ended up being on the same (all-tournament) team two years later."

He made the all-tournament team as a Hilltopper sophomore, while Dampier and Riley were still playing at UK as members of the famous Rupp's Runts. If Western Kentucky hadn't lost to Michigan in the Mideast Regional (where the Hilltoppers dropped a narrow 80-79 decision), it would have faced Kentucky for the regional championship. Chapman claims that WKU, which finished the season with a shining 25-3 record, would have stopped the Wildcats. "If Michigan hadn't beaten us, we would have beaten (Rupp's) Runts," he pointed out.

During his UK days, Chapman almost didn't finish his freshman year, feeling homesick. He wanted to leave the campus when the fall semester ended. His parents said no.

"They urged me to stay and stick it out," he said. "To be honest with you, I wanted to leave at Christmas and transfer. They talked me into staying until the end of the year and then (I) transferred that summer."

He emphasized that his departure from UK had nothing to do with Rupp and the team. He was satisfied as far as basketball was concerned.

"I was just intimidated by everything at that time," Chapman said of UK's large campus. "I was only 17 years old and the University of Kentucky just seemed like another world away because during that time we didn't have interstate (highways). It took you five or six hours to get there. The whole school was just so big coming from where I came from. I just felt lost. I was immature and that was basically the reason I went back to Western. It was closer to home. It was only 45 minutes to an hour away from home as opposed to five hours. That was really the only reason I left the University of Kentucky.

"I played every minute of every game. It (leaving) had nothing to do with that (basketball). And my grades were all right. It was just the fact that I was basically homesick. That sounds strange when you're only on the other side of the state but that's just the way I felt at the time. I was very young and I didn't turn 18 until that summer. It was just a tough situation for me so I decided to go back home."

Like UK with the legendary Rupp, Western Kentucky also had someone of similar stature in coach Ed Diddle. But Chapman's freshman season at Kentucky was the last of Diddle's remarkable 42-year coaching career at WKU. So, he didn't have a chance to play for Diddle, who posted an overall 759-302 mark as the head coach and sent three of his teams to the NCAA tournament and eight to the NIT (in the 1940s and 1950s the NIT was more prestigious than the NCAA). Diddle was popularly known as "the man with the red towel."

However, after his retirement in 1964, Diddle stayed around on the campus, attending team practices and games at E.A. Diddle Arena, named for the coach himself. And Chapman got to know him.

"When he was at the ballgames, you'd always look over at the box where he sat," Chapman said. "You'd always know where he was, except for one time. We were in a huddle and we all heard this crowd cheer go up, a loud cheer, and we were getting beat at the time. We just all kind of looked up out of the huddle and there he was, standing in the middle of press row, waving a towel at the fans. Standing there over the top of somebody's typewriter. (He) spelled out the words 'WESTERN.'

"At that time he'd already been sick for quite awhile but he still had that much energy. We went back out and kicked their butts. I don't know who we were playing but we beat them pretty good after that. But just knowing he was around was enough. I spoke to him and we lived in his house. He lived upstairs and we (players) lived down in the basement of the 'Dittle Dorm.' So, he'd come down, sit and talk to us and check on us every once awhile. It was nice having him around. He'd always tell you a good story."

After sitting out one year because of transfer rules, Chapman went on to have an outstanding career at WKU under the guidance of coach John Oldham. As a three-year starter, he helped the Hilltoppers compile an overall 66-13 record and earn two trips to the NCAA tournament. His well-known teammates included All-American Clem Haskins (who later became an NBA star, and head coach at WKU and Minnesota of the Big Ten Conference), and All-Ohio Valley Conference performers Dwight Smith and Greg Smith.

Individually, Chapman scored 1,292 points which ranks 12th among the school's all-time leading scorers. He played all 79 of his games, averaging 16.3 points a game and was chosen OVC Player-of-the-Year during his senior year. He had been drafted by the Philadelphia 76ers of the NBA in the fifth round after his junior season since his original class graduated. But he stayed on and received his bachelor's degree in 1968.

While in college, another important chapter began in Chapman's life. He met a pretty coed from Laurel County who was a Hilltopper cheerleader. He and Laura were married in January of 1967, right in the middle of the basketball season.

Following his senior year, he again was drafted by the pros. The Baltimore (now Washington) Bullets of the NBA selected Chapman in the seventh round, while the Kentucky Colonels picked him in ABA's second round.

He went to Louisville and signed a pact with the Colonels to begin his professional career. He had decided to stay home in Kentucky.

After his junior year at WKU, Chapman suffered one of the most shocking moments of his life in May of 1967. He learned that his ex-roommate, WKU star Dwight Smith, had been killed in a tragic automobile accident on a gloomy rainy day. Smith and his sister, Kay, were killed as their car plunged into a flooded ditch in Hopkins County. Their brother, Greg, managed to survive the accident. All three were students at WKU. About two months prior to the accident, the 6-5 Dwight Smith had played his last game for the Hilltoppers and was headed for a promising NBA career.

"He (Dwight) was coming back from Mother's Day down in Princeton, Ky., and he and his sister were killed in a car wreck during the spring of his senior year," Chapman said. "Greg was driving the car and he miraculously survived the wreck and went on to play on the NBA championship (squad) with the Milwaukee Bucks (in 1971). Dwight was getting ready to sign a contract with the Los Angeles Lakers.

"If he had done that, you would have never heard of Gail Goodrich (a former UCLA standout who played for the Lakers and the Phoenix Suns) because Dwight was, without question, the best basketball player on our team, including myself, Greg or Clem Haskins. He would have been a great NBA player and he was a great person."

At WKU, Dwight Smith was a three-time All-Ohio Valley Conference performer who often played in the shadow of Haskins, the team's top scorer. He had hoped to become a coach someday.

Without a national television contract, the young ABA was struggling with its identity. The league, in its second season, was fighting against the established rival NBA when Chapman first joined the Colonels, who played their home games at 5,072-seat Convention Center in downtown Louisville. At that time, Joseph and Mamie Gregory owned the club (with a dog named Ziggy) and Gene Rhodes was the coach. That was before well-known personalities like John Y. and Ellie Brown, Dan Issel and

Artis Gilmore arrived on the scene.

The Colonels, though, had outstanding players. Some of Chapman's teammates include Louie Dampier, Darel Carrier, Jim "Goose" Ligon, Gene Moore, Jim Caldwell, Bobby Rascoe and Oliver Darden, to name a few.

As a reserve guard, Chapman remained with the Colonels for two years, before he was shipped to the Denver Rockets (now Nuggets) in 1970. But he has fond memories of the Colonels and some of his favorite stories include playing a game in ice-cold conditions and a fight involving his squad.

"We used to play in the Long Island Garden (Arena) in New York (against the New York Nets)," said Chapman. "We got there one night. It was really cold. We walked inside the place and it was like 33 degrees. They had these electric heaters that were behind the bench and when you'd come out, you could put your hands down there and warm up.

"They (arena officials) were in a hurry, I guess, and they put the floor down on top of the ice rink without any insulation. So, water started coming up. It's not a great story but it shows you a little bit about the conditions. A guy named Levern Tart, who played for New York, went in for a layup, slid off the end of the floor and slid all the way to the end of the hockey rink and broke his jaw. The game was stopped. I remember we had a game called off there once and it could have been that night. So, we played in some adverse conditions."

But, as a Kentucky Colonel, Chapman said he probably remembered a wild incident at Indianapolis during the 1968-69 campaign more than anything else. "We were playing the (Indiana) Pacers," he said, "up at the old fairgrounds (9,111-seat Indiana State Fairgrounds) and a fight broke out between Jim Caldwell (of Kentucky) and George Peeples (of Indiana). They ran out underneath the stands all the way to the other exit and back under the floor again. Jim was chasing George. By the time they got back in, both teams were fighting. We went about four or five rows into the stands.

"The fans were into it. The owners were into it. The police were trying to break us up. I bet that fight lasted for 25 minutes. Fortunately, nobody was hurt. I remember Mamie and Joe Gregory owned the club at that time and

Joe, bless his heart, was getting the heck beaten out of him in the middle of the floor by somebody. Somebody hitting me over the head with a folding chair is the last thing I remember. It was an interesting fight.

"I guess, looking back, those were fun times but they weren't too much fun then. There were some great experiences in the ABA. Some of the people and characters you met there in the ABA are just life-long memories that you won't forget."

In 1970, Chapman did not have an opportunity to play with Dan Issel and Mike Pratt on the Colonels' squad as he was traded to Denver. Both of the former Wildcat stars had just signed fat contracts with the Colonels with Issel getting $1.4 million. Issel's deal with Kentucky matched the $1.4 million reportedly paid Lew Alcindor (now Kareem Abdul-Jabbar) by the NBA's Milwaukee Bucks as the largest amount ever paid an athlete in the age of growing financial war between the ABA and the NBA. Issel later said his contract was for much less than the amount that was reported by the news media. Pratt, meanwhile, reportedly received a $400,000 pact.

Although he was leaving his home state, Chapman was pleased because he figured that he would be able to see a lot more action for the Rockets. At Kentucky, he played behind the starting backcourt of Dampier and Carrier. They were both ABA stars.

The biggest thrill of his ABA career had yet to come. It would take place at Denver in January of 1971 when his mother saw him play.

"Oh, Lord," said Chapman, "my biggest moment in the ABA was, I guess, when my mother flew out to Denver and I think I got 38 (points). We didn't have television (coverage) back then so she didn't get to see me play very often. The All-Star game was the next week and I had a tough time explaining to her why I wasn't on the all-star team. I was glad that she got to see me play at least once in the pros. My dad never did get to see me. He died my senior year in college. So, he didn't know anything about my professional career. We won (the game), and that was probably the best game I ever had."

Referring to the trade that sent him to the Rocky Mountains, Chapman said, "I was very happy about it because I was going to be a starter. I'd always played backup. I got hurt my rookie year and I couldn't play (much). In my second year, of course, I played behind Louie and Darel. I wanted to be a starter like everybody. This was my opportunity. I played very, very well for the Denver Rockets and caught the eye of Bobby Leonard who coached the Pacers. (I) had some great games against them and they traded for me."

So, after 47 games with Denver, averaging nearly 10 points a game, Chapman went to Indiana while the season was in progress. He was back in a basketball-crazy territory where the fans, like their neighboring Kentuckians, adore the sport. He didn't mind, though. He went from a lower division club to a championship contender. "I was happy to get traded to the Pacers because they were going for an ABA championship," he said. The Pacers, who had the best record in the league with a 58-26 mark, didn't get it as the Utah Stars, led by former NBA star Zelmo Beaty, beat them four games to three in Western Division finals in the playoffs.

In 1972, Chapman's playing career ended on the advice of his doctors as he suffered a back injury. He only played seven games that season for the Pacers, who went on to capture the ABA title, defeating superstar Rick Barry and the New York Nets in the finals. "He had a back problem and he still has it," said his mother-in-law, Mayme Little Hamby. "They told him if he continued to play, he might become paralyzed."

If the cable television explosion had taken place in the early 1970s, instead of the early 1980s, the ABA could have been around today, enjoying the fruits of the explosive marketing success of pro basketball and featuring such stars as Michael Jordan and Isiah Thomas, according to Chapman.

"If ESPN (cable sports network) had been around, you might have two leagues now instead of just one," he theorized. "We would really have a great world championship."

However, ABA existed for only nine years before the NBA absorbed four ABA teams in 1976. The four teams — New York Nets, Denver Nuggets, San Antonio Spurs and Indiana Pacers — each paid a $3.2 million entry fee to join NBA.

"Well, the ABA survived anyway," commented Chapman. "We had all the great perimeter players. We had Dr. J. (Julius Erving) and we had Ice Man (George Gervin) and we had Donnie Freeman and we had Louie Dampier and we had Billy Cunningham. The only thing we were missing were the big centers. Then when we got (Artis) Gilmore and Dan Issel and those people, they (NBA) said,'Wait a minute, we better do something about that.' So, that's when the NBA went ahead and merged some of the teams in. They worked out an agreement.

"But it (the early years) was tough. We played in some pretty bad places sometimes. The clubs I played for really ran first-class organizations. Of course, two of them went on into the NBA. It's a shame that Kentucky never was able to maintain a professional franchise. I think the Colonels were very good for Louisville."

At sunny Miami, the Floridians franchise had ballgirls running around in skimpy swimsuits at their home games. The bikini-clad girls, including high school teenagers, would sit and stand on the edge of the playing floor, waiting for the red-white-blue ball to come in their direction. Some fans liked it and some didn't but it was a big attention-getter as the team received national publicity. In fact, the team's coach posed with five ballgirls in bathing suits for a photo that was published in a national sports magazine. One ballgirl remarked that the referees enjoyed watching them. They probably did and missed some calls.

Those were the crazy, but lovable ABA days. "Well, you call it strange, but now you've got the (L.A.) Laker Girls and the Dallas Cowboy Cheerleaders," Chapman pointed out. And, the red-white-blue basketball that the ABA used, he said, should have been adopted by the NBA. "I thought that was good for the fans," he said. "People used to ask me, 'How do you play with that red-white-blue basketball?' You don't look at the ball, really, you just play. It didn't bother the play of the game at all. You know, I think the ABA has got a lot to be proud of." The younger league also used the three-point field goal, which was later accepted by the NBA and the NCAA.

Throughout his ABA days, Chapman said superstar Julius Erving was the best player he had ever seen. "No question, hands down," he said of Dr. J.

Located near the Ohio River in the western part of the state, Kentucky Wesleyan College is a small Methodist school which has approximately 800 students. It has a student/faculty ratio of 11 to 1.

After spending seven years of teaching and coaching at three different high schools, Chapman joined Kentucky Wesleyan in 1981 as an assistant to coach Mike Pollio, who later moved on to Virginia Commonwealth of the Sun Belt Conference and Eastern Kentucky. In 1985, he was promoted to head coach and athletic director.

Known for his strong intensity, Chapman has been successful in his coaching career, both on the high school and college levels. Before resigning his post in the summer of 1990, he had directed Kentucky Wesleyan to a five-year mark of 128-29 for a winning percentage of .815, and a couple of national titles.

When his alma mater, Western Kentucky, searched for a new head coach in the spring of 1990, Chapman was one of the names that surfaced as a possible candidate. Instead, UK assistant Ralph Willard got the job. "Yeah, I was one of the names mentioned, but I don't think I was ever seriously considered for it," said Chapman. "That was a situation that probably could only best be explained by Western Kentucky. I don't always have the greatest success in the world but sometimes you wonder how people make decisions."

Prior to quitting his Kentucky Wesleyan job to pursue new career opportunities, Chapman had acknowledged that he would like to have a chance to coach at a major school in the future. Perhaps his time will come.

Interestingly, Chapman's resignation, coincidence or not, came at a time when his relationship with the local daily newspaper, the *Owensboro Messenger-Inquirer*, had been severely strained. He feuded with some of the sportswriters about articles on his son's basketball camp, and reportedly even threatened one reporter to stay away from him and his family. The camp received criticism when its advertisements had promised that NBA star Michael Jordan would appear and speak. But Jordan was nowhere to be seen.

As far as the Kentucky Wildcats are concerned, Wayne Chapman could be labeled as the Man Who Got Away. Just like his son Rex in 1988, he left UK before his collegiate eligibility expired. Although they left for different reasons, the Chapmans searched for new horizons.

Wayne wanted to be close to home. Rex wanted to play professional basketball. Perhaps, the younger Chapman, who is called by some "King Rex," had other reasons, too. Only they know for sure.

Anyhow, after departing the Wildcats, they continued to build on their successful careers in basketball, a sport they religiously love.

"They have a special tie (relationship)," said Rex's grandmother, Mrs. Hamby.

What would have happened if they had stayed on at UK? Wayne might have helped the Wildcats win the national championship in 1966. And Rex, as a senior, would have probably given coach Rick Pitino's first squad at Kentucky at least 20 victories, instead of a 14-14 record.

We'll never know.

4 LITTLE LOUIE

"...the (Rupp's) Runts captured the imagination not only of coach Rupp, but of everyone in the Commonwealth."

In 1975, when John Y. Brown, Jr. and his first wife Ellie were the owners of the defending American Basketball Association champion Kentucky Colonels, they sold the team's most popular star, Dan Issel, to the new Baltimore Claws franchise for a reported $630,000. Stunned by the unbelievable sale of Issel, the whole state of Kentucky was in a state of shock. The emotional fans and the media alike blasted the owners for this unthinkable action. Issel was The Colonels. He was The Franchise.

"That was one of the stupidest transactions ever made in pro basketball," recalled former Colonels star Louie Dampier who was Issel's teammate for five years. "It was turmoil the next year. I had one more year left (at Kentucky before the NBA absorbed the remaining ABA teams in a pro basketball merger) and we kept bringing in everybody trying to replace Dan. We even brought in high-priced ball players and we went through Tom Owens, Caldwell Jones and ended up with Maurice Lucas. Either the players didn't fit in with the team or had conflicts with (coach) Hubie Brown. We just had a poor season. It just wasn't a good move. The whole year was just a struggle."

The Colonels simply were never the same.

The Browns explained that the Issel transaction with Baltimore was purely a business decision, one of the most difficult they had made during their careers. Without the sale, they said, the Colonels couldn't have remained in Louisville for the next few years. The owners had also considered selling one of the team's other stars, Artis Gilmore, instead of Issel. But they decided Gilmore, being a 7-2 center, was more important to the team in the long run.

Without Issel, who eventually wound up with the Denver Nuggets as the Baltimore entry folded without playing a single game, the Colonels finished the 1975-76 season with a 46-38 record, their worst in five years. Meanwhile, at Denver, Issel helped coach Larry Brown and his new Nugget teammates post a 60-24 mark and reach the ABA championship series which they lost to New York four games to two. Interestingly, both Dampier and Issel are now a part of pro basketball history trivia. The former UK All-Americans are the answer to the following question: Who are the top two career scorers in the old ABA? Dampier scored 13,726 points in nine years for an average of nearly 19 points, while Issel gunned in 12,823 points, averaging almost 26 points in six seasons.

And the duo was inducted into the Kentucky Athletic Hall of Fame in August of 1990.

New York Knicks coach Pat Riley is one of the biggest names in sports. He was Dampier's roommate during their college days at UK, but they almost didn't room together. When they arrived in Lexington in 1963 as highly-regarded freshmen, they didn't get along. Despite their different personalities, Riley and Dampier were placed by the coaching staff as dormitory roommates.

The 6-4 Riley came to Kentucky from Schenectady, N.Y., where he was a high school football and basketball star, while Dampier was a 6-foot high-scoring guard at Southport High School in Indiana. "We had different personalities," Dampier said. "I wasn't very outgoing, just quiet and liked to be by myself. Well, not by myself, but just never one to be the center of attention. Pat was the other way around. He had a very outgoing personality. He fit in with (UK players Tommy) Kron and (Larry) Conley more than I did and so we had contrasting personalities and ideas. We had our problems our freshman year.

"It just came to a point where both of us went to (assistant) coach Harry Lancaster and said we wanted to change roommates and he refused. He said, 'No, you're going to room together.' I don't know if that's why he made a statement about 'You're both going to be All-Americans here and we're going to keep you together' or what. I don't know what it was. So, then we just grew to be friends. Actually, we became quite close after four years of rooming together and seeing each other almost year 'round. Unless you really have a bitter personality or whatever, you can't help but become close. So, I say we came out of UK the best of friends."

Riley, who served as an NBC studio host on NBA telecasts during the 1990-91 season after winning four league titles in nine seasons as Los Angeles Laker mentor, has a classy but expensive taste in clothes. A well-dressed sports personality today, he wears the latest styles. Just like when he was in college, according to Dampier.

"Somebody asked me a little while back if Pat was always a flashy dresser and I said, 'Yeah, he was always a modern dresser,'" Dampier said. "They asked because of the way he dresses now, always in the best of clothes. He was that way. He stayed up with the best of styles and whatever was in style he tried to get that for himself."

While at UK, Riley did not date a lot as he did not have a steady girlfriend. He liked to be free, spending some time at nearby lakes, shooting pool and dancing (especially in the summer when he wasn't working). That was not the case for his roommate. Dampier was seeing his high school sweetheart, Marty, whom he later married.

Asked if he ever thought Riley would be as successful as he is today, Dampier replied, "I always thought Pat would be successful. He always seemed to be the person in the right place at the right time. At that time, somebody coming all the way from New York to Kentucky, that wasn't heard of a lot like it is now. You can go from one coast to the other to attend school, but back then that was a long way to come. We had that one good year (1965-66 squad which was known as Rupp's Runts) so he was at the right place at the right time then. And then in the pros when he played with the Lakers, they won a championship (in 1972). He was traded to Phoenix, they were runner-ups to Boston (in 1976). Then, I think he went back to the Lakers and they won it again (in 1980 when Riley was an assistant to coach Paul Westhead). That's how he's always kind of been in the right place."

With 11 games gone into the 1981-82 campaign, Westhead was fired and Riley, along with former Laker star Jerry West, was named co-coach. That was only for a very short time and then Riley completely took charge of the show. "Pat and Jerry West took over as head coaches," Dampier said. "Pat had defense and Jerry had offense. Then Jerry West said, 'Now, I've had enough of this,' and that left Pat and he ended up coaching the Lakers.

"One thing that surprises me is how dedicated he's been, too. He is supposedly one of the hardest-working, if not the hardest-working coach in the NBA. He continually studied video tapes and had the players do it, but he also did it on his own. And he really just dedicated himself to coaching. I'm not surprised that he was successful, but I was surprised at how hard he worked at it."

At Kentucky, Riley didn't work that hard, especially in the classroom. At times, he was just plain lazy. "He practiced hard and played hard but he didn't hit the books," Dampier said. "He got by without having to apply himself like a lot of us did. Pat was pretty well-rounded and he came with confidence."

But not Dampier himself. He was not a youngster with lots of confidence. "I went down there (to Kentucky) as nervous as I could be because none of my family had ever been to college," he said. "I didn't know what to expect. I thought it was going to be a tremendous challenge. It was but I'm glad I went in with that attitude. I spent all my time studying the first semester of my freshman year because I was afraid of failure."

Dampier grew up as a middle-class Hoosier—not as a Wildcat. His hometown was in Southport, Ind., near Indianapolis. If things had gone his way, Dampier would've attended Indiana University where Branch McCracken was the successful head coach, a post he held for 24 seasons before stepping down in 1965.

However, when he was a sophomore in high school,

no one had expected Dampier to amount to anything in basketball. At 5-2, he was too short. And, going into the season, he had doubts about making the junior varsity squad. "Then as a junior I grew eight inches and I was 5-10 and fit into, all of the sudden, the team — going from doubts of making the reserve team to being on the varsity and a starter," he said.

Anyhow, Dampier felt the Hoosiers didn't really want him that badly. So, he opted for coach Adolph Rupp and his beloved Wildcat program.

"I was always a fan of Indiana," Dampier said. "I had dreams of going there but the coach, Branch McCracken, at the time wasn't really interested in me. My Uncle Louie, who is my godfather, was president of the alumni association and he took me to Indiana and visited with McCracken. While he (the coach) left me outside to walk around and look at the facility which was the gymnasium, he went in and talked with my uncle for about a half hour. When they came out, he (the coach) said, 'Okay, Louie, you have a scholarship here at Indiana.' My uncle had talked him into it. I really had always wanted to go to Indiana but after that visit I decided to accept a visit with Kentucky."

Unlike their earlier trip to Bloomington, the journey to Lexington turned out to be more enjoyable. Dampier felt wanted. "When I went down to Lexington, I enjoyed the people," he said. "They acted as if they really wanted me to come to school at UK. I watched some of the films that they had. They ran an offense a lot like my high school offense in Indiana. So, I made my mind up that I wanted to go to Kentucky."

Rupp became impressed with Dampier when he saw the kid play in a high school regional tournament in Indiana, shooting the lights out on a fast break. In that game Dampier hit nine of 10 baskets in the first half and that was all Rupp needed to see. The coach left at halftime. "But the second half I think I went one for ten or something like that so I was kind of glad he didn't stay for the whole game," smiled Dampier. "He came up to see me play and then I started getting letters and phone calls from (assistant) Neil Reed. Finally, I visited Kentucky. I kept turning them down until after I visited Indiana."

Although Dampier was a high school star and was

being recruited by one of the biggest names in basketball, he had doubts that he could play at Kentucky or anywhere else because some thought he was too small to play the sport. "I had doubts because of what people said," he said. "I always had confidence when I was on the floor, but when I was off the floor my mind would work then and I'd have some doubts." Even after his All-American days at Kentucky, some observers had the same lingering doubts about Dampier's size to play in the pros. Everywhere he went, Dampier had to prove himself on the court. He had to show that he could play with the big guys.

On his initial meeting with Rupp at Memorial Coliseum while visiting the UK campus, Dampier remembered that the Baron had a soft handshake. "It was interesting. The first thing I noticed about meeting coach Rupp was his handshake," Dampier recalled. "It was real soft. I thought, after hearing some of the stories about coach Rupp and how hard he was on people, he'd have a real, real tough grip. When he had the soft handshake, right away it kind of changed my opinion of him. At least my immediate reaction was, 'Well, he doesn't seem to be that tough.' He didn't promise me anything. He did say that he wanted me to come to Kentucky. He wanted me to play there and thought that I could fit in with them."

As far as college basketball is concerned, Dampier had a good rookie season, averaging almost 27 points a game for the freshman squad. But life off the court was tough on him. Besides adjusting to his new college life, he had to deal with the death of his parents. His father had passed away the summer before Dampier came to UK. His mother died previously while he was a high school sophomore.

"To make it a little more difficult, Dad died during the Kentucky-Indiana high school all-star games," Dampier said. "I was away practicing and preparing for those games when he died. I was a little fearful of it (going away from home to UK), but once I got down there I got used to the situation and settled in. My sisters and brother took care of me anyway. They were like parents because they are a lot older than I am. They looked after me and gave me my needs and everything worked out well. My oldest sister is 15 or 16 years older than I am and my brother, who is the youngest of the four (Dampier has three older sisters and one brother), is eight years older than I am. That helped with them taking care of me after my parents died."

After his father died, Dampier even had to work at the family's dairy bar for one summer. Eventually, the business was sold.

Oddly, it was his father who once told Dampier that he thought participating in sports was a waste of time, even though the elder Dampier had played sports in high school. "He didn't really support me in sports and follow the games or even come to very many games until after my mother died," commented Dampier, who now lives in La Grange, Ky., near Louisville. "Then he started to back me. So, I really got close with him the two years after my mom died.

"I was real close to my mother. She was the one who took me to my games and supported me and came to all my games. My dad, of course, had to work."

Although he was one of the team's top players throughout his UK tenure, Dampier once thought his collegiate career was about to come to an end when he almost had words with Rupp in a practice session. Actually, he was going to offer a suggestion about game strategy to Rupp.

"There was a time that I became very nervous," Dampier said. "We were preparing to play Tennessee. I can't remember which year it was. It was my sophomore or my junior year. We were going over their offense. We were on defense and they ran this one play. Each time my man would score and coach Rupp would yell at me. So, after the second or third time, he got on me again after that play worked again. I said, 'Well, ...' and that's the only word I got out of my mouth. I was going to say, 'Well, I think he should switch.' He informed me that no one ever talked back to coach Rupp and he said, 'Go take bomb,' which meant go to the showers.

"So I went in there immediately and I could see my career crumbling and I wondered if I was going to get to play in the Tennessee game or get to play in any more games ever. I took my shower and when the other guys came in, I went out to talk to coach Rupp. I apologized. He said everything was alright, accepting my apology. That's when I was really nervous because I didn't know what he would do."

Dampier and many of his teammates were never really close to Rupp and Lancaster. The players didn't go to them a lot if they had problems. "We went through the channels. Coach Rupp and Lancaster would be the last ones we'd go see," said Dampier. But that doesn't mean the players didn't have good relationships with the coaches. They just tried to avoid them if possible, preferring to go to other staff members for help.

After Rupp's retirement at Kentucky, he and Dampier became close. Dampier would drop by and visit the Baron at his Lexington home. "I really didn't stay in contact (with Rupp) a whole lot until his forced retirement," said Dampier, one of several ex-Wildcats who signed a petition in support of Rupp to stay on as Kentucky mentor. "I started visiting him at his house and especially when he became ill. His wife, Esther, is a beautiful woman. She was always nice to the players. So, every time I'd go visit, I'd visit her, too. It wasn't just coach Rupp and me.

"He became involved with the Memphis Tams (and later Kentucky Colonels as a club executive). At that time Issel was on the (Colonels) team and he was really close to coach Rupp because they had camps together after Dan was finished playing at UK. Anyway, we'd go out to eat with him after the games or have a drink. I really got to know him a lot better and the type of person he was. It was on a more even basis because he didn't have to have the 'coach attitude' with us."

Dampier doesn't think Rupp is a lot different from what the fans read in the newspapers or magazines about the legendary coach. "I really don't think so," he said. "He was a very strict disciplinarian on the floor. He did have strict rules about what we couldn't do. He always kept a wall between himself and the players. He didn't allow himself to get close. I think sometimes he felt he might be getting that way with some of the players and he would purposely find a reason to disillusion them again, make them feel that if they thought they were getting to be his buddy or something, he'd give them a reason to feel like he was their enemy again.

"He was very tough to play for. That's why a lot of

players didn't stay. If a free spirit would come in, they (coaches) would have their ways of trying to change that person or the person would decide on his own to leave. If a player came in and wanted to play basketball and was serious about it and getting his education, there weren't any problems."

Dampier had his best game as a Wildcat in 1966 when he pumped in what would be his career-high 42 points, leading Kentucky to a 105-90 victory over Vanderbilt in Nashville. It was the year of Rupp's Runts.

"One of my happiest moments was during that season when we were ranked No. 2 and Vanderbilt was ranked third in the country," said Dampier. "We went down there to play for more or less the conference championship. I had my best game as a college player. I still have the audio tape of that game with Cawood Ledford calling it. I listen to that every once in a while because it's something that I can relive through the eyes and the voice of someone else. I didn't realize quite what was going on and what the fan would feel just listening to the game or being able to see it."

Dampier also has the audio tape of another game that season, a very important one. It was a semifinal of the NCAA tournament where top-ranked Kentucky was meeting No. 2 Duke in College Park, Maryland. The Wildcats won that contest 83-79 to advance to the national championship game. On listening to that game on tape, he said, "I don't remember very many things that happened. I guess I was just so caught up in all the emotion of that being the number one and number two teams in the country playing against each other. It was a strange feeling. It was almost like a game I didn't really play in even though I heard my name mentioned." In the victory, Dampier led UK with 23 points with Riley adding 19.

Then came the third-ranked Texas Western (now Texas-El Paso) Miners on the next night. They were Kentucky's opponent in the NCAA title game. Unlike Kentucky which had no blacks, coach Don Haskins' Miners club featured an all-black starting lineup, turning the matchup into a hardwood battle between the whites and the blacks. And underdog Texas Western, hitting 28 of 34 free throws, pulled a major upset, shocking the foul-plagued Wildcats and the world by winning 72-65. The loss deeply hurt Rupp as he knew his favored Wildcats had the better team.

Dampier didn't see or hear Rupp cry after the setback. But he could tell that Rupp was grieving inside.

"Right after we got beat, it was more like we were stunned," he said. "Coach Rupp was crushed. He was going after (his) No. 5 (NCAA championship) and we were really wanting to get it for him and for us. To see the disappointment on his face was the crushing blow that you talk about. He showed how he felt. He was very sad and you could see it. It was almost like he aged a few years that night. He never cried but you could just tell how hurt he was and how much he wanted that victory. I was more or less angry that we lost but then it set in, what we'd missed out on in the days and years to come."

Claude Vaughan, who worked as an academic advisor/trainer for the team, agreed that Rupp was devastated. "I think it was the toughest loss he had ever faced," he said. "I think that team, the (Rupp's) Runts, captured the imagination, not only of coach Rupp, but of everyone in the Commonwealth (as the tallest starters were Kron and Thad Jaracz, both 6-5). I was in the locker room as soon as the game was over. I was there with the team and coach Rupp and coach Lancaster. Coach Rupp looked over at me and said, 'Claude, you don't get many people in the dressing room when you get your ass beat.' He then went out to do the toughest thing probably he ever had to do, speak to the press and do his show with Cawood (Ledford) on the radio."

On UK's ailing players who struggled to stay ahead in the game, Vaughan said, "I looked down at Pat Riley's foot and it looked almost like hamburger meat. It was just as raw as it could be — this athlete's feet had gotten completely out of control. Then Larry Conley was sick (with flu) although he played a great game against Duke in the semi-finals. It was an awful, awful, awful loss for us. It's something that I don't guess any of us have ever gotten over."

Kentucky finished the season with a 27-2 mark, with the other loss coming at the hands of coach Ray Mears and his Tennessee Volunteers in Knoxville in the next-to-last game of the regular season.

About 20 years later in the late 1980s, the starting five of Rupp's Runts participated in a radio call-in show in Louisville. They reminisced about their college days, including that bitter loss to Texas Western.

"I remember (Tommy) Kron making that statement (on the radio) that it's a shame that we're remembered for our loss rather than for winning," Dampier commented.

According to Dampier, Rupp said he might have called Rupp's Runts his best team ever if they had won that national championship. "Since we didn't accomplish what four other of his teams had done, which was to win the championship, he couldn't say that we were the best team he had coached," Dampier said.

On Feb. 13, 1991, members of Rupp's Runts celebrated their 25th anniversary as they were honored in a special pre-game ceremony at the Kentucky-Tennessee game in Rupp Arena. Portions of the nostalgic affair were shown on TV as part of the halftime report of the regionally-televised matchup which ironically was called by none other than Conley, a Rupp Runt, and Lexingtonian Tom Hammond.

The next season Rupp saw his team compile a 13-13 mark, his worst at UK. Riley could not play up to par, after he suffered back pains as the result of a summer water skiing accident at Herrington Lake near Danville, Ky. But UK students even heard fascinating stories or rumors on the campus — probably untrue — that Riley injured his back when a go-go dancer at a Lexington bar threw out the 6-3 Wildcat star.

Although it was a poor season by Kentucky standards, Dampier and Riley, nevertheless, posted fairly good statistics as seniors. Dampier led Kentucky with a 20.6-point average, while Riley averaged 17.4 points, despite his nagging back injury.

And, when the pros came calling in 1967, both Dampier and Riley went separate ways. Dampier signed with the Kentucky Colonels in the ABA, which was preparing to begin its first year, while Riley ended up on the west coast, going to the San Diego Rockets, one of the NBA's two expansion franchises. Riley was San Diego's first-round pick, the seventh overall NBA selection.

The Cincinnati Royals of the NBA drafted Dampier in the fourth round. But he balked at the Royals. "The reason I didn't really even consider signing with them is because they had a three-day rookie tryout camp," Dampier said. "Even their number one draft choice, which was Mel Daniels, had to come up and try out and he ended up signing with the ABA, too." A 6-9 All-American from the University of New Mexico, Daniels inked with the Minnesota Muskies and went on to have an outstanding career in the ABA. He later was traded to the Indiana Pacers.

So, rather than risking an injury or a poor performance in Cincinnati's tryout camp, Dampier decided to stay in Kentucky and received a one-year contract for $15,000, including a bonus of $2,500, from the Colonels. The team officials thought his name association with the Wildcats would sell tickets. He became the very first Colonel in the Louisville franchise history.

"The Colonels offered me that contract and I took the security of that rather than taking a chance on going with Cincinnati," Dampier explained. "I was real excited to sign that contract. To get paid to play basketball, I thought that was great. I thought maybe I'll last three years or six years and continue to play."

Not so. When Dampier retired in 1979, he had played a total of 12 seasons in pro basketball, nine years with Kentucky in the ABA and three with the San Antonio Spurs in the NBA.

The Kentucky Colonels made pro basketball history on Nov. 27, 1968 when they hired a woman to make a brief appearance as a player. In becoming the first female to play pro basketball, Penny Ann Early, a blonde jockey, made a one-second appearance by throwing in an in-bounds pass during the second quarter of Kentucky's 111-107 setback to the Los Angeles Stars. The event drew a near-sellout crowd of 5,345 at Louisville's Convention Center. But the Kentucky players didn't like the publicity gimmick the team officials had put on. In fact, they were somewhat embarrassed about the event, especially Dampier, who scored a game-high 30 points.

"Thumbs down," said Dampier, pointing his thumb downward. "It was just explained to us that it was to draw some people in and get some publicity. She was a jockey who rode at Churchill Downs and they brought her in. She warmed up with us, sat on the bench and came in for Darel Carrier." Such an event was not uncommon in the early days of the ABA. The struggling league used all kinds of attractions to generate publicity, including ballgirls in bikinis who were employed by the Miami franchise. When the ABA was established in 1967, the league introduced a couple of radical innovations which eventually became popular, the three-point field goal and the red-white-blue "beach" ball. Actually, the ABA was not the first league to use the three-point field goal as the old American Basketball League, which lasted just over a year in the early 1960s, also utilized it.

In his pro career, Dampier had several coaches, including a couple of Wildcat legends. His mentors at Kentucky and San Antonio included John Givens, Gene Rhodes, Alex Groza, Frank Ramsey, Joe Mullaney, Babe McCarthy, Hubie Brown and Doug Moe. Both Groza and Ramsey had been All-Americans at UK.

Dampier said he didn't really have a favorite coach. "I feel like I'm a coachable player because I go along with whatever they want," he explained.

Early in the 1970-71 season, which was Issel's rookie year, the Colonels dismissed Rhodes as the coach and Ramsey was hired by club president Mike Storen to guide the team on the floor. (In the interim, Groza, the team's business manager, coached the Colonels to two victories). Ramsey was returning to basketball after a six-year absence. Upon his retirement from the NBA in 1964, he had entered private business in his hometown of Madisonville, Ky.

Ramsey had a successful pro coaching debut when Kentucky defeated the Carolina Cougars 122-112 in Charlotte, N.C., as Issel and forward Cincy Powell each pumped in 28 points. The duo also grabbed 15 rebounds apiece. For the remainder of the regular season, the Colonels managed to post a 32-35 mark under Ramsey before catching fire in the playoffs. Kentucky advanced to the ABA championship series, but it lost to the Utah Stars in seven games. In the regular season, Kentucky posted an overall 44-40 mark with a second-place finish in the Eastern Division. And Issel captured the ABA scoring title with a 29.9-point average, edging New York Nets superstar Rick Barry by a fraction of a point. He also shared the league's Rookie-of-the-Year honors with Virginia's Charlie Scott, a former pupil in coach Dean Smith's North Carolina program.

It was Ramsey's only season at Kentucky. Joe Mullaney, the former Los Angeles Lakers coach, took over the helm the following season. Watching Ramsey on the hardwood floor, many fans had the impression that he did not enjoy or care about his coaching job. Dampier said that wasn't the case. "I think he enjoyed it," he said. "He's just such a laid back kind of guy that he wouldn't show it. One thing is that he didn't have pressure on him. That wasn't his goal in life to be a pro coach. He was approached (by the Colonels) and he had other things to fall back on that were probably more important to him — his businesses in Madisonville — rather than worrying about coaching."

Later, in 1974, Hubie Brown came to Louisville where he was named the Colonels coach, his first head coaching job in pro basketball. A disciplinarian, he had been an assistant with the successful Milwaukee Bucks of the NBA. When the 1974-75 season ended, Brown was a happy man as he guided the Colonels to their first league championship, defeating arch-rival Indiana in the finals. According to Dampier, that was the most fun season of his college or pro basketball career.

"The 1975 championship was the only championship I'd had at any level," he said, pointing to the championship ring on his finger. "After coming close a few times before, we finally did it. That was the happiest (moment), as far as pros or really through my whole career, because I finally got the championship.

"I personally had better seasons in scoring and assists, but we were in such complete control the whole year. Hubie Brown made it that way. He had a very analytical mind when it came to basketball and he programmed what we did and what we would do. Sometimes it wasn't the most pleasant of circumstances because we got a little tired of continuous scouting reports, day to day, on the teams that we already knew quite well. He programmed us and he stuck to what he had scheduled for us and that proved to make us a very dominant team even though the Nets gave us a chase for a while. Toward the end of the year we were one of the strongest teams in basketball and I think that showed in the way we went through the playoffs. Each of them (playoff series) was four to one. It was just an enjoyable season, even though we worked a little harder than we were used to. It paid off and everything was fun when you were winning."

Speaking of Brown, he later became head coach at a couple of NBA stops for the Atlanta Hawks and the New York Knicks. Currently a TV analyst for Turner Network Television (TNT), Brown said the 1975 Colonels were the best team he's ever coached in his career.

Before the playoffs began, both the Colonels and the Nets had ended up in a first-place tie for the Eastern Division title with 58-26 record. But Kentucky won a special playoff game for the division championship, beating Julius Erving and the Nets 108-99. In a losing cause, Erving poured in a game-high 34 points.

When the Colonels passed up an opportunity to join the NBA in 1976, Dampier obviously was very upset. Club owners John Y. Brown, Jr. and his wife, Ellie, said the price tag to join the established league was way too high at $3.2 million. They also thought the Louisville market was actually too small to support a pro basketball franchise, even though the Colonels had been among the ABA's leaders in attendance figures for several years.

"I was real disappointed because we could have been an NBA member," said Dampier. "I don't think they (owners) used the right or honest excuses for why we didn't do it. We knew the money was there, but they said that we didn't have a large enough market or good enough place to play in, which wasn't accurate. Freedom Hall is one of the nicest places there is to play basketball. Even before it was remodeled, it was a great place for players because the background was dark. It was a good shooting arena and sat almost 17,000.

"The interest would have been there (in the NBA) because teams only came in two times a year and that would have brought in all the stars. People could have seen a different star every game and wouldn't have to do like they did the last year in the ABA when we had seven teams. You might see the Virginia Squires twice in a week or once every two weeks. So, going with the NBA, (the league) would have had well over 20 teams. You know if a Magic Johnson was coming in once, people would be there and you'd have a big crowd. If the Phoenix Suns only come in once, you'd have a big crowd. I think the attendance would have been there. The money was there. The people would have supported it and we would have had a good competitive team, too."

So, as the result of the so-called NBA-ABA merger, Dampier went to San Antonio where he played three more years primarily as a key reserve guard. However, things weren't the same. Texas was not home to Dampier. Kentucky was where he belonged. But there was nothing he could do.

"I was not as happy as I would have been staying in Louisville," he said. "It was a good situation if I had to go to another team because I knew all the players on San Antonio. It was an ABA team. I knew the coach (Doug Moe). It was probably the best thing that could have happened to me that I did go down there. It's a beautiful city and I enjoyed it. But after three years of San Antonio, I was ready to go somewhere else."

Dampier retired in 1979 as one of the all-time NBA/ABA leading scorers with 15,279 points, many of them coming from his patented three-point bombs, with an average of 15.9 per game.

In its policing of its member schools, Dampier doesn't care for some of the NCAA's rules or investigative methods.

"I don't always agree with the NCAA," he said. "I think they overstep their bounds and try to control too much. Their rules are vague and there are too many of them. I know there has to be some organized body that controls college basketball but they have so many rules that are (ridiculous). I don't know why they have some of their rules. For instance, recruiting. Former players can't talk to recruits when they come in (not) like they did when I was being recruited."

Dampier explained that if his local school, Oldham County High, had an excellent recruit, he could not even talk to him about Kentucky unless he was authorized by the school. He finds this rule absurd. "(That's) the way I understand the rule," he said. "Supposedly, they took a recruit out to Dan Issel's farm. He wanted to meet Dan Issel. What's wrong with that?

"It's almost like they think Dan is going to put money in his pocket or something. When I was recruited, they had the former players and present players. I think that present players can talk to them and recruit them but not former players. But the former players would be there if you had questions about the program or how they felt when they were there. Like how they felt about Rupp or the school itself. That's usually a good clean recruiting method.

"When I came down, I met a couple of the former players and I had questions about (the program). The coaches had talked to me, but I wanted to know, what's the story with the players? How do they feel? Now you can't do that. For example, Oscar Robertson can't recruit for Cincinnati. That's a rule I don't understand."

On Kentucky being placed on a severe three-year probation by the NCAA in 1989, Dampier said, "I don't know everything that was involved. They did have some (rules violations). I think they (NCAA) wanted to set an example. They wanted to make a point, (saying) 'If we (NCAA) can do this to Kentucky, we can do it to anybody,' and I disagree with that. Why treat Kentucky any differently than another school just because they are one of the top programs, if not the top program in the country?"

Dampier generally agreed the Wildcats were just caught with rules violations. And he pointed out that they are not the only ones who broke the rules. "I agree with that for the most part," he said. "Even though coaches like Bobby Knight and Digger Phelps say that their programs are perfectly clean, they don't have control over the businessmen in the community or anyone else. They (schools) don't have complete control over what these people do. In programs like that, there are going to be people out there doing favors for the players. Some coaches turn their heads. Some, I think, are like Bobby Knight and really don't think it (violations) is going on, but they have to know. To a certain degree, they all break the rules. But, like I said, it's not hard to break the rules when you have so many little petty ones."

Considered a homebody, Dampier, now a 47-year-old grandfather, enjoys the quiet life out in the country in Oldham County. Located fairly close to I-71, his modest home is within easy driving distance of three metropolitan areas — Cincinnati, Louisville and Lexington. And he operates an audio-visual tape distribution business from his home. His family includes his second wife, Judy, whom he married about six years ago. In addition to his two stepsons, he has two grown children from a previous marriage — Nick, who played basketball for Oldham County High in the late 1980s, and Danielle, a recent UK graduate who is now an elementary schoolteacher.

"Little Louie," as he is affectionately known to many Wildcat fans, still goes to UK games at massive Rupp Arena as he has season tickets.

"The main thing (about Rupp Arena) is how much different it is from Memorial Coliseum," he said. "How many more people there are and how much more elaborate everything is. I say (to myself), 'Look at all of these people in this big arena and how things have changed in 20 years.'"

Yes, times have changed. Dampier, of course, is older, too. He may be a grandfather, but he is still "Little Louie" in the hearts of thousands of Wildcat faithful.

5 Rupp's Unorthodox Trainer

"I can't imagine anyone asking coach Rupp if they had to come to practice on Friday or Saturday..."

Adolph F. Rupp and Paul "Bear" Bryant are two of the biggest names in the history of college sports. Yes, while they both were coaching at Kentucky at the same time in the late 1940s and early 1950s, they supposedly didn't get along very well. They were men with big egos and Kentucky had room for only one. They wanted their sports program to be No. 1 in the eyes of Kentuckians. Eventually, Bryant lost out and left the Bluegrass for Texas A&M and later Alabama.

While at Alabama, Bryant, however, said in the mid-1970s that he and Rupp were fairly close even though a lot of people didn't think so. Bryant explained that they just did not chat in public very often.

Dr. Claude Vaughan, who served as the team's trainer and academic advisor for Rupp at UK for several years, agrees that Rupp and Bryant were friends. "In spite of what you read in certain places, he (Rupp) was a great friend and admirer of coach Bryant," he said.

Sometime in the late 1960s in Tuscaloosa, Ala., Kentucky was practicing and shooting around on a Monday morning, preparing for its game against Alabama that night. Vaughan was retrieving and kicking some balls back to the players, and both Rupp and Bryant were chatting on one end of the court.

Rupp called his trainer over and said, looking at Bryant, "Paul, I want you to meet my trainer. This is Dr. Vaughan."

Vaughan and Bryant greeted each other and shook hands. The trainer said, "I'm so glad to meet you. We have a mutual friend, Dude Hennessey (who played football at UK under Bryant and Blanton Collier). We grew up together over in Paris (Kentucky)."

"Oh, yes, yes," Bryant nodded. At that time, Hennessey was an assistant coach for Bryant at Alabama where he served from 1960 to '76.

Then Rupp said, "Now, Paul, I want you to understand that Dr. Vaughan has a Ph.D. in economics. I'm the only coach in the United States that has a Ph.D. in economics for a trainer. Now, I'm just wondering when you're going to get one."

Bryant just smiled.

In late October of 1968, somewhere in the Eastern Kentucky mountains, when Rupp was on his way to make a speech at Lynch, he heard a news bulletin on the radio that the former First Lady, Jackie Kennedy, had just married a hedonistic shipping tycoon from Greece by the name of Aristotle Onassis. And naturally Rupp made a sarcastic remark about her marriage.

"Well, I could imagine why she would marry some young graduate student at Harvard, but marry a G__d____ old Greek? It's beyond my ability to understand!" Rupp told Vaughan who accompanied him on the trip. They had spent the night in Hazard and were going to pick up one of Rupp's former players living in that area, William "Bill" Sturgill, who lettered in 1945 and '46. Currently, Sturgill, a wealthy businessman, serves on UK's Board of Trustees.

Now a respected professor of economics at Eastern Kentucky University in Richmond, Vaughan became involved with the Wildcat basketball program in the fall of 1958 when he was a student at UK. Before coming to UK, where he eventually received all three of his academic degrees, he had served four years of active duty with the U.S. Navy.

"My economics professor asked me after class if I would like to do some tutoring and work with some of the basketball players," Vaughan said. "So, I went over (to the Coliseum) and met with coach Rupp and coach (Harry) Lancaster."

Vaughan continued to work as a professional tutor, except for brief tenures at Ford Motor Company in Louisville and the Tennessee Valley Authority, until 1966. During that time, Rupp had also utilized a trainer to head the academic program for his players and Vaughan assisted the trainer.

In 1966 Rupp and his staff signed a bunch of high school All-Americans, including Dan Issel of Batavia, Ill., and Mike Casey of Simpsonville, Ky., and assembled what would be one of UK's greatest freshman teams in history. The 1966-67 "Super Kittens" finished with an 18-2 mark and had more fun than the varsity team which struggled with a .500 worksheet that season.

During the season, Rupp became concerned with some of his players' classroom performance and he contacted Vaughan. "The whole group (23 players, including the freshmen) wasn't performing very well," Vaughan recalled. "So, coach Rupp called me over and put me in charge of the academic end of it on full-time basis. If you remember, that's the year in which we were 13-13; that was a very, very difficult year for everybody who had any association with the basketball team."

When the season ended, the trainer resigned and Vaughan was asked by Rupp to fill the vacant spot. Vaughan, however, had reservations.

"Claude, you need to take this thing over full-time until we get us a new trainer," Rupp said.

"Well, coach," said Vaughan, "I don't finish my (doctorate) degree until December and that's a bad time to be in the job market — in the middle of the academic year. So, why don't you just make me trainer and everything (including the role of academic advisor), the whole works?"

His comment surprised Rupp, who leaned back in his chair and looked at Vaughan in the eye. "Claude, what do you know about training?"

"I don't know a G___ d____ thing about it, coach," said Vaughan.

"By Gawd, you're hired," Rupp said. "I can't stand those damn trainers. Every one of them thinks they're a medical doctor."

Even though Vaughan did not actually have the proper credentials to be a trainer, he had learned enough to do the basic things required in the job after being with the program for nearly 10 years. "I'd been in the training room and had gone on enough trips with the freshmen; I had learned how to do some things just by being curious; I taped ankles and one thing or another.

"Nobody really helped me get the job. I just sort of evolved into it. Probably, I think Mr. Rupp always did trust me because my cousin had been the team physician for a number of years and coach was very close to him, and I had been fairly successful with running the academic program. Rupp knew that I would be able to do the job."

A number of people helped Vaughan get his feet wet as a team trainer. That number included assistant coach Joe B. Hall, who eventually took over Rupp's post at UK in 1972.

"Joe had been the head coach out at Regis College (in Denver, Colo.)," said Vaughan. "He was also the athletic director. He took care of the laundry, the swimming pool and anything else that had to be needed, including being trainer. So Joe was very helpful to me.

"I read several books. I suppose one should, to be a success in whatever you do, learn what your limitations are. Believe me, I never tried to practice medicine. We had plenty of doctors available at all times."

Besides his other roles as academic advisor for the team and economics instructor at UK, Vaughan managed to stay on as trainer for four years. He quit the team the year before Rupp retired to concentrate on teaching.

Surprisingly, Rupp once offered Vaughan a shot at a coaching career. "Do you want to get into coaching?" Rupp asked his trainer one day. "If you want to get into coaching, I'll get you a good assistant job some place."

"No, coach, I don't think so," said Vaughan who, by the way, never played basketball in high school.

According to Vaughan, Rupp was a strong believer in academics. The coach wanted his players to make good grades, but in the right way. He had even taught a class or two himself at UK. And just to avoid a potential problem that could arise from certain situations, the coach ordered Vaughan not to put any of his players in a class that was taught by the trainer himself. "We never did have any basketball players in my class," Vaughan said. "Coach Rupp was that straight-laced about things. That's why he never got into any trouble."

Rupp had told Vaughan, "I want to tell you this. I'm sure you're smart enough to figure this out yourself but I don't want any of the basketball players in your class."

The trainer/instructor agreed, "Yeah, I didn't intend for any of them to be in my class."

"I thought so," said the coach without false modesty. "And I think it's a shame, because you've been around me long enough that maybe you'll be a great teacher. You've learned it all from me. It's a shame they can't be exposed to that but we're not going to have any conflict of interest."

Said Vaughan, "One of the things that has gotten out of hand lately is that you see and read about so many youngsters today that go to college and play basketball or football and don't manage to graduate. Well, I think the vast majority of the players who played for coach Rupp graduated. Most of the problem is that sometimes they get an ornery spell and don't want to go to class. When I caught them missing class, they only wanted to make one trip to see him (Rupp) during their career. That was enough. If I took them to see coach Lancaster and coach Rupp in tandem, that was about all *anybody* could deal with in one career. No one would want to go through that again.

"I can't imagine anyone asking coach Rupp if they had to come to practice on Friday or Saturday as they wanted to go home. The students would come up to me and say, 'Are you going to do anything important (on Friday)?' I'd just say no, nothing important, go ahead. But no one had the courage to do that to Rupp. I mean he would have blown the roof off the Coliseum.

"We have a group of people today that I find very,

very irresponsible. I was telling my former (department) chairman the other day that some of these people, including faculty, should have to do an internship with Mr. Rupp for about a year and they would find out what responsibility was all about. He was a stickler for doing what you're supposed to do, on or off the floor. It didn't make any difference to him. When you put on a Kentucky uniform and you played for him, you had a certain set of standards — table manners, going to class or behaving yourself — that you had to uphold. It was made perfectly clear to you when you came there that this was expected of you. And I think if you look at the record, the youngsters who stayed and played for him for four years — and most of them graduated — are very, very substantial people. Not very many of them are in jail."

Rupp, who had a very active interest in farming, and Vaughan once traveled to a cattle show. The coach was a good farmer and served as president of Kentucky Hereford Association for many years. At the show someone asked Rupp, "Coach, do you use artificial insemination?"

"No," Rupp shouted back. "I want my bulls to enjoy their work."

This was just one of many funny stories that Vaughan was able to recall about the Baron. "He had a unique sense of humor," Vaughan explained. "He tried to get a message across with humor. I never did hear him say anything derogatory or facetious to a person unless he was trying to get their attention."

According to Vaughan, Rupp did not project the same image to the public as in private life. It was almost like day and night.

"I don't think he gave the same image publicly as he did privately," he said. "Coach Rupp was a big man. He was about 6-4 and he was a pretty towering figure when you were up next to him, unless you were somebody like Dan Issel or Alex Groza. But he had this commanding presence about him.

"I suppose the last 15 years of his life I was as close to him as anybody around. He was very warm, understanding, very bright, articulate, very well read. He was telling me one day about reading Nazi leader Albert Speer's memoirs on organizing the economy of the Third Reich. Well, I had to run out and get the book to read it so I could discuss it with him. We very seldom talked about basketball. We talked about more serious things. He was a very well-educated man. He had a great sense of knowledge of history and we had more intellectual discussions than anything. Occasionally, we talked about the days when he was an undergraduate at Kansas (where) he majored in economics and history. We always had something to talk about.

"He was a very strict disciplinarian, which you saw publicly, but privately he was a very warm and loving person. Of course, my relationship (with Rupp) was unique. He was more of a father image to me than anything else, although I never did try him and I never did test him. He had a great respect for loyalty. Loyalty to him was not being a "yes" man. He also used to say about me, 'If you don't want to know what Claude's thinking, don't ask him because, by God, he'll tell you.' He never got upset with me about anything I ever told him."

On a road trip in January of 1968, upon beating Vanderbilt 94-78 in Nashville, the Wildcats — who were led by heralded sophomores Mike Casey, Dan Issel and Mike Pratt that season — journeyed to Tuscaloosa, Ala., where they were to meet the Crimson Tide. And there, Vaughan felt like a "real" coach during the game, as he sat on the bench near the coaches. Alabama was playing in its old facility; less than a month later, the Tide moved into the new arena named Memorial Coliseum (now called Coleman Coliseum).

"Very seldom did I sit down on the end of the bench where he (Rupp) was," Vaughan said. "We were in Alabama and Russell Rice (who was the school's assistant sports information director at the time) got sick and didn't come to the game so our (student) manager kept the scorebook. So, I sat down and kept the water (cooler) covered up. We had to keep the water covered up because we were playing in the old Foster Auditorium and the birds flew around and defecated in it if you weren't careful.

"But, anyway, coming off a great victory (over Vanderbilt), we were playing very poorly. But we took a run at them, got ahead five, six or seven points and with about five minutes to go in the ball game, he (Rupp) looks over at me."

Rupp said, "You think we ought to put it (the game) in the freezer?"

"Yeah, if you want to get your ass beat," said the trainer.

Rupp's eyes got as big as saucers.

Overhearing the conversation, Lancaster, who was sitting next to Rupp, said, "Well, G__d___ it, Adolph, he's right."

Continuing its running game, Kentucky stopped Alabama 84-76 as 6-2 junior guard Phil Argento scored 24 points. After the contest, Vaughan told the coaches, "Well, you always said that basketball is a game of momentum and I didn't think we ought to risk breaking up the momentum."

In 1971, when Gale Catlett came to Kentucky as an assistant on Rupp's last coaching staff, Rupp said that he wanted him to be like Vaughan, who had resigned from his staff position on the team to devote more attention to teaching on the campus.

"The best advice I can give you, Gale, is to be like Claude Vaughan," Rupp told the new assistant.

Catlett, now head coach at West Virginia, said to himself, "Who is Claude Vaughan?"

So, he sought Vaughan and asked him what Rupp meant by being like Vaughan.

"Well, Gale, he meant that when he asks you something, he wants you to tell him exactly what your opinion is — what you think, not what you think that he wants you to tell him," Vaughan replied, explaining the type of loyalty Rupp expected from his staffers. "He's perfectly capable of making a decision. So, don't worry about that. He's paying you to be honest and straightforward."

Catlett only stayed at Kentucky for one season as Rupp retired the following spring. He went on to the University of Cincinnati where he was named the head coach.

Vaughan, who once babysat ex-UK star Larry

Conley when the trainer lived in Ashland, Ky., as a youngster, was a key participant in the infamous Joe B. Hall-St. Louis episode in 1969, which only lasted several days. Hall, then Rupp's top assistant, had left Kentucky to become the head coach at St. Louis University, only to return to the Commonwealth about a week later with a promise that he would be the next coach at UK when Rupp retired.

At about 1:30 a.m. on a Saturday morning, Vaughan received a phone call from Hall, who had come back to Lexington for a weekend visit with his family. It may well have been the most important phone call of Hall's life as he later got the head coaching job at Kentucky. The trainer had just returned from a trip to Lima, Ohio, with Rupp and assistant Dicky Parsons where they assured a new UK recruit, 6-11 Jim Andrews, who was signed by Hall, that everything would work out. Andrews reportedly had become concerned when Hall left the school.

"We went up to Lima to talk to Jim to make sure that he wasn't too despondent about Joe leaving," Vaughan said. "We gave him some reassurance and when we got back Joe called me on the telephone."

Hall said, "Claude, I'm miserable. (Hall's wife) Katharine's miserable. None of us want to go to St. Louis. Do you think coach Rupp would take me back?"

"Well, I don't know," said Vaughan. "You just left the other day. Joe, I'll tell you what. I'm going to take him (Rupp) to the airport in the morning. He's got a 7:30 a.m. flight — he's going down to Orlando (Fla.) to speak. I'll just pick you up and then I'll pick him up and we can see if we can get you back together."

En route to the airport, Hall and Rupp talked things over and Hall told the Baron that he wanted to come back to UK. But Rupp wasn't ready to say yes before he boarded the flight to Florida.

Upon arriving in Orlando, Rupp dialed Vaughan and said, "What do you think?

"Well, I think Joe made a mistake and he wants to come back as your assistant and that's all there is," Vaughan replied. "He was just a little bit premature in his decision and he wants to get out of the decision and come back as coach."

The next day, which was Sunday, Hall called

Vaughan, saying that he had talked to Rupp (who was returning to Lexington that day) and that he would be leaving town Monday for St. Louis with attorney Harry Miller to try to get a release from Hall's new contract. But Hall wanted a favor from Vaughan — asking Rupp to make a public statement supporting Hall when the assistant returned from St. Louis.

Vaughan recalled, "I talked to coach Rupp and he said, 'Yes, I want Joe Hall to come back as my number one assistant and furthermore, when I retire I would be pleased if he would replace me.' That was the end of Joe's short-lived tenure as head coach at St. Louis. He came back and carried on very well in the Kentucky tradition."

In Vaughan's last season as a member of Rupp's staff in 1970-71, the Wildcats had an abundance of outstanding guards. They were Mike Casey (a senior who sat out the previous season due to a broken leg suffered in an auto accident), Jim Dinwiddie, Kent Hollenbeck, Terry Mills and Stan Key. They were all good enough to start, but Rupp settled on Casey and Hollenbeck as starters for most of the season.

Dinwiddie didn't like it as he thought he outshone Casey in practices, and he felt that Rupp should have chosen him for the starting five. A 6-4 guard from Leitchfield, Ky., who had started in the previous season on a team that included Issel and Pratt, Dinwiddie criticized Vaughan for causing him to lose his starting position, believing the trainer had influenced Rupp to go with Casey in the lineup. Several weeks later on a road trip, Dinwiddie and Vaughan argued in the airplane, engaging in a short brawl.

Despite some dissension on the team, Kentucky captured the SEC championship, and finished with a 22-6 mark and a No. 8 national ranking. The Wildcats also placed five players on UPI's All-SEC teams — Casey (first team), forward Tom Parker and 7-2 center Tom Payne (second team), and forward Larry Steele and Hollenbeck (third team).

Generally speaking, Rupp enjoyed a good relationship with the news media. When they wrote articles that Rupp didn't particularly like, he didn't take them personally. And he treated all reporters the same whether they were from the *New York Times* or the smallest weekly newspaper in the state of Kentucky or even the school newspaper. He was a good copy for the sportswriters who would pick up many of his colorful quotes.

And Rupp once gave advice to Vaughan after the trainer got upset over a story about himself and the team. Appearing in a Louisville newspaper, the 1970 article, dealt with six Wildcat players getting caught drinking at a bar near Starkville, Miss., earlier in the week when they faced the Mississippi State Bulldogs. On Sunday night, assistant coach Hall and Vaughan saw the players violate team training rules for visiting the bar. Moments after UK's 86-57 victory over Mississippi State behind Mike Pratt's game highs of 26 points and 18 rebounds, Rupp told reporters that two of the players involved in the tavern incident — senior Randy Pool and junior Bob McCowan — were dismissed from the squad. Previously, they both had been suspended for missing curfew. Rupp had warned them that if they got into more trouble, they would be kicked off the squad. Other players involved in the tavern incident were Art Laib, Clint Wheeler, Randy Noll and Hollenbeck.

"A sportswriter made some sort of derogatory remark about me," Vaughan commented. "So, I walked into coach Rupp's office that morning after the paper came out and I showed him the article. I was upset."

Leaning back in his chair, Rupp said, "Now, Claude, don't be thin skinned about something like that. Wait until you pick up the paper and read where some s_o_ b___ is suing you for $25 million."

On his players drinking in that Mississippi bar, Rupp said, "Boys will be boys." He didn't get too excited about things like that.

McCowan, who returned to the team a year and a half later as a senior, publicly criticized Vaughan, describing the trainer as overbearing and a "hawk." The player admitted that he had made some poor judgments, but did not like the way Vaughan was doing his job, "hawking" the team by keeping a very close eye on the players.

Vaughan understands why Rupp was basically successful in his dealings with the press, even though the media in New York City were especially harsh on him.

"I think that was one of his great attributes," he said. "He didn't take things personally and I think that's one of the reasons he got along well with the press. He was great copy but he didn't let things get to him. I don't see how he coached as long as he did. I think that's one reason he coached as long as he did because he could stand the pressure better than anyone I've ever encountered."

Married to Carol, his wife of nearly 35 years, with three grown children, Vaughan says today he still misses Rupp as a close friend. He was one of the 10 pallbearers in Rupp's 1977 funeral.

"There's never a day in my life that goes by that something happens that I don't reflect upon the many things that he taught me," Vaughan said. "I would venture to say that most of the people associated with him very long have the same feeling. His loss was very tough. I miss him very much and I loved him very much. He was a great influence in my life."

6 A WILDCAT POLITICIAN

"I don't think it (being an
ex-basketball player) will get
you elected, but...
it will help..."

Many of Adolph Rupp's former players are or were involved in state politics, including George Atkins who became state auditor, and Jim LeMaster who is state representative from Paris, among others. And Scotty Baesler is another one. He is perhaps the best known politician among ex-Rupp players.

"I like politics. I enjoy it," Baesler smiled.

The hard-working Baesler admits that he is not the most "colorful" person in the Bluegrass. He does not have a lot of charisma, but he seems to be satisfied with himself. When he runs for office, he doesn't appear to be too concerned about his lack of appeal to some potential voters. He feels the people will look at his qualifications, not his lack of charisma. But, what if Kentucky's charismatic coach Rick Pitino decides to run for something? Well, that's a whole new ball game.

Baesler, who has been elected three times (1981, 1985 and 1989) as mayor of Lexington, was running a political race for Kentucky governorship as a 1991 Democratic candidate when the interview for this book took place. By the way, one of Baesler's opponents in the governor's race favored the legalization of marijuana.

A former Wildcat starting guard in the early 1960s, he acknowledges that name recognition from his playing days certainly doesn't hurt when he is on a campaign trail.

"I don't think it will get you elected, but I think people sometimes refer to it," he said in his downtown office in Lexington. "If I walk door to door in Lexington and Fayette County, which I did, seven out of 10 people talked to me about basketball when I played, although it's been 25 years. So, I think basketball makes for a real warm spot. UK basketball is a warm spot for a lot of people. It will help obviously, but it won't get me elected.

"It will get my foot in the door and a lot of people identify with it. The good thing about being an ex-basketball player, you get better as you get older. You get better than you actually were," he smiled.

Former Kentucky coach Joe B. Hall has helped Baesler in the gubernatorial race. He accompanied the Lexington mayor on several campaign swings throughout the state. Hall does not shy away from politics. Previously, he was involved in several other campaigns, even during the time he coached the Wildcats.

When Baesler was a youngster growing up on his parents' farm in Athens, a tiny community located in the southeastern part of Fayette County, he followed basketball very little. He enjoyed baseball. That was in late 1940s and early 1950s.

"I liked baseball players quite a bit," he recalled. "Warren Spahn (who was elected to the Hall of Fame in 1973) pitched for the Boston Braves. Spahn was my favorite and also Henry Aaron (the home run king who became a Hall of Famer in 1982). Those were the two I primarily liked at that time as far as baseball players were concerned."

Later, his interest in basketball grew and Baesler became a roundball hero at Athens High School and then as a senior at the newly-established Bryan Station High where he was the valedictorian of his class.

In 1959, Baesler sort of made history when he became the first Bryan Station High athlete to be given a major athletic scholarship at Kentucky. Baesler tried to downplay the feat.

"Yes, that is true, but you have to keep in mind that

was the first year of Bryan Station High School," he pointed out. "So, that would be sort of misleading. We had closed a small school (Athens High) where I went."

Before selecting Kentucky, Baesler was also being recruited by a couple of other schools — Western Kentucky and the Citadel.

While at UK, Baesler and his steady girlfriend, Alice Woods, whom he had met during the summer before his senior year in high school, planned to get married. The couple were the very first Mr. and Miss Bryan Station High.

"When I was a sophomore, I was going to get married but according to Rupp you could not be married and play," he said. "So, I didn't get married. We just waited two years and got married after college."

Rupp once complained that if he allowed his players to marry, they would not be concentrating on basketball as they should. The coach explained that they would worry about their families, finding ways to buy clothes and putting food on the kitchen table. Not to mention their homework assignments or studying for exams. So, basketball would be a low priority on their list, Rupp bemoaned.

Like Baesler, his wife is a UK graduate. They own a 375-acre farm in Fayette County, raising tobacco and beef cattle. His wife "runs the farm. It's a fairly large farm operation," said Baesler. "I haven't moved from the place I was born .... on the same farm, but we live in a different house." They also have two grown children who are in their early twenties. Baesler's father, Henry, was a tenant farmer, while his grandfather served as janitor of a local school at one time.

During his playing days at Kentucky, Baesler was not a superstar, but he was a competent performer. The 5-11 floor general was well respected by opposing coaches.

In his last two seasons, Baesler averaged in double figures and had a single-game high of 26 points against third-ranked Southern Cal in a 79-77 setback at Memorial Coliseum during his junior year. The loss was only one of three that UK suffered in the 1961-62 campaign. That 23-3 squad finished the year with a No. 3 national ranking in the final Associated Press poll, just ahead of No. 4 Mississippi State. The Starkville, Miss., school at that time was guided by Babe McCarthy, who later coached the Kentucky Colonels in the ABA.

Baesler, who was described by some of his former teammates and teachers as being quiet, determined and smart, said his relationship with Rupp was not a real close one. But he admired the coach.

"Coach Rupp was a very strict disciplinarian," said the mayor. "Everything we did was very organized and my relationship (with him) was very businesslike. I came in from high school and everybody else that came to UK had also been a basketball star. So, we had to get adjusted to not being a star any longer. My relationship was very good because he was a person you respected. You learned to be disciplined and you learned to devote all your time to basketball."

At a practice or a game Rupp often used cutting remarks directed at his players when he got angry, Baesler recalled.

"Coach Rupp used sarcasm as a way to motivate you," he said. "He could make you feel very small when he criticized you because you didn't do the right thing. Criticism in a sarcastic way encouraged you to do better.

"But one thing they (teammates) always told me was, 'If they (the coaches) didn't get after you, they didn't like you.' So, then you better start worrying if they didn't get after you because they didn't care what you did. You kind of kept that in your mind."

Although many of the players were intimidated by Rupp's presence, Baesler said, "He wasn't an intimidator. He was more of a motivator by sarcasm. If you couldn't take the criticism, you weren't going to play."

When Baesler was a senior, the Wildcats ran into difficulties on the hardwood floor as they went 16-9, drawing tons of criticisms from the news media and impatient fans. Some furious fans even questioned Rupp's coaching ability at the age of 61.

"That was the worst record in the history of UK at the time," commented Baesler who was also the team captain. "Since that time, there have been worse (records). There was a lot of criticism because nobody at Kentucky accepted the fact 16-9 was a very good year and it wasn't. We should have won more games.

"The year before we were loved and the next year we weren't loved as much. We had plenty of experience. We just did not have a good year. I don't think I did as well as I could have. I think (Cotton) Nash did not have as good a year."

Speaking of Baesler's star teammate, Nash was not able to match his blazing sophomore success that season as a junior. (As a sophomore, Nash had led the SEC in scoring with a 23-point average and was named a consensus second-team All-American.) The 6-5 center/ forward simply did not receive enough help as he was double or triple-teamed by opponents. And the Wildcats did not have a deadly sharpshooter from the outside to force the enemies to play honest defense as they had lost 6-1 All-SEC guard Larry Pursiful to graduation. However, Nash — whose high school coach in Indiana was Cliff Barker, a member of Kentucky's "Fabulous Five" — again became All-American, an honor he would repeat the following season. (As a senior, Nash became the school's all-time leading scorer with 1,770 points. He held the record until 1970 when Dan Issel finished with 2,138 career points, a feat which still stands.)

Reflecting on the 1962-63 campaign, Baesler said it helped him handle all kinds of adversities later in life. "That season prepared me for anything that might follow. Nothing could be tougher," he said.

After graduation from UK Law School in 1966, Baesler found work as an attorney. But he continued to play his favorite sport for several years for the local YMCA and Jerry's Restaurant teams. Later, he became player-coach of the Lexington Marathon Oil touring squad, which was a perennial national contender in AAU (Amateur Athletic Union) competition. The team included several standouts like former UK stars Jim Andrews, Mike Pratt,

Jimmy Dan Conner and Larry Stamper, and former Eastern Kentucky University stars George Bryant, Boyd Lynch and Daryl Dunagan.

Baesler, who also holds a bachelor's degree in accounting from UK, held several public offices before becoming mayor of Lexington in 1981.

Many basketball fans have suggested that "Kentucky just got caught as all schools do it" in regard to UK's three-year probation placed by the NCAA in 1989 for rules violations. Baesler doesn't agree with this theory.

"No, I don't believe the theory that everybody does it so it's OK," he said. "I think that's behind us. I think coach Pitino has done an outstanding job along with (athletic director) C. M. Newton. I think we need to go on from here and not worry too much about the violations and whether they were right, wrong or indifferent. They're imposed and we should quit dwelling on them and move on."

7 FROM HAZARD TO LEXINGTON

"At the press
conference here, I said
it was un-American for the
NCAA to tell us that we can't
sell a subscription to
our newspaper."

During the days of the Vietnam War, a young newspaperman in Hazard, Ky., wrote a column about a sportswriter from Louisville who was critical of Kentucky coach Adolph Rupp. And Rupp somehow read that article which appeared in a weekly newspaper in eastern Kentucky, about 150 miles away from Lexington. The author of the column, Oscar Combs, a promising editor, was astonished to find out that Rupp was among those who read the column.

The Baron liked what Combs had to say. "I got a letter in the mail one day from Adolph Rupp, thanking me for my column supporting him and I was just on cloud nine!" Combs recalled. "He said if I ever came to Lexington, to drop in and visit with him. I left in about 15 minutes."

Sitting in his cluttered office in Lexington where he is presently the publisher of the highly-successful *The Cats' Pause* magazine, Combs said that letter from Rupp is one which "I will cherish the rest of my life."

Combs, a Perry County native who began writing sports stories at the age of 15, said his association with Rupp was very limited. Especially when Rupp was coaching.

"I didn't know him that well," Combs said. "I did cover a lot of the (UK) games, thanks to Russell Rice, who was the school's sports information director at that time. I started coming to the games around 1967 and I always went to five or six a year.

"I didn't go back into the locker room. You weren't allowed in the locker room when Rupp was here. He would come outside and give you two or three quotes. He would say, 'Cotton Nash thinks that we didn't rebound very well tonight.' And if you want to know what Louie Dampier said, (Rupp would say) 'He said he just couldn't hit the long shot tonight.' That was as close as you got to a player to get a quote from him. He handed you what he said they said."

After Rupp retired from UK, Combs' relationship with the Baron grew. He saw Rupp in a different light, as a changed person.

"I got to know him fairly well when he was with the (Kentucky) Colonels because he would come to Hazard quite frequently," Combs said. "He would always come to visit (businessman and politician) Willie Dawahare. Willie was a good friend of mine and whenever Rupp was coming to town, Willie would always call me and invite me out to lunch with them.

"When I moved to Lexington in 1976, I got to spend quite a bit of time with him (for nearly two years before Rupp died in 1977). I got to know him a lot better. I can't say it was Adolph Rupp as he was when he coached because I am sure he changed. He was a very hurt person late in his life. He felt ignored, unwanted, and that hurt me a lot. He had done so much."

One day Combs conducted an interview with Rupp which he will never forget. It involved the former coach's unflattering comments about Dr. Otis Singletary, who was UK president from from 1969 to 1987.

"He really did not like Singletary," Combs said. "He hated him. The parting of ways came when he (Rupp) had to retire. I'll never forget I was doing an interview with him once at his home. He had his radio tuned to WVLK and, suddenly, there was a news bulletin and it said that Singletary was considering an appointment to the Carter Administration in Washington, D.C. He turned to me and said, 'That damn Singletary, hell, he ain't leaving here. He's just trying to get a new contract.'

"Singletary probably wasn't the villain he was made out to be but coach Rupp was old and I think he deserved a more gentle way of going out, although I don't know how a gentle way could be made. When it is time for a person to leave and he doesn't want to, then nothing is rational to him. But I think it was sad that there couldn't have been a better way to end it, and I am not saying any particular person is at fault."

During the hot summer days of 1988 when the NCAA was investigating Kentucky's basketball program, Combs was one of the people they wanted to talk to.

Combs said he would be glad to discuss things with them because he had "nothing to hide."

Among the subjects that the NCAA reportedly wanted to discuss with Combs included a talent scout from Columbus, Ohio; prep star Lawrence Funderburke, also of Columbus; and Combs' two publications — *The Cats' Pause* and *Big Blue Basketball*.

For a few years, Combs ran a full page called "Big Blue Penetration" in *The Cats' Pause* which the readers could use to buy gift subscriptions to be sent to high school libraries throughout the state. The NCAA officials cried foul, saying it created a big recruiting advantage for Kentucky. Also, they don't want to believe that his two publications are financially independent.

"They just can't believe that there are enough people paying for this to make it go, so they think that some big supporter of the basketball program is writing us a secret check to keep this going," Combs explained. "Now, if this is true, we are part of the university and we shouldn't be allowed to write all this recruiting stuff."

But the NCAA balked at meeting with Combs when he demanded that their conversations be tape recorded. According to an NCAA policy, their investigative conversations should not be recorded. (NCAA has since changed that policy, allowing the recorders to be used during interviews.) Combs subsequently held a press conference to explain the circumstances surrounding the NCAA's investigation of his publications and UK.

"At the press conference here I said it is un-American

for the NCAA to tell us that we can't sell a subscription to our newspaper," Combs recalled. "They were trying to tell me that I could not sell subscriptions for gifts to high schools out in the state. (They said) it was illegal and an unfair recruiting tool for UK. My comeback was that this was First Amendment rights. We can sell a newspaper to anybody we want to."

Combs says no one, including UK and NCAA officials, can tell him what to do, except for his faithful subscribers. He has about 18,000 bosses.

"Some of the people at the university don't like me," he said. "If I had one big advertiser and that advertiser said, 'Oscar, you print this and you are finished.' But I have 18,665 owners or bosses. No 10 of them would break me. Now, if all 18,665 decide I'm no good then I'm out of business. If they say that, I should be out of business. But as long as they hold together, I'm safe."

The Cats' Pause doesn't carry many advertisements. Instead, it derives most of the revenue from subscription sales. Combs generally agrees with the theory that many universities commit rules violations and that Kentucky just got entangled by the NCAA in 1989.

"I think there is a great deal more truth in that than a lot of people want to believe," he said. "I agree with (the theory), but it should be qualified. The qualification is that it doesn't make any difference. There are murders committed every day, but that doesn't give me a license to go out and commit one tomorrow.

"I think Kentucky was guilty and they were penalized and probably penalized fairly. The sad part is that most of the people who commit the crime are not going to get caught. We hear every day that crime doesn't pay. If crime really didn't pay, people wouldn't be committing it. Whether it is robbery or murder or whatever, for most of the people crime does pay. It only doesn't pay if you get caught.

"Now I think the thing that hurts me most and I admit that I was wrong, is I badly misjudged (former Kentucky president Dr.) David Roselle. I really, really believed in him, but now when I look back I see that he served Kentucky's head on a platter and said 'Here, NCAA take it.' He's not become a hero to those people who want to clean up college and make it pure. That ain't going to happen. You are not going to clean up the medical profession, the legal profession, the mechanic profession. You are not going to clean up any profession.

"There was a great one-hour documentary on ABC-TV. A news documentary called 'Lying, Stealing and Cheating in America.' If you watched that, it told you what is wrong with America. It took big business. It took religion. It took sports. It took government. Kentucky was part of it (the moral decay in society). What it said was it's everywhere. There are still a few good people, but the moral fiber of our country has deteriorated so quickly they are hard to find.

"I think basically that Kentucky is no worse or better than the others. In the Eric Manuel thing (academic fraud case), they would have never known if Roselle hadn't told them. I'm not advocating that Roselle should have hid it, but he did hide it for two years before he turned it over to them. He knew in the fall of his (Manuel's) freshman year. He did nothing about it 'till the NCAA came in.

"My personal feeling is that Roselle, after about a year, decided he wanted to get rid of (coach) Eddie Sutton because of Sutton's personal problems but he couldn't do it because people would say, 'Well, why didn't you get rid of him last year?' So, he had to wait till something happened and when the NCAA came in, it became very convenient. It is obvious because Oklahoma State hired him (Sutton) and the NCAA said they had no problem with him. If the NCAA had no problem with him, why did Roselle fire him? He did fire him!"

Practically all of his life, Combs, the fifth of eight children, has been associated with a publication in one capacity or another. First, he sold the *Hazard Herald* when he was six or seven years old so he could buy a bicycle, among other things.

"I wanted to buy a bicycle in the worst way," said Combs, who is now in his late 40s. "You won't believe this but bicycles back then were $52.00, higher then than they are now. I wanted one to deliver papers."

Combs' father, who ran a post office and a small general store, purchased the bicycle with the promise that the youngster would pay for it. It was his father's way of teaching responsibility.

"You can have one but you have to pay for it," the father told the boy. "You have to sign this agreement and you've got to pay for it out of the paper sales."

Combs continued selling newspapers on his route and paid $2.50 every week on the new bicycle until it was paid for.

"It took almost a year (to pay off) because there were some finance charges involved," Combs smiled. "That was my first link with the paper."

Years later, Combs started to write sports articles for the local newspaper. And, as a sophomore at Dilce Combs High School in Perry County in 1960, he worked for the *Louisville Courier-Journal* as a prep correspondent for the 14th Region. The sports editor of the *Courier-Journal* at the time was Earl Cox, who some 30 years later did a statewide radio show with Combs and wrote a weekly column for *The Cats' Pause.*

On a recommendation from *Hazard Herald* editor Fred Luigart, Jr., Combs was approached by Cox at a high school regional basketball tournament about a writing job and the kid tried to downgrade his talent, lacking confidence to send in scores and write for a big, established newspaper

"I can't write for the *Courier-Journal*," a shaken and surprised Combs told Cox. The *Courier-Journal* at the time was regarded as one of the top newspapers in the country.

Cox turned deaf. "You just do the best you can and we will doctor it up," he said.

"So, I did and Earl would clean it (the story) up," Combs later said.

Ironically, Rupp was at the game, scouting a couple of players. "They (Luigart and Cox) introduced me to Rupp and I was in heaven," Combs laughed.

Combs will always remember his first paycheck from the *Courier-Journal.*

"The very first month I got a check from them," he said, "and it was $65.00. That was a lot of money."

Combs thought there was a mistake in the amount of the check. He called Cox and asked him about it.

"Mr. Cox, I've got this check here and there must be some mistake," Combs said.

"What do you mean?" Cox wondered.

"It is for $65," Combs said.

"Whose name is on it?" Cox said.

"It says Oscar Combs," said the youngster.

"Well, it is yours," said Cox. He abruptly hung up the phone.

Like any high school kid, Combs was just "tickled to death" to get the check.

A few years later at Cumberland College, a small Baptist school located in Williamsburg, Ky., where Combs was majoring in English (the school didn't have a journalism program), he continued to work part-time for the *Courier-Journal*, submitting scores and articles. But, an honest Combs had a question about another paycheck.

"The first week that I started doing it in college, I got a check for $200," Combs said. "I knew there was a mistake on that."

So, Combs called Cox again, repeating almost the same episode he had when he was in high school.

"Mr. Cox, I know there is an error this time," said Combs. "I can't afford to pay you back if I cash it. I need to send it back and get the right amount."

"How much did you say it was for?" Cox said.

"Two hundred dollars," said the kid.

"Whose name is on it?" Cox questioned.

"Oscar Combs," said the kid.

"Well, then, it is yours," said an irritated Cox. "What are you bothering me for?" He abruptly hung up.

Looking back to his younger days when he didn't have a lot of money, Combs said he is very thankful to Cox.

"It never really dawned on me until I got out of school what he was doing for me," Combs recalled. "So, I owe an awful lot to Earl Cox. He helped me when I needed it the most."

In 1962, when Combs graduated from high school, Cox wanted the youngster to attend the University of Kentucky. But Combs never did because he was scared to death of UK.

"When I was a senior in high school, Earl kept wanting me to go to UK," he said. "I kept using the excuse of saying I couldn't afford to. I told him so and he said that's not a problem."

Actually, Combs said the excuse was "people in Eastern Kentucky have always been told that they are not as good as other people, that we are not as talented, that we can't compete against them, and that we're backward and inferior to other people. I bought that and I was afraid of failure and afraid to go to UK.

"I wanted to go to either Eastern Kentucky or Cumberland. I couldn't afford to go to Eastern. I couldn't really afford to go anywhere unless I got a scholarship. Cumberland never turned a person away if they wanted to go to school.

"Dr. (James M.) Boswell (who was president of Cumberland at the time) was the greatest humanitarian that ever lived. So, I went over to Cumberland with my father and met Dr. Boswell. They gave me a half scholarship and a half workship. I didn't have to pay anything."

Combs never did finish college, lacking 16 hours for his degree. He departed to take a $90-a-week position at the *Hazard Herald* as news editor to support himself and his wife, the former Donna Alexander who was his high school sweetheart. "That was big, big money," Combs said.

Also, he didn't really care for school.

"I was itchy to get out and, quite frankly, I never did like school that well," Combs admitted. "I really went to school because I like sports. I was the sports information director for three years at Cumberland and did some work in the public relations office."

By the time Combs started to work for the *Hazard Herald*, there was an editor who was just leaving. The fellow's name was Gurney Norman who today is a well-known Kentucky author. He had left the mountains for sunny California to join the peace movement in the Vietnam War era, according to Combs. "He wasn't a hard-line protester," commented Combs. "He was a little calmer than most of them. He was a great writer." Norman is currently a faculty member in the English Department at UK.

For the next 10 years, the Combses stayed in the

Hazard area, managing and publishing various newspapers. In 1975, they sold one of their two publications to a big newspaper chain from Virginia. *The East Kentucky Voice* was sold for a sizeable profit.

Later, Combs thought of moving to Cumberland where he also owned a small newspaper, *The Tri-City News*. But things didn't pan out and the publication was eventually sold.

With the help of a generous profit from the sale of *The East Kentucky Voice*, the Combses moved to Lexington in 1976 to launch a new weekly magazine devoted to UK and Southeastern Conference sports called the *The Cats' Pause*.

Because of an agreement Combs made with the Virginia company, he could not reveal the selling price of *The East Kentucky Voice*. However, according to various newspaper reports, the purchase price was nearly $230,000. He had purchased *The East Kentucky Voice* for $25,000 in 1972.

Several times Combs had refused to sell his newspaper but the Virginia-based Worrell Newspapers chain would not give up.

Finally, in a negotiating session, Combs "wrote out a figure that I thought was about three times what it was worth. I wrote it on a piece of paper, turned around and handed it to two fellows who were there together. One was with the company and the other was their lawyer. They looked at it and looked at each other and then at me. They said, 'How do you want it?' I said, 'What do you mean?' They said, 'How do you want the money — do you want it all right now or do you want it in three years or what?' I said, 'You have to be kidding.' So, we cut the deal.

"I will never forget it because it happened during the 1975 Cincinnati-Boston World Series. I went out and told Donna we've made a deal, I've sold it (the newspaper) and we are going to the World Series in Cincinnati."

After driving to Cincinnati, Combs bought his wife a new automobile. "I bought her a Lincoln Continental and in less than 24 hours we were watching the Reds beat the Red Sox," he said.

So now, after both newspapers were sold, Combs had become an early retiree at the age of 32. But he had an interesting venture in the back of his mind.

One day, in 1976, he received a phone call from his good friend, UK public relations official Ray Hornback.

"Hey, Oscar, we've got an alumni excursion to New York for the NIT (where Kentucky was to participate)," said Hornback. "You and Donna ought to go. You have nothing to do. You can't say you have to work."

The Combses took a bus to Cincinnati and they flew to New York. It was his wife's first flight. Understandably, she was rather uneasy. "Donna was scared the whole time flying," he smiled.

During Kentucky's first game in the NIT against Niagara at Madison Square Garden, the Combses met three interesting men who were sitting in front of them wearing fancy three-piece suits. It was pretty obvious that they were not from Kentucky, but they were big Wildcat fans.

So, by Kentucky's third game in the NIT, Combs began to ask these three men some questions, like a nosy reporter.

"Where are you all from?" asked a curious Combs.

"I'm from Manhattan," said one fellow.

"Where are your buddies from?" Combs asked.

"Well, we are all here but he is from Connecticut and I'm from Manhattan and he's from upstate New York," said the man.

"What is your Kentucky connection?" Combs asked.

Combs was surprised to learn that they did not have any ties with Kentucky.

"We're just big Kentucky fans," said the man.

How did they become Wildcat followers?

"Well, we've always listened to them on WHAS (from Louisville)," the man said. "We've heard a lot about them since the fifties but we have never even been to the state of Kentucky."

That was the beginning of a special but risky project soon to be called *The Cats' Pause*.

Combs said, "That got me to thinking. If I run into three people at Madison Square Garden who are big

Kentucky fans, there might be something for this magazine."

He reasoned that if there were Wildcat fans 750 miles away from the Bluegrass, surely there were plenty more of them in the rest of the nation.

So, the rest is history. The first issue of *The Cats' Pause* was published in September of 1976, with a cover photo of UK linebacker Jim Kovach in color. In the first year, the magazine's circulation figure hit about 400 before it mushroomed to over 20,000 subscribers several years later.

At first, it appeared the magazine might not make it. Times were bleak. "After the first two months I questioned whether we could survive three months," Combs said. "In fact, there was a period of four or five months where I sat down and asked 'What have I gotten myself into?' I came to believe I was stupid to do this because things weren't taking off."

The independent magazine is now the oldest tabloid of its type — publications which cover a particular team or school — in the nation.

Before Combs actually began his publication, he contacted UK's top sports officials — athletic director Cliff Hagan, basketball coach Joe B. Hall and football coach Fran Curci — about his new venture. He wanted their approval.

Curci was somewhat cool toward the project. "Fran was sort of lukewarm about the idea," Combs said. "Not against it but lukewarm."

Then Combs wrote a letter the following week to Hagan and Hall, telling them that he would like to meet with them individually.

Like Curci, Hagan expressed some reservations. But Hall had other ideas. "I went and talked to Joe and Joe was just sky high," Combs recalled. "He said, 'What can I do for you.' And he didn't know me from Joe Blow."

Since Hall liked the idea of a publication about the Wildcats, Combs decided that he would go ahead with his magazine even though Hagan and Curci did not actually give their approval.

"Joe was all for it and I had already decided that unless someone was totally against it, I would pursue it, without anything in writing," Combs said. "If one was against it, I would think about it. If two were totally against it, I would just back off and not pursue it. Well, nobody was against it. And Joe was strongly in favor of it, and I thought that was the key factor because basketball is the big thing. Curci was sort of for it, but he wanted to make sure that he was going to be able to control me."

Combs received national attention in July of 1981 when he and associate editor Gene Abell broke a story in *The Cats' Pause* that Kentucky Gov. John Y. Brown Jr. wanted former Washington Redskins coach George Allen to replace Curci as the head football coach at UK. Both Gov. Brown and Allen later confirmed the article.

Allen, who was 59 at the time, said he was very interested and indicated that he would like to be the Wildcat mentor when the position became vacant. He had been visiting Gov. Brown and his wife, Phyllis George Brown, and was a guest of theirs at the Kentucky Derby.

Some say the rift between Brown and Curci had started a couple of years before when Brown asked the coach to campaign for him in the governor's race. Curci refused. So Brown began to apply pressure to remove Curci from the job. Brown also had been unhappy with Kentucky's embarrassing off-the-field problems and its lack of success on the field.

But Curci won the power struggle as he still had four years remaining on his contract and the faithful support of UK president Dr. Singletary and former Kentucky Gov. A. B. "Happy" Chandler. And Allen backed out of the highly-publicized affair.

Just over four months later, Curci was gone after his Wildcats compiled a 3-8 mark, his fourth consecutive losing season at UK.

Speaking of the Brown-Allen-Curci episode, Combs said it marked one of the most disturbing moments of his journalism career.

"The time of Curci's departure, or that period when Fran's future was being determined, was disturbing because it was the first time in my life in journalism I ever felt the sword being stuck in me because I was a messenger," Combs said. "You always hear, 'Shoot the messenger.' We found out about the story and we broke it even though we were in the summer editions where we only printed once a month. We sat on it for two weeks and then wrote the story.

"I don't know that Ourci has ever forgiven me. He felt that I had broken allegiance to him and the program by printing that story but all we were doing was printing a legitimate news story. I guess maybe as time goes along, you change. I guess maybe I can sense a little bit of how he felt at that time toward me, even though I thought it was unfair then and I think it is unfair now. Putting myself in his shoes, I can see how he may have felt at the time but I didn't do it to harm him. I did it as a news story but he really was upset."

Throughout his journalism career, Combs has met a lot of interesting characters and become friends with some of them. LSU basketball coach Dale Brown is one of those people.

"Dr. Jekyll and Mr. Hyde!" Combs said of Brown. "Dale is the type of fellow who, after two or three meetings, is a great guy or the biggest hypocrite you ever met. One or the two. There is no in-between."

Sometime during the late 1970s, Combs once wrote a column that Brown didn't appreciate. In fact, Brown was angry enough to call the sleepy-eyed Combs at one o'clock in the morning from an SEC town where his traveling Tigers had a national television date with an SEC rival the next day.

"He brings up this column that had been written months and months earlier," Combs said. "He was on the phone for about an hour just ripping me. Quite frankly, I'm sure he did not know me by sight. He goes on and on, and says he is never going to speak to me again. He would never allow me to do an interview. If I'm in a room while he is doing a press conference, he will stop talking until I leave."

Combs said, "O.K."

However, after a silent pause, Brown had a change of heart.

"Oscar, you are a nice guy," said the LSU coach. "Let's forget about all the past and let's be friends again.

Let's have dinner sometime."

Combs said Brown's sudden attitude change caught him off guard. "That blew my mind," he said. "We did chat two or three times after that and we got to be pretty good friends over the years."

During the 1986 SEC Tournament in Lexington, Combs' wife and eight-year-old daughter Amy were relaxing and enjoying the festive atmosphere at Rupp Arena and Brown happened to be sitting in front of them. Amy had a book with her. She was reading it since the Wildcats were not playing.

Brown noticed that and struck up a conversation with her.

"Why are you reading a book?" Brown wondered.

"Well, I have to go to school tomorrow and I have to do some studying," said Amy.

"Do you read your book when Kentucky plays?" Brown asked.

"No, I root for Kentucky," she said proudly.

And Brown later sent her a surprise gift. He gave Amy a T-shirt.

In the following year, during the SEC Tournament in Atlanta, Brown recognized Amy at a press conference, even though she was sitting in the back, away from the spotlight. Amy and her mother had made the trip with Oscar, who was covering the tournament.

"Dale gets to talking philosophy and he turns around and hollers at Amy," remembered her father. "He asks her to come up there and he starts talking to her. So, she wrote him a letter and he wrote her a letter. They (the writers) wrote a column on how even Dale Brown has a fan in Kentucky.

"The point is, I guess, is that he struck up this conversation (with Amy at Rupp Arena) and he remembered her and he recognized her. Brown is real good about this. He is a master motivator, master mind reader and he knows these things. I tend to think that there is a lot of good in Dale Brown. He came from a tough background (in Minot, N.D., where he did not have a father, resulting in an impoverished childhood). Everything he's done he had to do on his own. Nothing can keep you down if you really want to get ahead. I admire Dale."

The Sporting News, the St. Louis-based weekly, has been called by many fans "the sports Bible." However, some people, especially Kentucky Wildcat followers, didn't like the magazine's apparent "negative" journalistic attitude toward Kentucky in the 1980s. Combs, once a faithful subscriber to *The Sporting News*, didn't like its journalism style, either.

"I want to plead guilty to something that most people wouldn't," Combs said. "I probably shouldn't. I've not read a copy of *The Sporting News* in about five years. It is a terrible thing to say. For years, from the time I was probably 16 up until about five years ago, *The Sporting News* was the Bible in my house. I got every issue. In fact, I've got some old ones at home. But about five years ago I came to the realization that in their guidelines they have a list of people that they like and a list they don't like. Whenever they write about someone, they use that narrow view.

"For years I thought they really picked on Notre Dame football. I don't know why. They also jumped on the Eddie Sutton story real big when it (the Mills-Casey-Emery incident) happened. And that was the same Eddie Sutton that they glorified when he was in Arkansas. When he came to Kentucky, they started talking about all his personal problems.

"Well, those problems started in Arkansas, but they didn't expose them then. I think this is one of the things Eddie had a hard time dealing with. He had this illness (alcoholism) but it wasn't a problem with people until he got to Kentucky.

"For example, my own daughter was sitting at the table when we were eating and she threw some mashed potatoes. First time she has ever done it, and we all laughed and had a big time, and she giggles. The next night she does the same thing. We jerk her up and wham, wham, wham. Now, she is puzzled because the first time it made us laugh and have fun, and the second time she gets a spanking. Her mind was all mixed up.

"I think this is what happened to Eddie. He was a good guy at Arkansas and when he came to Kentucky, he was a bad guy. I think this is *The Sporting News'* way.

There are certain groups of people who are bad guys. And there are certain people who are good guys and can do no wrong. If the good guys do something wrong, they just ignore it and don't record it. If the bad guys do something right, well, they should have been doing things right all along."

Combs enjoyed *The Sporting News* because he loves to read the gossip, but "the next day after I read it I wondered if I could really rely on it. I knew some of it was not truthful. When they tell me a negative story about Texas A&M, how do I know that they are not just upset with them? Once you lose your credibility, you have lost everything."

The Sporting News, however, has somewhat changed its tune in the Pitino Era at Kentucky. Pitino graced the magazine's cover early in 1991 as he revived the Wildcat fever in the Bluegrass. With the Wildcats ineligible for post-season championship, Pitino also wrote columns as a guest for the magazine during the 1991 NCAA tournament.

From time to time anywhere, there will always be somebody upset about a particular item in a newspaper or a magazine. For years, Joe B. Hall had problems with the news media. Hall generally had a good relationship with *The Cats' Pause*, but he once confronted Combs about something he didn't like.

"He never really got after me a single time except once," Combs said. "We were on a plane flying somewhere, probably around 1983 or '84. It was after one of those years when they got upset in the (NCAA) tournament. The fans were really down on Joe and they were writing those letters (to *The Cats' Pause*). We were getting on the plane and he said, 'Oscar, come up here and sit with me awhile.' We sat down and I said, 'Come on, Joe, what is on your mind?'

"Why do you run all those stupid letters?" said an angry Hall.

"What do you mean?" Combs replied.

"They are all stupid," Hall said. "They don't make any sense."

"Joe, I agree they are stupid," Combs remarked. "But don't you think everybody knows they are stupid?"

"Yes, but why do you run them?" Hall asked.

"Well, if you know they are stupid and the readers know they are stupid and I know they are stupid, then what is the problem?" Combs asked Hall. "Let me explain. Aren't I good to you? Am I not fair to you? There have been a few times I have written some things you probably didn't like. But weren't they true?"

Hall said, "Yes."

"Well, that is why you didn't say anything, wasn't it?"

"Yes," said Hall.

"If I don't run these letters about you even if they are wrong and I try to defend you, nobody is going to believe me. They will say he is just prejudiced."

Hall turned around and lifted up his glasses and rubbed his eyes. "I hadn't thought about it that way," he told Combs.

"To this day, he has never said another word," Combs said later.

Combs — who underwent successful open-heart surgery in the fall of 1990 — is very appreciative of his success in the sports publishing field. He does not take success for granted. He remembers where he came from ... a struggling, but strong family in the coal mountains of Eastern Kentucky.

"I don't know that there is really a highlight," Combs said of his career with *The Cats' Pause*. "There have been a lot of low things but when I came here 15 years ago, I told somebody, 'If God took me today, I have lived a wonderful life. I can't complain about anything. I have had much more than I deserve. I basically started out with nothing, had a lot of lucky breaks and a real good wife to help me along and we've been happy.' I can't see anything that would happen in the next 15 years that would change anything. There have been some low times, but that's life. I can look at lots and lots of people who have had it much, much tougher."

8 A DREAM COME TRUE

"I was the last sub
that he ever made in
Memorial Coliseum."

March 6, 1972.

For thousands of Wildcat fans as well as the players and coaches, it was a historical night. That evening saw Adolph Rupp appear in what would be his last home game as a Wildcat mentor before a sellout crowd of 11,500-plus emotional fans at Memorial Coliseum. When the final buzzer sounded, Kentucky had whipped Auburn 102-67 with All-SEC senior Tom Parker's 29 points and 11 rebounds. The victory kept alive UK hopes of a SEC title with one conference game remaining.

But that evening was an extra special one for a little, scrappy guy from Lexington named Kirk Chiles. That's because he finally got a chance to play for the very first time in his Wildcat uniform. He saw action for nearly two minutes and that was it. It turned out to be the only appearance of Chiles' Wildcat career.

Rupp didn't give Chiles a roundball scholarship. At 5-10, Chiles was considered "too small" to play on a major college basketball level. But Rupp liked Chiles because the youngster had a big heart and the coach kept him on the squad along with two other walk-ons, Larry Miller and Greg Smith, both from Daviess County.

Chiles was the same 5-10 guy who once played on coach Al Prewitt's squad at Lexington Henry Clay High

School as an "eighth" player during his senior year. He never started a game in high school. And several years later, Chiles became a walk-on member of Rupp's last Kentucky squad as a fifth-year senior.

"I was not a great athlete by any means," Chiles reflected in a 1986 interview with Somerset's *Commonwealth-Journal*. "I was little. Somehow, coach Rupp took a liking to me. I did hustle. I was hard-nosed and I was able to make the team in that manner.

"It is an interesting story in that coach Rupp always told me that I'd get to play sometime. Well, I kept wondering when he was going to come across with that promise because the season kept going down and down and down. But, true to his word, I played in the last (home) game of the season against Auburn. I could say in a trivia game that I was the last sub that he ever made in Memorial Coliseum. Also, when he got ready to put me and the other two walk-ons in with a minute and 39 seconds left in the game, he said, 'Don't throw the damn ball away.' It was an honor just to be on the team."

Three days after the Auburn game, Kentucky invaded the Big Orange Country to meet flamboyant coach Ray Mears and his league-leading Tennessee Volunteers. The Vols held a one-game margin over second-place Kentucky going into a regular season finale for both teams. With Kentucky Gov. Wendell Ford on hand at Stokley Athletics Center, the Wildcats spoiled Tennessee's plans for a post-season NCAA party, as they won the thrilling matchup by one point, a 67-66 decision. With a 14-4 SEC worksheet, the triumph gave Kentucky a share of the league title. And the Cats earned the NCAA tournament bid since they had defeated the Vols twice in the regular season. So, this would be Rupp's last chance to shine in the NCAA tourney. Although unlikely, he would be gunning for his fifth national championship.

Several months earlier, Chiles showed up in Rupp's office at Memorial Coliseum, sporting long hair and a moustache. The youngster wanted a chance to play for the Wildcats. But Rupp wasn't too crazy about the youngster's "hippie-like" appearance.

"The idea (of trying out) was put in my mind by a friend of mine," Chiles recalled. "We were together one night and out of the blue, he said, 'Why don't you go out for the team?' He said that they (the Wildcats) don't have very many players. (Tom) Payne had left and gone to the pros. (Kent) Hollenbeck broke his leg, and this and that. They needed some more players just to scrimmage. Well, I had never given that any consideration, although I had made the (UK) freshman team out of high school as a walk-on (under the direction of coach Harry Lancaster). But to tell you the truth I don't think anybody remembered me four years later from that time. So, I said, 'What the heck.'

"I had long hair. I had a moustache. As I went into coach Rupp's office, I put my hair behind my ears. I asked him if I could try out. The first thing he asked me was what year I was in. I said senior. Well, he laughed but I believe he really admired the guts that I had to walk into his office and ask him for the opportunity to go out, especially as a 5-10, 22-year-old fifth-year senior. So, he said, 'I'll tell you what, if you think you can play with these guys — they play out there every Monday, Wednesday and Friday — come on out. They'll tell you if you can play or not.' Then he said, 'If you make the team, that moustache is going to go and you are going to get a haircut.' Well, he didn't know but if he had asked me to shave my head, I would have done it."

But Chiles almost blew his life-long dream of becoming a member of the Wildcat squad.

"The night I tried out for the team, we went through his famous guard offense," he said. "It was an offensive drill in which you run all these fundamentals. It was beautiful. Red Auerbach (of the Boston Celtics) used to say he'd rather watch coach Rupp's teams do that in practice than watch most college teams play. The first time I touched the ball, it went right through my hands and I kicked it. My hands were dripping wet with anxiety and nervousness."

An angry Rupp, who was a perfectionist himself, didn't like what he saw.

"Shorty, if you kick the ball again, you can just follow it right on out through the door," Rupp told Chiles.

After two weeks of grueling practice, Chiles was still wearing his old gear, while other players had the university-issued practice equipment. Then, one day, Rupp interrupted the practice and he told the kid, "Shorty, tomorrow I think we'll get you some better equipment."

And, at that moment, Chiles knew he had made the squad. "I just wanted to yell and scream out," he said. "Of course, I couldn't do that as it was right in the middle of practice. I had to be cool. That was one of the biggest thrills I've ever had in my life."

Like his teammates, Chiles had a chance to observe an awkward and difficult situation that took place during Rupp's last season at UK. Rupp was fighting a mandatory retirement rule which stated that he must step down from his post since he was 70 years old. His assistant, Joe B. Hall, was preparing to replace the legendary Baron. The coach still didn't want to leave UK. At that time, Rupp saw Hall as his biggest problem. Rupp supposedly didn't have a kind word for Hall all year and any praise often went to another assistant, Gale Catlett.

"It was obvious that they had problems," Chiles said. "As far as I know, those two men didn't speak to each other that season. I believe coach Rupp confided in coach Catlett. Catlett was just there for one year and he had to take sides. He probably wisely — profession-wise and career-wise — took coach Rupp's side. He left that year to become the head coach at the University of Cincinnati. Catlett did have a relationship with coach Hall. I believe it was handled as professionally as the situation could have been handled by all three men. It was tough on everyone concerned. There was no outward animosity that we saw.

"When the ball went up, coach Hall wanted the Wildcats to win as did everyone else concerned. And I have always admired him for that. The team just went out and took care of the business at hand — just like coach Rupp had coached the game, the way it was meant to be played, for 41 years (not including the 1952-53 season which was suspended by UK officials in the wake of a point-shaving scandal)."

Another assistant on Rupp's last coaching staff was Dick Parsons, who was a starting guard at Kentucky in the late 1950s and early 1960s. During his playing days, Parsons led both Wildcat basketball and baseball squads as the captain. After Rupp retired, Parsons stayed on to become Hall's top assistant.

During that season, some of the team members felt that Rupp was getting a little old for the game, according to Chiles.

"You knew the man was not in good health. Any time you are around someone who is not in good health and who has reached 70 years of age, you might tend to think, especially after the losses, that maybe the game has passed him by. But about the time you got to thinking that about the old man, he would raise hell and spur the team on to a victory. Maybe make a key substitution. Maybe change a defense. Maybe call for a certain play at the right time. So, he'd fool you.

"In my opinion, coach Rupp did one of the finest coaching jobs that year of all his 41 seasons at UK. I don't think we had a whole lot of talent and we won the SEC. So, I think that if he had coached another year or two, he would have continued to do the job that he had always done for UK."

After upsetting coach Al McGuire and his favored Marquette Warriors 85-69 in the NCAA Mideast Regional, it marked Rupp's 875th and final coaching win. Two nights later, the Cats faced Florida State in what would be Rupp's last coaching appearance. It was a game that every Wildcat faithful would just as soon forget. Florida State, guided by young coach Hugh Durham, a Louisville native who happened to be a big Wildcat fan, whipped UK by 19 points. Kentucky finished the campaign at 21-7 and the 6-7 southpaw shooter, Tom Parker, was chosen SEC's Player of the Year by the Associated Press.

"It was a very emotional ending to a very trying season," said Chiles. "It was tough to see coach Rupp go out with a loss."

Many people have assumed incorrectly that Rupp was a coach who didn't like having black players on his team.

While at UK, Chiles' teammates included two black

players from the football team — Elmore Stephens and Darryl Bishop. And after observing Rupp's attitude toward them, Chiles became convinced that Rupp was not the racist that people made him out to be.

"I remember all the accusations about coach Rupp being such a racist," he said. "I can tell you right now that he would have bent over backwards to make Darryl and Elmore feel welcome on the team. He treated them as equals from the start.

"I got to make one trip during the season. The day we worked out at Mississippi State, he stopped (the practice) and asked the squad if any of us knew why Babe McCarthy, in the old days when he won the SEC, would not participate in the NCAA tournament. There was Darryl and Elmore standing right there. I remember that very distinctly."

During McCarthy's 10-year regime at Mississippi State, his Bulldogs captured or shared four SEC championships in the late 1950s and early 1960s. However, Mississippi State had to decline the NCAA tournament bid three different times because of its racial stand. The Mississippi legislature did not allow its state schools to play against teams that had black players. In 1963, the Bulldogs finally made their first-ever appearance in the NCAA tourney after winning the school's fourth SEC title.

After Chiles received his degrees from UK and Eastern Kentucky University, he went on to have a successful coaching career. He is now the head basketball coach at Marshall County High School in western Kentucky where he was hired in the spring of 1991. In his previous stops, Chiles had coached at Kentucky Business College, Cawood High School (where he had Phil Cox who later became All-SEC performer at Vanderbilt), Somerset High and Lyon County High. Going into the 1991-92 campaign, Chiles has compiled a 15-year coaching mark of 305-149. While at Somerset, he led the Briar Jumpers to a Sweet Sixteen appearance in 1985.

9 THE MAN WHO REPLACED THE LEGEND

"I was his successor,
so naturally I fell into
the category of the
bad guy."

When Kentucky Athletic Director C. M. Newton announced the retirement of jerseys honoring Adolph Rupp and Joe B. Hall in a special pregame ceremony at Rupp Arena, Hall turned sentimental.

The ceremony took place before a then-record crowd of 24,301 spectators on the emotion-filled night of Feb. 15, 1990. It was a high time that Hall will never forget, and Kentucky fans will also long remember that SEC game itself that night, when first-year coach Rick Pitino's undermanned, scrapping Wildcats stunned ninth-ranked LSU 100-95 and sent shock waves throughout the country.

Said a grateful Hall, "Being from Cynthiana, about 30 miles north of here and growing up as a Kentucky basketball fan, and later playing at Kentucky under coach Rupp, coming back and being his assistant for seven years, and having the responsibility of the program for 13 years, the university could not have done anything that would have meant more to me."

Hall later informed Pitino, "If the school had put a million dollars in my pocket, it wouldn't have meant more to me than that recognition."

Sitting in his office at Central Bank and Trust Company in Lexington where he has worked since his 1985 retirement from coaching and is now senior vice-president of correspondent banking, Hall emphasized that he really appreciated the honor.

"I wrote C. M. Newton a letter and thanked him for the honor and the way it was presented," he said. "When you think about where I've been and how I idolized Kentucky basketball as a young lad, to be put into that classification in Kentucky basketball history means more to me than anything that could possibly happen to me in my life."

Needless to say, Hall was one of the most successful coaches in the nation. His record proves it. He guided UK to eight SEC titles, three trips to the NCAA Final Four (including 1978 championship) and one National Invitation Tournament (NIT) title in his 13 seasons at the Wildcat helm. Named SEC Coach-of-the-Year four times, he is ranked fifth among the all-time victory leaders at SEC schools, behind Rupp, Dale Brown (LSU), Newton (Alabama and Vanderbilt) and Harry Rabenhorst (LSU) in that order. Hall posted a 297-100 overall record at UK.

However, off the court Hall had his share of troubles with the NCAA. But, to his credit, he was probably no worse than most of the coaches from major powers. Still, he doesn't like to talk about them. His first brush with the NCAA came in late 1976 when the Wildcat program was placed on a two-year probation for various rules violations. The NCAA restricted Kentucky to giving only three new basketball scholarships for each of the next two seasons.

Hall's program wasn't the only one at UK penalized by the NCAA. Football coach Fran Curci's program was charged with other NCAA rules violations as the Wildcats were banned from post-season bowls for two years and from live television appearances for one season.

Approximately a year after Kentucky won the NCAA championship in 1978, the NCAA, bowing to pressures from other jealous schools, ordered UK to "redecorate" or "tone down" its luxurious Joe B. Hall Wildcat Lodge, a new dormitory which housed the basketball players. Many schools had been crying foul, claiming the Wildcats had an unfair recruiting advantage when they showed their new plush building to wide-eyed recruits. So, a new rule was passed to prohibit such types of housing that were not available to other students. The lodge was built in 1977 at a cost of $700,000 with private donations by Wildcat faithful.

"I don't believe there is another school in the country that has a place like this," marveled UK senior guard Dwane Casey in a 1978 interview. "A lot of things were donated by the fans."

In October of 1985, about seven months after Hall announced his retirement, the *Lexington Herald-Leader* dropped a bombshell when their investigative reporters — Jeffrey Marx and Michael York — revealed in a series of articles that cash payments and other benefits were distributed to former Kentucky players during their playing days under Hall, apparently violating NCAA rules.

But the NCAA did not place Kentucky on probation as its officials were not able to obtain enough hard evidence to indict UK for breaking regulations. Instead, the school was reprimanded by the NCAA for not cooperating with the probe.

As far as NCAA rules violations are concerned, Hall doesn't agree with the attitude of some Kentucky fans that "all schools do it and Kentucky just got caught."

"Absolutely not," Hall commented. "My dealings with the NCAA have always been on a very high plane. I respect them. Your dealings with the NCAA include legislation, arbitration and defending yourself. You always have to do that because there are accusations made that are erroneous and absolutely absurd. You have to defend yourself in those cases. And defending yourself is some- thing that they certainly expect and want because they don't appreciate the black marks that have been placed on schools."

Major powerhouses, such as Kentucky, Louisville and Indiana, have no need to cheat to stay ahead of their chief competitors, Hall said.

"I think that there is less need for a school like Kentucky to be involved in going against NCAA rules than there is for a school without the tradition that Kentucky has," he said.

Despite his past problems with the NCAA, Hall is still proud of the way his program was run.

"I think we have done an excellent job in keeping Kentucky basketball where it should be with the student-athlete in mind, with a very high graduation rate," Hall said. "I remember CBS came in here and did a lengthy, very positive report. Lem Tucker, a black columnist, came in and stayed about one week with us. They had about three investigative reporters who talked to everybody on our squad. They talked about the negative things in college athletics.

"They interviewed Bob Bradley, who was in charge of academics (for UK basketball players and other athletes), and witnessed the fine job that we do in seeing that our players do meet the academic requirements and that most of them do get their degrees."

The television report, titled "The Basketball Machine," was aired on CBS in 1983 and Tucker served as the on-camera reporter. Tucker said that his crew shot about 100 rolls of film in Lexington for the special one-hour documentary on high school and college basketball. The segment on Kentucky's program lasted 15 minutes. Other segments on the program covered blue-chip basketball camps and a high school all-star game.

Before the show aired, many fans and the news media speculated that the Wildcat program would be cast in a negative light in the special report, portraying the Wildcats as one of the cheaters in the world of amateur athletics.

But Hall and his Wildcats came away with a clean bill of health.

At a news conference in 1972 when school president Dr. Otis Singletary introduced Hall as the new head basketball coach at Kentucky, Hall's predecessor, Adolph Rupp, was noticeably absent. Rupp was bitter because he had been forced to retire at 70. Asked if Hall was disappointed in Rupp for not offering congratulations, he said, "No."

"I had talked to coach Rupp prior to the announcement," Hall said. "He just did not show up at the press conference and if you knew coach Rupp, you would understand why. He was a disciple of (coach) Phog Allen at Kansas. He played under Allen and Allen probably had as much influence on coach Rupp as any other single person in the world.

"I remember reading the accounts of Allen's retirement (in 1956 at the age of 70). They said they bodily carried him, clawing and scratching, out of his office when they forced him to retire.

"Coach Rupp was much the same. Coach Rupp fought it every step of the way. I was his successor, so naturally I fell into the category of the bad guy at that time.

"But that soon passed. And in the seven years that I was his assistant, we had a lot of great experiences. We had a lot of good times together in our travels and in our coaching. I think he appreciated the recruiting job that I did for him and the help that I gave him on the floor.

"He never, in any way, demonstrated any lack of appreciation to me for what I did for him. His absence the day that I was named at the press conference was understandable to me because I knew him well."

In Hall's first year as the Wildcat boss, he became the league's first rookie coach to be named SEC Coach-of-the-Year. He was selected by the coaches for the award sponsored by *The Knoxville* (Tenn.) *News-Sentinel*. Under Hall's direction, the Cats posted a 20-8 record in winning his first of many SEC titles and a trip to the NCAA tournament.

Hall pointed out that many people loyal to Rupp wanted to see the new coach fail in his mission to maintain Kentucky's basketball greatness, a way to make their old hero appear "Godly." Rupp still had his own TV show on WLEX (Channel 18) in the first year after his retirement, while Hall's program aired on another Lexington station WKYT (Channel 27), creating an awkward situation in the UK camp. There were three groups of fans — Rupp supporters, Hall supporters and Wildcat supporters. "There was such a sentiment for coach Rupp and what he had done for Kentucky basketball. Not only Kentucky basketball, but basketball in the south and all over the world," said Hall. "I'm sure there was an underlying feeling that in order to really pay tribute to coach Rupp, the coach following him should fall on his face. I just know there were a lot of people that were hurt seeing coach Rupp leave and not having a coach Rupp clone step in to take his place. I never was as colorful. I never had the opportunity to grow in the program like he did and get the credit for building the program. I took over a successful program and my job was to keep it successful and I don't think that was exciting to the fans."

Well, the fans are excited today. They are going bonkers over Pitino's running style of basketball, creating old flashbacks of Rupp's famous fastbreaking offense.

"I think that it is (exciting) now," Hall said after the conclusion of Pitino's extraordinary first year at UK in which the young Cats posted a surprising 14-14 mark. "I think Rick Pitino — after the pendulum had swung in one direction — is the guy to bring it back to new heights. And if he brings it back to where it was when I received it, then he will be a big hero in this state."

When Hall returned to Kentucky in 1965 after successful coaching stints at Regis College in Denver and Central Missouri State College, he worked for Rupp as assistant coach and head recruiter. His first year as a Wildcat assistant saw the team, which was known as Rupp's Runts, compile a remarkable record of 27-2. They went all the way to the NCAA Final Four where the ailing Cats dropped a 72-65 heartbreaker to Texas Western in the championship game.

Hall said that season (1965-66) was probably the most enjoyable one he had while an assistant under Rupp. The starting five of the legendary Rupp's Runts included guards Louie Dampier and Tommy Kron, forwards Pat Riley and Larry Conley, and 6-5 center Thad Jaracz. It was a small team which was not ranked in some pre-season Top 20 polls. "That team went all the way to the final game and (it) was a very memorable experience for me," Hall said.

"Coach gave me a lot of responsibility (in my first year). I ran the pre-season conditioning program which they had never had at Kentucky. I was also given a lot of responsibility on the floor, with practice and game coaching. I really appreciated the confidence that coach Rupp showed in me as a young assistant. I enjoyed having that relationship with coach Rupp and coach (Harry) Lancaster."

Back in the late 1940s at UK, the 6-1 Hall played one year of varsity competition for Rupp as a little-used sophomore reserve before transferring to the University of the South in Sewanee, Tenn. Hall wanted more playing time and had gotten weary of sitting on the UK bench even when watching standouts such as Alex Groza, Ralph Beard, Wallace Jones, Dale Barnstable and Cliff Barker lead the 1948-49 Cats to a 32-2 mark and their second consecutive national championship crown.

While at the University of South, Hall set a school single-game scoring record and was team captain. Hall's coach at South, Lon Varnell, later rated Hall as the No. 1 player he ever coached.

But before Hall left UK, he had gotten the taste of what Rupp and the program were like.

"Everyone who played for coach Rupp was intimidated by him," Hall remembered. "Even the servicemen that came back, mature men who had been through prison camps, wars and everything else were intimidated by coach Rupp and those who weren't completely intimdated by Rupp were intimidated by Harry Lancaster. The 1-2 punch just about got everyone.

"I was intimidated by coach Rupp. He was very distant. You never saw him except on the floor. Occasionally, you might run into him in outer offices or somewhere on campus but rarely would he bother to even speak to you. You showed up for practice and did what was expected of you. That was all the contact you had with coach Rupp.

"Of course, on the trips in those days (often by train), we had an opportunity to get to know him better and in a different way. Usually he had (athletic director) Bernie Shivley, (radio announcer) Claude Sullivan and close friends around him and not so much the players."

Rupp had developed a reputation of being strict and mean. His practices were very long and demanding. The players, understandably, weren't too thrilled about them. But they accepted the rules if they wished to don a famous Kentucky uniform.

"Coach Rupp was a disciplinarian and he came down on us very hard for little things," said Hall, who once played on an all-star squad which journeyed with the Harlem Globetrotters on a 1951 European tour. "I think he did that in an effort to demonstrate what would happen to you if you were involved in something very bad. He was a perfectionist both on and off the floor. I think that was very good for us while we were growing up and being away from home, having that pressure of coach Rupp's discipline."

There were rumors years ago when he was coaching that Hall kept a "hate file" of certain sportswriters whom he did not like. He said that was not true.

But Hall did keep a different type of "hate file," which was composed of letters from angry fans, criticizing his team or his coaching tactics.

"I never will forget what my secretary, Jane Rollins, asked me the first day that I was the head coach," Hall said. "She said, 'Coach, what do you want me to do with your hate mail?' "

I said, "Jane, what is hate mail?"

"Well, coach Rupp always got letters, and you will, too, of criticism from people who disagreed with him," she said. "I always screened his mail and trashed those."

"No, Jane, I want to read those letters," said the new coach. "I have to develop a tough hide if I'm going to survive in this job."

During his tenure at Kentucky, Hall read every letter whether it was positive or negative. He felt like it was part of his job.

"I read every letter and answered every letter," he said. "I did face the public and did understand their concerns. I sympathized with them and, in some cases, I used their suggestions.

"So, if you want to survive, you have to have a love for the program. You have to feel deep inside that you are doing a good job yourself and that you can look in the mirror and be satisfied with what efforts you are giving and what you're accomplishing."

Rollins retired in 1980 after spending 25 years as a trusted member of the UK basketball office as administrative secretary to coaches Rupp and Hall.

Hall had several big games and he cherished all of them. They include Kentucky's 94-88 victory over Duke in 1978 which gave him his national title; the Wildcats' stunning 92-90 upset of top-ranked Indiana in the finals of the 1975 NCAA Mideast Regional tourney; and the 1978 miracle at Rupp Arena which saw Kentucky surprise fifth-ranked Kansas after being down by six points with 31 seconds remaining in overtime.

"Certainly, the most memorable game to me was the Duke game in St. Louis when we won the championship," said Hall. "That one will always have a warm spot in my heart. Not necessarily because it was the best game we played but because it was the most important in my career while I was at Kentucky.

"One of the finest was in 1975 in Dayton Arena in the finals of the Mideast Region against Indiana, which at that time was undefeated and ranked number one in the nation. They had beaten us by 24 points in Bloomington earlier in December. That comeback win, which put us in the Final Four in San Diego, was probably the most exciting game I've ever been a part of, even the national finals."

Hall feels that wild Kansas game is the one "that initiated or baptized Rupp Arena into being the official floor for the Kentucky Wildcats because of the excitement that was generated with that comeback."

The newly-constructed Rupp Arena, the major portion of a $53 million Lexington Center complex, had been the home of the Wildcats for only two years.

On the Kansas game, Hall said in 1978, "We really struggled and those guys just didn't give up and the effort in making up seven points in 31 seconds was almost unbelievable."

It was junior guard Kyle Macy's free throw with four seconds left in overtime that gave Kentucky a dramatic 67-66 win. Macy got the free throw when the Jayhawks were whistled for a technical foul because they had already used all of their available timeouts as the sellout Rupp Arena crowd went wild.

Visibly-shaken Kansas coach Ted Owens blamed the officials for the loss.

"We made some mistakes at the last, but when we were ahead by six points with 31 seconds to go, the officials eased up," Owens told the reporters. "They had called a fine game up to that point. The game went down to the last half-minute. If they had continued to call the game the way they had earlier, we would have won.

"I am tremendously proud of our players. These boys (Kansas) deserved to win. It was an absolute crime they didn't. That's all I have to say."

Those games were not the only memorable ones in Hall's coaching career. He had many more thrills.

For instance, the nationally-televised regular season finale with red-hot LSU at Rupp Arena in 1981. The nationally-ranked Tigers, 17-0 in conference play at the time, were about to become the first SEC team to go undefeated in a round-robin conference schedule. Before the eyes of NBC sportscasters Al McGuire and Billy Packer, the Wildcats denied LSU that chance, winning 73-71 and snapping the Tigers' 26-game winning streak. The victory also avenged an 81-67 setback UK experienced earlier in the season.

That same LSU squad, behind Louisville native Durand Macklin and 6-9 intimidator Greg Cook, finished the campaign with a 31-5 mark, captured the SEC regular season championship and made a trip to the NCAA Final Four.

"We had great fan excitement in that game," Hall said of the 24,011 vocal fans who attended the Sunday afternoon game.

McGuire agreed. He said the crowd was the most electrifying he had seen in his long basketball career.

Furthermore, Hall mentioned a 1976 contest with Mississippi State. The matchup was significant because it was the last Wildcat game played at Memorial Coliseum, affectionately known as "The House That Rupp Built," and ended the storied 26-year history of the UK gym. After trailing by seven points with a minute and half left in the contest, Kentucky, which had already been invited to the NIT, bounced back to force the game into overtime and defeated the Bulldogs 94-93.

Hall also faced some difficult moments. For one, he had trouble finding ways to beat arch-rival Tennessee and failed numerous times, especially in Knoxville. And how about that devastating 53-40 loss to eventual champion Georgetown in the semifinals of the 1984 NCAA Final Four in Seattle?

The Georgetown game "was a great disappointment because I really felt we had the caliber of team that could have won the championship," Hall said of his 29-5 team which included 7-foot senior stars Sam Bowie and Melvin Turpin. "In the second half, nothing would fall for us and it was almost a freakish-type shooting exhibition (the ice cold-shooting Cats hit only three of 33 second-half shots).

"We had already beaten Houston (74-67 earlier in the season), which would have been our next opponent in the final game. I felt we matched up very well with them. That second half was something that I would not want to experience again."

Six years later, former UK player Bret Bearup, who was a junior on that 1983-84 squad, said, "To this day, I have not looked at that tape (of the Georgetown game). I cannot stand to look at it."

Meanwhile, at Stokely Athletics Center in Knoxville, Hall could only manage to beat the Volunteers once in 13 games during his UK career. His 1978 NCAA championship squad was the only group that could stop the Vols in K-town. They beat host Tennessee by 11 points, a 68-57 verdict. Overall, Hall's 13-year record against Tennessee was a poor 11-16, including a 1979 SEC tournament loss in Birmingham, Ala.

But in 1985, with Kentucky Gov. Martha Layne Collins in attendance at Rupp Arena and a regional TV audience looking on, Hall did come up with a lopsided victory over Tennessee coach Don DeVoe's club. It was Hall's last game against the hated-rival Vols, which took place on an emotional Senior Night, featuring UK seniors Bearup and Troy McKinley. Kentucky won 92-67, the biggest victory margin Hall ever posted against Tennessee, as junior Kenny Walker gunned in 33 points and grabbed 18 rebounds.

As it turned out later, that game also marked Hall's

last coaching appearance at Rupp Arena.

On Hall's Stokely Center jinx, former Tennessee coach Ray Mears once remarked that Hall was totally "psyched" by failing to beat the Vols in Knoxville. Mears thought the jinx really worried Hall.

Unlike many other coaches, Mears was fairly successful against the Cats, posting an even 15-15 mark for the Vols from 1962 to '77. Against Rupp, Mears was 8-12. And against Hall, he was even better, compiling a 7-3 mark.

When Mears had superstars Bernard King and Ernie Grunfeld in the mid-1970s, the Vols were a force to reckoned with.

"Ray Mears had the best Tennessee teams in history when he was there," Hall said. "I guess his team with King and Grunfeld was probably as good a team as I ever competed against."

Mears is the sixth winningest coach of all time in the SEC with an overall record of 278-112.

During Hall's coaching days, especially in the early 1980s, he received a lot of criticism from the fans and the news media. Many armchair critics were after his head, especially after embarrassing losses to Alabama-Birmingham and Middle Tennessee State in the NCAA tournaments, both in the first round.

But Hall had friends in high places.

In an August 1984 column that the author wrote for Somerset's *Commonwealth-Journal*, it was reported that Hall apparently was getting more popular than ever with the UK Board of Trustees. Here are excerpts from the column:

Do sports and politics mix? Apparently so.
And Joe B. is smiling these days.
It looks like a safe bet to say that Joe B. Hall, who will be beginning his 13th season this winter as the head basketball coach at the University of Kentucky, will be directing the Wildcats for many years to come unless he himself decides to retire early for fishing. That's because Hall's popularity with the UK Board of Trustees (not to be

confused with the UK Athletics Association Board) has probably reached an all-time high.

That's bad news for Joe B.'s armchair critics. But great if you adore him.

As you may know, Gov. Martha Layne Collins appointed two of Hall's close associates to the university's Board of Trustees earlier this summer. They are wealthy horseman Cap Hershey, 40, who owns Hillbrook Farm in Fayette County, and 45-year-old James L. Rose, a London businessman who operates a coal firm and holds controlling interest in banks in London, Danville, Nicholasville, Manchester and Lexington.

The appointments were announced to the state news media and, of course, Hall's close connections with the two board members was not revealed. But many observers close to the UK program, including Oscar Combs of The Cats' Pause magazine, were already aware of Hall's ties with the appointees. Combs wrote of the situation in his weekly tabloid last month.

Hall frequently can be spotted fishing on the Kentucky lakes and rivers with Hershey, who is from the state of New York. And Rose is one of Hall's best friends. The London business executive often provides Hall his private plane for use on recruiting trips.

Also, Terry McBrayer, a member of UK's Board of Trustees who unsuccessfully ran for the Democratic nomination for governor several years ago, is a good fishing partner of Hall's. In June they were spotted, sitting together, at the Kentucky-Indiana All-Star Basketball Classic in Rupp Arena. McBrayer, who practices law in Lexington, also goes hunting quite often with some of Hall's players.

While Hershey and Rose were chosen to the board, Bill Sturgill, who was serving as the board chairman, was not reappointed by Gov. Collins. Obviously, it was mainly because Sturgill did not support Collins in her quest for the Democratic nomination in the governor's race. Instead, he politicked for Louisville Mayor Harvey Sloane, who was the losing candidate.

Anyhow, Hall, who last spring received a new five-year pact from the UK Athletics Association Board, is probably glad that Sturgill is no longer a force in the board's smoke-filled room.

Against Hall's wishes, Sturgill and the Board of

*Trustees last year forced the UK Athletics Board to order
the Cats to play the University of Louisville. Because of
that, it is generally thought that Hall's relationship with
Sturgill has deteriorated.*

*With the addition of Hershey and Rose on his side,
it is certain that Hall's influence will now have a greater
impact on the board's actions when it comes to his pressure-
packed cage program.*

On the subject of his dealings with the news media,
Hall said that was part of his job. Were they tough on him?

"I don't think that the media was any tougher on me
than it is on people all over the country," Hall replied, "not
only in athletics, but in politics and other areas. As I watch
television, I see talk shows and the comedy hours and the
fun that they poke at the President, at the governor, at
political leaders, at scholars, at the heroic feats of athletes.

"I can understand them taking some shots at me. I
was certainly not above that and that is the way of the
media today. You're just gonna have to live with it."

But he certainly had his share of problems with the
press. Oscar Combs of has an interesting theory about
Hall's relationship with the media.

"The media hated Rupp, but they respected him,"
Combs said. "That is all a coach can ask for and I think this
was one of Joe Hall's biggest problems. They hated Rupp
badly because he was God and they would not dare challenge
him in this city. So, I think when Rupp left and Hall came
in, the media subconsciously said, 'Hey, we are going to
make sure this fellow never gets control of the public like
Rupp did.' I think this was part of Joe's problem."

Soon after he quit coaching, Hall moved over to the
other side of the microphone, interviewing players and
coaches. He became a television commentator for the ABC
network in 1987, ironically making his network debut at
Rupp Arena where Kentucky was hosting LSU. For his
performance, he received good reviews.

"I had no idea how I would could come across (on
TV)," Hall said in 1987. "I had no experience. I didn't really
know what I should and shouldn't do. The biggest problem

I had was the timing which is very difficult for a color person on television. Only experience can help you solve that problem.

"I was surprised (by the reviews)."

Columnist Billy Reed wrote a piece for the *Lexington Herald-Leader*, suggesting that Hall should have been given the role of ABC's top commentator over the loud-mouthed Dick Vitale.

"I didn't see that article," Hall said at the time. "I heard about it, though. I'm very pleased with the article and all that the critics had to say."

Hall's partner at the contest was veteran play-by-play announcer Al Michaels.

For the record, LSU destroyed hapless Kentucky 71-46 in Hall's debut, the worst loss by a Wildcat squad in Rupp Arena history.

Hall was asked if the colorful Vitale is too outspoken. "Dick Vitale is probably the most identifiable, controversial person in the media covering basketball in the world," Hall said. "Yes, he is too outspoken but he always has an opinion, and says it very forcefully, and you can take it or leave it. People are interested in what he says. There are people who like him very much and those who don't. He is knowledgeable and has a style and personality that come across in an exciting way."

Thus far, Hall has not worked with Vitale in a basketball game.

"I did a halftime (show) with him," he said. "I don't think they will ever put us together again. I have never worked with Vitale in a ball game. I admire him for what he's done and what he's accomplished in his career."

Since UCLA's famed coach John Wooden retired in 1975, the Bruins have not been able to secure a stable force in their roundball program.

People like Gene Bartow, Gary Cunningham, Larry Brown, Larry Farmer and Walt Hazzard have tried to take the Wizard's place. They all failed. Former UCLA assistant Jim Harrick is the boss today. In all, there have been six coaching changes since the glory days of Wooden.

By comparison, Hall succeeded as he took over

Rupp's program and stayed on for 13 years. How did he manage it?

"I think the difference is that I had no place else to go," said the ex-Wildcat mentor. "There was not an opportunity for me to leave Kentucky and go to some other school. Bartow, Brown, Farmer and Hazzard all had some place to go to after leaving UCLA. Kentucky was my home. It was where my family lived, where my wife's family lived, where my children lived, where my brothers and sisters lived. I couldn't pack up and leave, and leave my troubles behind because I had failed. I would have left all those problems for my family. So, I had to stick around and develop a tough hide."

If Hall could have had his way, he would have retired after Kentucky's appearance in the 1984 NCAA Final Four.

But things didn't work out as the Wildcats left Seattle with an embarrassing setback to Georgetown coach John Thompson's squad.

"I had originally planned to retire when I was 55, which would have been after the Georgetown game," he said. "We were graduating a big group of seniors and coming back with a very young team, and I did not feel good after the Georgetown loss. I did not want to leave the following coach a weak team after having a team at the Final Four. So I decided to coach one more year. But I was almost certain that I was going to retire at that time."

During the next season, rumors about Hall's possible retirement persisted off-and-on and the talk intensified during the last week of the regular season and the SEC tournament in Birmingham.

Hall finally announced his decision to retire during his radio show with announcer Cawood Ledford following Kentucky's loss to St. John's in the NCAA tournament in Denver. His announcement was also televised live back to the state of Kentucky. Hall said regretfully he had lied to some people during the Wildcats' 18-13 campaign, telling them that he would not retire, just to avoid distractions on the team.

"I had already discussed it (retirement) with some

of the members of the Central Bank's board and talked to them about a position," recalled Hall. "They had pretty much agreed (on a position) before I retired. So, I had laid some plans, and pretty much decided that was what I was going to do. When I got into coaching, I decided I did not want to be an old coach. I said my coaching days would end at about 55. I would seek some other employment that was a little more suited for that stage in my life."

Hall retired at 56, fulfilling a long-standing promise — although a year late — to his wife, the former Katharine Dennis of Harrison County, whom he met during his college days at UK.

Ironically, Hall's last coaching appearance was at none other than UK's Memorial Coliseum several days after Kentucky's loss to St. John's. In the midst of the 1985 NCAA Final Four hoopla in Lexington, he coached in a college all-star game before a friendly home crowd of over 11,000. When the buzzer sounded, Hall was carried off the floor by Alabama's Bobby Lee Hurt and Florida's Eugene McDowell, his former SEC opponents.

His coaching days were over.

In earlier days, Hall and his Wildcats took many timeouts to visit local hospitals in the Bluegrass area without much fanfare — especially around the Christmas holidays. They made the patients' stays at the hospital more bearable and brightened their lonely days.

Oscar Combs said he will never forget the times Hall and his players spent in local hospitals. It made Combs appreciate them more than anything else they had done.

"The most eye-awakening experience I have had in Kentucky came in the early 1980s when Joe Hall was coaching," Combs recalled. "During the Christmas break when the players had nowhere to go, he would take them around to all the pediatric wards here at the local hospitals a day or so before Christmas. We went along and shot some pictures and went into these wards where kids were anywhere from two years old to 8 or 10 years old. You've got a kid with one arm, another with no hair because of cancer, another with leukemia. They've got a right to be upset with life and I'll never forget one year when Dirk Minniefield went over to a couple of other kids. They just broke down; they cried all over the floor. We often take everything for granted. We never see it until it comes home to roost. I guess this taught me more and gave me more respect for Joe than anything he has ever done.

"This was a ritual; every year he took them out there. He did little things like that and he didn't do it for fanfare. He didn't call in all the TV stations. There were times when they would end up finding out about it and come out. But it was that type of thing that made the program so special to so many people in the state.

"I can't tell you over the years the number of things that UK coaches from Curci to Hall to Eddie Sutton to Rick Pitino have done such as writing out a letter to a little kid who has a terminal illness. Those people would rather have a Kentucky Wildcat or Kentucky coach autograph something for them than have a good day."

The summer of 1988 was a time that Hall would like to forget. But that would be impossible because he had a life-threatening situation.

He had cancer. He had a tumor in his colon. While on a fishing trip in Canada in early June, Hall first discovered he had rectal bleeding. And it was in a Canadian hospital that the doctors detected the cancer. The following week, Hall underwent surgery in Lexington for removal of a cancerous tumor. Although cancer can spread in mysterious ways, the operation was declared a success. It was similar to a tumor that was taken from President Reagan several years ago.

Hall said he was shocked when he learned he had cancer. "I don't guess you could have a bigger shock than to look up at your doctor and hear him tell you that you have cancer," he said. "We all fear that word. I guess when I found out, I said, 'Well, Doc, what do we do next?' I wasn't bitter. I wasn't hurt. I wasn't afraid. I just knew something — surgery or chemotherapy — had to be done."

His faith in God helped Hall to remain strong during this difficult period. He was already very much at peace with himself when he found out about cancer. And that made the whole ordeal easier.

"I did reflect that my life had been a good life," said the former coach. "I had a great family. I had a sensible childhood and grew up in a most enjoyable atmosphere. I had the opportunity to participate in sports and spend my life doing something that I liked to do. Upon that reflection, I couldn't do anything but smile at my situation and go forward in whatever direction I was guided by my physician and accept whatever came.

"I guess it does make you think a little bit more about the time you have left on this earth, in this world, in this life and that your life is in the hands of a greater power than you can possibly understand. My faith in God, and living and following the life of Jesus Christ, has given me the strength to face whatever comes. I totally feel that."

Herky Rupp and his family at a UK game during earlier days.
Photo by Alen Malott, *The Cats' Pause*

A frustrated Joe B. Hall does his famous sideline act with a rolled-up program in the 1984 Kentucky-Tennessee game at Stokely Athletics Center in Knoxville. Hall could only come up with one victory against the homestanding Vols in the "House of Horrors" during his 13-year Wildcat head coaching career.

Photo by Jamie H. Vaught

Rex Chapman shares a laugh with his father Wayne Chapman, Kenny
Walker and his sister Jenny Chapman at a 1989 reception held in honor
of his late grandfather at London's Sue Bennett College. They were
looking through old photographs and newspapers from the days of Rex's
grandfather who played and coached basketball at the college.

Photo by Susie Bullock

Rex's Granny, Mayme Little
Hamby, enjoys playing the
piano.

Photo by Susie Bullock

ABOVE: Retiring Joe B. Hall is being carried off the floor by Alabama's Bobby Lee Hurt (left) and Florida's Eugene McDowell in an all-star game held at UK's Memorial Coliseum. It was Hall's last game as a coach.

Photo by Jamie H. Vaught

OPPOSITE TOP: "Praying" coach Eddie Sutton drops to his knees as he watches host Kentucky defeat Northwestern (La.) State 77-58 in his successful Wildcat debut in 1985. Behind Sutton is assistant James Dickey.

Photo by Jamie H. Vaught

OPPOSITE BOTTOM: Television broadcaster Joe Dean, now LSU athletic director, interviews Kentucky's James Blackmon after a Wildcat victory as teammate Rex Chapman waits for his turn.

Photo by Jamie H. Vaught

"Rupp Runt" Larry Conley interviews Eddie Sutton on ESPN after Sutton's Wildcats edge Tennessee in a 66-65 thriller in 1989. It was one of Kentucky's few highlights of the scandal-marred campaign.

Photo by Jamie H. Vaught

New Yorker Rick Pitino meets the press after he was officially named the head coach at UK as then-UK president Dr. David Roselle, sitting in his chair, listens.

Photo by Jamie H. Vaught

New coach Rick Pitino and his wife, Joanne, look at each other prior to a news conference held at Patterson Office Tower on the UK campus as the school announces the hiring of Pitino.

Photo by Jamie H. Vaught

Former Gov. A.B. "Happy" Chandler sings *My Old Kentucky Home* during UK Senior's Night pre-game festivities at Rupp Arena.

Photo by Jamie H. Vaught

The spotlight on the Wildcat players shone brightly during the pre-
game introductions in UK's last regular season game at Memorial

Coliseum before moving to spacious Rupp Arena. Kentucky won the 1976 contest in a come-from-behind 94-93 victory over Mississippi State.

Photo by Bruce Orwin

10 MOUNTAIN BOY

"I always got the feeling
he (Rupp) liked the
country boys -- kids from
the mountains."

The 1973-74 campaign wasn't a very pretty season. The Wildcats started poorly with a 1-3 mark. After winning the season opener against Miami (Ohio) 81-68 at home, they dropped three consecutive games, losing to Kansas, Indiana and North Carolina, all of which later finished in the final Top 10 rankings. Kentucky just couldn't seem to get the ball rolling as the Wildcats struggled to finish with a 13-13 worksheet in Joe B. Hall's second year as the head coach at UK. The season would eventually mark Hall's worst year as the Wildcat boss.

The team had plenty of talent despite the loss of 6-11 star Jim Andrews to graduation the previous year. But there had been some dissension on the squad and they just could not play well together. Some players were pointing fingers, blaming others for mistakes.

On the squad, Kentucky had four junior standouts in Kevin Grevey (co-SEC Player of the Year as a sophomore with Alabama's Wendell Hudson), Bob Guyette, Jimmy Dan Conner and Mike Flynn, and 5-10 senior captain Ronnie Lyons. They all had big high school reputations. Grevey was a prep All-American from Hamilton, Ohio; Guyette was from Ottawa, Ill.; Conner, from Lawrenceburg, Ky., where he guided Anderson County High to state tournament runner-up title as Kentucky's "Mr. Basketball";

Flynn, from Jeffersonville, Ind., where he earned the state's "Mr. Basketball" title; and Lyons, who was Kentucky's "Mr. Basketball" at Mason County High and the state's leading scorer with nearly 36 points a game.

Plus, the Wildcats had a key substitute by the name of G. J. Smith, a 6-7, 185-pound stringbean from the southeastern Kentucky mountains. The junior forward was a two-time All-Stater from Laurel County where he played at legendary Hazel Green High before moving to Laurel County High for his senior year. Hazel Green, located in the northern part of the county, and three other high schools (Lily, London and Bush) were consolidated into Laurel County High in 1970.

During that dreadful season in February of 1974, one of Smith's roommates at UK was Grevey. They lived at Holmes Hall, a dormitory which was within walking distance of Memorial Coliseum. One night Grevey, who later starred for the Washington Bullets and Milwaukee Bucks in the NBA, was nowhere to be seen in the dorm. He had disappeared after the team returned from a long, grueling bus trip from Starkville, Miss., where the Wildcats dropped 82-70 to Mississippi State. Alarmed about Grevey's absence, coach Hall decided to stay overnight at the dorm.

"I spent one night in Kevin Grevey's empty bed sharing the room with G. J. Smith," Hall recalled. "Kevin had skipped curfew. I just waited up for him. I wasn't upset. I was worried. I was always concerned about the health of my players. We had made a long trip from Mississippi that afternoon by bus. We got in about two o'clock Sunday morning and we had another game the following Monday. I told the players to go right to bed — no one to leave the dorm. I got over to the Coliseum and I was worried a little bit about them. I hadn't really checked to see if they were alright, so I went back to recheck them and Kevin Grevey was out."

Said Smith, "Coach Hall came in checking the rooms and he (Grevey) wasn't in yet. Coach Hall then checked all the other rooms and came back and Grevey still hadn't come in. Coach Hall laid down in Grevey's bed and he slept there the whole night waiting for Kevin to come in but he never did come in." According to Smith, Grevey showed up in his room at about nine o'clock the next morning.

Because Grevey had violated curfew, Hall suspended the player for one game against LSU, the team's next opponent. The Wildcats, however, managed to beat the visiting Tigers 73-70 without the help of Grevey's scoring machine.

Hall later said Grevey didn't offer any reasons for missing the curfew. "There wasn't any excuse that would take care of a situation like that so he didn't even bother," Hall pointed out. "There wasn't any excuse that would be justifiable so he didn't offer one."

Grevey finished the season as SEC's top scorer with a 21.9-point average and was named All-American.

Smith grew up in an athletic-minded family in rural Laurel County. His father Charles, now a retired farmer, played on the 1940 state championship team at Hazel Green High and later made the All-State team in 1942. The elder Smith was good enough to play on the college level, but he turned down several scholarship offers. His mother, Muriel, is a retired schoolteacher who was a cheerleading sponsor at Hazel Green. His older sister, Charlie Jean, was a high school cheerleader in the mid-1960s. "We were real close and had a very athletic family," said G.J. Smith, who is now married and a family man himself. "We have been going to the games for as long as I can remember."

Before Hazel Green closed in 1970 due to consolidation, the Bullfrogs had a long-storied basketball tradition as the tiny mountain school made several trips to the Sweet Sixteen. For the record, the Bullfrogs had a total of eight appearances in the state tournament, including one championship. In Hazel Green's last year Smith lead the Bullfrogs to the 1970 state tournament as a junior. He was also named to the All-State team.

"The last year (at Hazel Green), we had a real nice ball team," Smith commented. "We went to the state tournament and reached the quarterfinals and had a record of 33-3. Making a trip to the state tournament was quite satisfying for the last year. Losing the last game at Hazel Green was sad. We were pretty pumped up that final year. We wanted to do real well because we knew it was the end. We always had good teams and we sure wanted one that year.

"My father played in the first game in the gym at Hazel Green and I played in the last game there. So, that was kind of a unique thing. My dad was an All-Stater and I was an All-Stater. If one of my two boys can make All-State — if they are good enough to play — that will make three generations in my family to play as All-Stater.

"It was just a real close knit community school and everybody knew all the basketball players. There was a lot of tradition and they had a lot of great teams. It was one of the larger schools in the county. Hazel Green had grades one through 12. The elementary school kids were all there with the high school in one building which made it a unique situation."

In the following season at Laurel County High, Smith again starred on the hardwood floor and guided the new school to a trip to the Sweet Sixteen in Louisville. Named to various All-State squads for the second year in a row, Smith did not play at full strength in the state tourney. He reinjured his foot in the pre-game warmup drills in regional tournament's championship game. However, while wearing a special brace on his broken foot, he did well enough in two games to be selected to the All-State tournament squad. Smith's future teammate at UK, Jimmy Dan Conner of Anderson County, was the crowd favorite as he led all scorers in the 1971 state tournament with 94 points in four games. Conner's Anderson County squad lost to Louisville Male for the coveted state crown.

All of SEC's 10 schools — Alabama, Auburn, Florida, Georgia, Kentucky, LSU, Ole Miss, Mississippi State, Tennessee and Vanderbilt — expressed strong interest in Smith's roundball skills. But the Laurel County star was only interested in Kentucky schools. During the recruiting process, Smith eventually narrowed his list of schools to Kentucky, Louisville, Western Kentucky, Eastern Kentucky and Morehead State.

"Some schools sent me as many as eight to ten letters every day from all over the country," recalled Smith, who currently doubles as the athletic director and head baseball coach at Laurel County High. "But I basic-ally narrowed it down to schools in the state in the last part of the recruiting season. I told the rest of them (other schools) that I was going to stay in Kentucky. So, that was over for them.

Smith said he received a lot of recruiting mail from Kentucky's rival in Knoxville, a 90-minute drive from his hometown. Tennessee coach Ray Mears wanted his services. "I received some kind of letter everyday," Smith remarked. "They like to come up here and get a Kentucky boy when they can."

But he didn't really appreciate the circus atmosphere that the Vols put on for their halftime show. "I didn't like that," he said. "It was a show. I'm old-fashioned, I guess. I don't like to put on a show or anything. Keep the game very simple. Keep it very traditional."

"The last two schools I had to choose from was Morehead and UK. I wanted to stay close to where my parents were. The first time my parents missed seeing me playing a ballgame was my freshman year at UK (at a time when the freshmen were not eligible to play on the varsity level) when the team went to Florida. I remember that night real well. It was on the radio that night and my parents had to keep driving because the radio kept fading out. They had to drive all the way to Berea (Ky.) because nobody down here (in Laurel County or surrounding counties) carried the freshman games on the radio except for the Lexington station."

That UK freshman squad, popularly known as the Kittens, went through the entire campaign undefeated with a glittering 22-0 mark. And a national basketball magazine selected the Kittens as the country's No. 1 freshman team in 1971-72. An excellent jumper, Smith surprised many observers with his outstanding play. He led the team in rebounding with an average of 10.3 caroms. He was also the Kittens' fourth-leading scorer.

While he was being recruited by Kentucky, Smith went to the UK Medical Center in Lexington. No, he wasn't sick, he just wanted to meet ailing coach Adolph Rupp. "The first real meeting (with Rupp) was in the hospital," Smith said. "He was having problems with his foot. I had a broken foot also and I remember him commenting that we both have bad feet.

"I always got the feeling he liked the country boys — kids from the mountains. I think he had a special feeling for them. One thing that I really admired about him was my first practice at UK. He had the varsity out there practicing at 3:00. He told the freshmen they could come in earlier if they wanted to. I was sitting there and he hollered at me and had me practice with the varsity and I was only a freshman. I think his reason for doing this was because he knew I was nervous. He wanted to work me in there with the varsity and that settled me down and soothed my nerves a little bit. I really believe he did that for a purpose."

Smith never had a chance to play for Rupp. The legendary coach was forced to retire from his UK job at the end of Smith's freshman year. But Smith remembers one story about Rupp. The coach could be funny at times.

"He had a strange personality," he said. "I remember one time they were scrimmaging — the varsity against the freshmen — and after (junior forward) Larry Stamper made a mistake or the referee made a bad call, Larry was angry and threw the ball up in the stands.

"The coach didn't like what he saw. 'That will cost you two of your four complimentary tickets next time,' Rupp told Stamper.

" 'Well, take all four if you want to,' replied the furious player.

'I did,' said Rupp who in his mind had already taken away the tickets.

On Rupp, Smith said, "I was only with him for one year. If I had been with him for four years, I probably would have picked up a lot more stories. But we spent most of our time with coach Hall who was our freshman coach and only went into the locker room at halftime during the varsity games."

Smith has always been a quiet person. But he may have been too quiet.

"I think G. J. lived with his roommate for three

years before he ever said his first word," quipped coach Hall. "His roommate, at one time, was Kevin Grevey. Kevin said he was in there about a month before he even found out what his name was."

Smith admits that he is "actually a little backward. Because of my personality, I'm not really outgoing and friendly to strangers. I'm sure sometimes I come across as an arrogant, conceited person. I don't want to come across that way. But the people who know me personally know I am not like that. Since I've had a little success at UK, they think, 'Well, he's arrogant and stuck-up.' That is not really true.

"I would like to think I am a fair person. I like to treat people the same way I would want to be treated. I try to treat people fair. At one time I was probably considered to be a little hot-headed. I think I have settled down quite a bit now. I'm not as bad as I was. I think having a family has probably done a lot for that. "

When Hall became the head coach at Kentucky, he was not the same mentor the players saw when he guided the freshman team or served as an assistant on the varsity team. Smith was a sophomore in Hall's first year at the UK helm. "He was a different man from when he was a freshman coach," Smith said. "He treated me a lot differently. I'm sure that's because of the pressure (from his new post). No man alive could replace Rupp. There was no need in trying. I think Rupp was the greatest coach that's ever been. Coach Hall wasn't going to try to replace him. He was going to try to make a reputation for himself. There had to be a lot of pressure on him. He was a very intense person. He was so serious so much of the time that when he tried to have a little sense of humor you didn't know how to take him."

While at Kentucky, Smith never considered transferring to another school. He accepted the fact he wouldn't see a lot of action, especially during his sophomore or senior years. He was a key substitute. Playing or not, his goal was to get an education and become a coach.

Smith never had a chance to show his full potential as a Wildcat player. In his sophomore year, he hurt his knee during the University of Kentucky Invitational Tournament and had to sit out the remainder of the season. "I had my knee operated on and I missed a lot of practices," he said.

Hall said of the injury, "He never seemed to recover from that. G. J. was a very slender young man. When you hurt a knee like that, it takes a lot of muscle mass to protect it in the future. But G. J. was a full-time contributor while he was at UK. G. J. was a player we called a Long Rifle. He could hit the outside jumper and the pro three-point line wouldn't have meant anything to him. He was an excellent shooter— a good, aggressive, hard-nosed player."

Unlike his junior year when he saw a lot of action, starting several games, Smith's playing time dropped considerably during his senior year of 1974-75. He played behind the super freshman class of Rick Robey, Mike Phillips, Jack Givens, James Lee and Danny Hall. Smith played 18 games that season, averaging only 1.9 points.

His best game as a Wildcat came on the road during his junior year. The contest was regionally televised and host Alabama, coached by former UK player C. M. Newton, was the opponent. Smith scored 15 points and grabbed seven rebounds, but those figures weren't enough as the Cats lost 81-77. And the Crimson Tide — who later defeated Kentucky again 94-71 in Lexington — shared the SEC regular season crown with Vanderbilt that year.

"I never wanted to transfer," Smith said. "I wasn't going to do that. I went there and I was going to stick it out. I was going to do my little part. They had a real good recruiting year my junior year that brought a lot of good freshmen in and he (Hall) wanted to give them some experience. If it hadn't worked that way, I might have gotten a lot more playing time. You may think it's your time (as a senior) to play and then he goes out and recruits a bunch of good players and you just drop a little farther behind.

"But it's a big business. You have to grow up and face the facts that your career has to end sometime. Everybody's going to have to face reality somewhere along the line that your basketball career is over and then you have to move on to something else. And that's the whole thing about getting an education. Go out and get an education so you can be prepared when it does end so you can go on and do something else. I had already made plans and I knew what I was going to do. I wanted to become a coach. I'm happy at what I'm doing right now. I'm just tickled to death."

Incidentally, Smith's most memorable moment of the intense Kentucky-Tennessee rivalry came in 1972 when he was a spectator in the stands as a Kentucky freshman. Played on a Saturday afternoon in Lexington, the regionally-televised matchup was marred by orange-throwing incidents directed at head coach Ray Mears and his Tennessee players.

"I remember coming in that Saturday to watch Tennessee warm up. They came out a lot earlier than the other teams and put on their own show," said Smith, who had played against UT's freshman team the previous night, beating the baby Vols by nearly 40 points. "And, all of a sudden, I see one orange come out of the top of the stands. And they (spectators) just bombarded him (Mears) with rotten oranges. The floor was soaked with orange juice. They had to mop the floor before they could start the game. The TV broadcast was delayed and everything to get the floor ready. That's probably one of the more memorable things I can remember about it (Kentucky-Tennessee rivalry)."

Kentucky narrowly won that contest 72-70 on Jim Andrews' winning basket. Tennessee's promising star, 7-foot sophomore Len Kosmalski, scored a game-high 30 points.

Another time Smith will never forget was Kentucky's exciting trip to San Diego for the 1975 NCAA Final Four during his senior year. Although his parents did not see him play in San Diego, several of his hometown friends and supporters from Laurel County were there to cheer the Wildcats.

Smith barely saw action in the Final Four, playing only in semifinals against Syracuse in which the Wildcats triumphed 95-79. He missed his only field goal attempt. He did not play in Kentucky's heartbreaking 92-85 loss to UCLA in the championship game. It was UCLA mentor John Wooden's last game as a coach. The 64-year-old Wizard was calling it quits.

Did Wooden's surprise announcement, after his team's 75-74 overtime victory over Louisville in the semifinals, that he was retiring affect the outcome of Kentucky-UCLA matchup?

"I think we would have had a lot better shot at it (winning NCAA title if Wooden hadn't made the announcement)," Smith said. "Sitting there watching the game, and you hate to sit and cry about the officials, obviously they were not going to give him (Wooden) any bad breaks that night. I'm not saying they gave us a rough time, but I don't think they gave us any breaks. I don't think they were going to jeopardize taking the blame for him losing the last game he coached. I thought they got the breaks—you get breaks during a ballgame. The official is going to miss some calls. But I think they bent over backwards to make sure they did not give us any breaks or blow any calls against UCLA.

"And the announcement that he was going to retire pumped his kids up because they didn't want to be remembered as the team that lost the last game for John Wooden. So, that was the advantage. But I thought we had a better team."

Of his UK career, Smith likes to point out that he witnessed two of the college basketball's biggest moments in history. "I had the opportunity to see coach Rupp coach his last game and also to see John Wooden coach his last ballgame," he said. "So, I thought it was kind of a special thing to be able to witness those two great guys coach their last ballgames."

Shortly after his college basketball career at Kentucky came to an end, Smith played some baseball for the Wildcats as a pitcher. And he found time to return a favor to his hometown by participating in an exhibition basketball game at Laurel County High which featured UK seniors against the Marathon Oil AAU squad. The two teams were on a barnstorming tour throughout the state. The game attracted a near-sellout crowd of 5,000 fans.

Local community officials honored Smith in a pre-game ceremony. The player received a plaque as well as a portrait. "We came back my senior year to have a scrimmage and they had a little thing for me before the game started that night," recalled a modest Smith.

Since leaving UK in 1975, Smith has taught and coached at Laurel County High. The school has produced several basketball standouts for UK, namely Paul Andrews and Todd Bearup for the men's team as well as Bonnie Sizemore, Sharon Garland, Lisa Collins and Stacey Reed for the Lady Kats. Not many rural schools can match that feat, if any.

This mountain boy is a quiet, unassuming person who returned to his home devoting his time and attention to the training of other mountain boys.

11 Mr. Cool

"...the greatest guard in the nation."

During his pro career, Kyle Macy found Italy to be a very interesting place as well as a valuable cultural experience.

Dubbed by some as the most popular player ever to wear a Wildcat uniform, Macy played pro basketball for 10 years, including three adventurous seasons in Italy. After seven years in the NBA where he played for the Phoenix Suns, Chicago Bulls and Indiana Pacers, he journeyed to Europe in 1987 to compete in the Italian League before he called it quits in 1990.

It is the same league which once signed American stars Danny Ferry and Brian Shaw to fat contracts with Ferry getting about $2 million plus a free house and automobile for one year. And, in early 1991, the league featured several ex-NBA standouts in Michael Cooper, Bob McAdoo, Michael Ray Richardson, to name a few, as well as Brazilian star Oscar Schmidt, who recently became the Italian League's all-time leading scorer.

In Macy's first year of Italian competition, he played for a squad based in Bologna. He later moved on to Treviso where he played for a couple of years. Both cities are located in the northern part of Italy.

Macy finds the level of competition in the Italian League fairly tough. He respects their players. "The

Italian League is supposedly the second strongest (professional) league in the world and obviously, the NBA is the first," said the former two-time UK All-American. "It's improving, I think, each year. (Speaking of) the Americans, or foreign players as they are called, you're allowed two per team. There are few players from other countries. I know one is from Brazil and another player is from Argentina. But most of the foreign players are Americans.

"The Italian players are paid okay. They're not paid obviously as well as the foreign players who come in. But, they're paying very good money now. You read about Danny Ferry and Brian Shaw and the big contracts they signed with Rome. There are other players who are making a lot of money, too. So, it's not just one or two players. But, as a foreign player coming in, I think it's pretty safe to say I was making as much playing there as I was making my last year in the NBA. So, it's good money."

However, don't get the impression that Italian players make relatively nothing. "They make anywhere from $100,000 and up," Macy said. "It just depends on how good the player is."

During the 1989-90 season, Macy experienced some bizarre moments as an overseas player — something unheard of in the United States.

"Normally, you hear about a player disappearing, not coming to practice or not showing up for a game," he said. "Well, our coach disappeared two different times. We were ready for practice and no one knew where he was. The people in the office, the general manager and the president had no idea where the coach went. But, instead of firing the coach or taking any (disciplinary) actions, the following day he returned and things picked up as normal. That happened not just once but two times during the course of the season. So, needless to say, it was a little confusing and it was kind of bizarre. I've heard of players disappearing but never coaches."

Macy was not the only ex-UK player you could find in Italy during the 1989-90 campaign. After one year of limited NBA action with the lowly Los Angeles Clippers, former Wildcat standout Rob Lock has participated in the Italian League since 1989. He faced Macy a few times.

Lock played for the club based in Pavia and his teammates included Schmidt, the same guy who practically defeated the U.S. all by himself in the 1987 Pan Am Games. Although their Italian teams were stationed about 150 miles apart, Macy and Lock occasionally got together and traveled for relaxation. "When we'd have off days, sometimes we'd get together and make trips, maybe outside of Italy," Macy commented. "We went to Stuttgart (in Germany), Innsbruck (Austria) and Zurich (Switzerland). We got together and talked in English and just had a good time."

For the American players like Macy and Lock, the language barrier can be very difficult to overcome in a foreign country, both on- and off-the court. But Macy did manage to learn to communicate in various situations such as game strategy, ordering a dinner, or buying goods at a store.

"I was fortunate that most of the players on the team did speak some English," Macy said. "Usually they will have an assistant coach that will translate. A lot of times the head coach can speak some English. So, you get a little bit of both and the longer you're there, practicing everyday and hearing all the different things in Italian, you get to where you understand Italian, probably more in a basketball sense than out on the streets. My Italian first improved in basketball terminology and later just being out on the streets talking to people. If you have a problem, they usually have a translator for you."

The more successful an Italian squad is, the more it travels, playing in tournaments in other European countries. Macy's Treviso squad was one of the more competitive clubs in the league (whose members often play only one regular season game per week, usually on Sunday afternoons, besides tourney action). Because of his team's success, Macy did see a lot of interesting and historic sights in other countries.

"It depends on how your team does. If you have a lot of success, you can play in other countries more — Austria, France and Spain," Macy said. "It just depends how your team has been doing the past few years. You qualify for other tournaments each year.

"I know this past year (1989-90) we played in Yugoslavia and played in a tournament in Berlin

(Germany). In fact, we were in Berlin about a week before they started to knock the Berlin Wall down. So, that was real interesting."

How is the Italian press different from the American? Are they more critical of the players? Can Macy read their articles?

"I've learned to read enough to understand, but the Italian press is very critical of the players and they're not a very knowledgeable press," he said. "They are really more interested in the points scored by a player than anything else. They don't really know the game enough to understand the other aspects — rebounding, passing and defense. So, their only concern is how many points a player scores. If he scores a lot of points, even if he takes 50 shots, then they think he's a good player. They're very opinionated and they're not very knowledgeable.

"They have roughly six newspapers and it's a very small country so one paper itself is just all sports. They have to find things to write about so they try to stir up rumors and gossip and get things going."

Unlike the basketball-crazed states of Kentucky and Indiana, basketball is not Italy's favorite pastime. Soccer is the country's No. 1 sport. The government-controlled television network carries many soccer games. Demonstrating Italians' love affair with soccer, Macy used a two-hour TV sports program that airs on Sunday night as an example.

"I'd say an hour and 45 minutes are devoted to soccer and maybe five minutes for basketball and maybe 10 minutes for the other sports of the day," he said of the TV show. "That's kind of how the comparison comes down with soccer being the dominant sport."

With the exception of post-season playoffs, Macy also pointed out that when a basketball contest is being nationally televised, the game is not shown in its entirety. Instead, Macy said, "It's a little bit different. They'll show the second half of the game; they don't televise the whole game until the finals of the playoffs."

As an NBA rookie during the 1980-81 campaign, Macy enjoyed playing for the Phoenix Suns. He had been selected by the Suns in the first round of the 1979 draft as a "junior eligible" because his original class had graduated and was the league's 22nd pick overall. But he opted to stay at Kentucky for his senior year and later signed with Phoenix shortly before the 1980 draft. If Macy and the Suns hadn't agreed to a contract before then, he would've been eligible for the draft again.

At Phoenix, it was a fun time for Macy. With a glittering 57-25 mark, his team captured the Western Division title, beating out Kareem Abdul-Jabbar and the defending champion Los Angeles Lakers by three games. The Suns, however, were not able to advance very far in the playoffs as they dropped to Kansas City in the Western Conference semifinals which went seven games. Playing behind rising NBA stars Dennis Johnson and Walter Davis in the backcourt as a first-year pro, Macy did not win any major individual awards. However, he contributed significantly to the team in a reserve role, seeing action in all of the squad's 82 games and averaging 8.1 points a game with a high of 21. Some of the NBA's top rookies at that time featured Joe Barry Carroll of Golden State, Darrell Griffith of Utah and Kevin McHale of Boston with Griffith winning the NBA Rookie-of-the-Year honors.

During his five-year stay at Phoenix, Macy did well as a part-time starting guard. In Macy's second year (1981-82), he was the league's top free throw shooter with a nearly 90 percent average. Also, he ranked third in the league in three-point field goal shooting with 39 percent, hitting 39 of 100 shots. For the season, he averaged 14.2 points a contest with a game-high of 31, both of which eventually ended up as his NBA career highs. And, in 1984-85, he captured his second NBA free throw title, converting nearly 91 percent of attempts.

"We had some very good teams in Phoenix and it was a lot of fun playing there. In my first year as a rookie, we won the Western Division and that was an exciting time. I think probably some of the most exciting moments were in the playoffs against the Lakers in 1984. In the Western Conference finals, we took the Lakers to six games (before losing) with a team that had really been struggling even to make the playoffs. But we kind of peaked at the right time and the crowds really got behind us. That was a lot of fun." The Suns had compiled a mediocre 41-41 record before catching fire at the end of the season.

As time passes, Macy begins to appreciate his good days in the NBA and the individual awards he has received. "I won two NBA free throw shooting titles and that's something I'll look back on later," he said. "They can't erase that. It will always be in the record books, so it means a lot to me. It's kind of nice to think about that sometimes and if you ever have kids or grandkids, see here what dad or granddad did way back. It didn't mean anything, maybe, at the time, but the older I get I think it's kind of nice to have.

For a couple of years, Macy also had his former college teammate — 6-10 Rick Robey — on the Suns squad.

But toward the end of Macy's tenure at Phoenix, the Suns began to falter. After posting a .500 mark the season before, their 1984-85 record dropped to 36-46, the worst in eight years. It was Macy's last year as a Sun. In the following season, Phoenix was even worse with a 32-50 mark. The winning attitude had just disappeared. The once-proud franchise was in a big mess. And something else was happening off the floor as well. The Suns later found themselves in a very embarrassing court case which attracted national attention. Seven former or present players of the team were involved in a highly-publicized drug scandal which rocked the franchise and the entire NBA.

"I've heard some talk of those years where other players on the team may or may not have been involved in some drugs," Macy said. "If it's true that they were using drugs, then you kind of have a bad feeling about those times. You wonder what would have happened if they'd not being doing those things. We could have maybe beaten the Lakers and gone on and won the NBA championship.

"I think as a professional athlete you have an image to uphold to the young people. If guys are messing with drugs or doing things that they should not be doing and setting a bad example, then that is disturbing."

In his final two NBA campaigns, Macy played for the Chicago Bulls in 1985-86, leading the team in assists and averaging around nine points, and the Indiana Pacers the following season. For the Pacers, guided by veteran coach Jack Ramsay, Macy logged only 1,250 minutes, the least of his NBA career. He averaged 4.9 points in 76 games.

But a few years later in 1990, Macy felt that he still can compete in the NBA as a key reserve player, if not a starter. He said he was not given the opportunity to play his team-oriented style of basketball when he was with the Pacers.

Born in 1957, Macy grew up as a Hoosier, having lived in the northern Indiana cities of Fort Wayne and Peru. Fort Wayne once had an NBA franchise called the Fort Wayne Pistons but they moved to Detroit in 1957, when Macy was an infant.

At Fort Wayne, he became what you call a "gym rat." "I grew up in Fort Wayne and my father was a coach at a small college there at Indiana Tech," Macy said. "For me, the guys who were my heroes — the ones I really looked up to — were the players on his team. If I'd name the players, no one would know their names other than the people from that school.

"I'd go to practice with my father and watch. Afterwards I'd go out and shoot. The guys would stick around and play with me a game of horse or sometimes one-on-one. For me, I'd go home after practice and go either down in the basement or outside, and try to imitate everything they did on the court. I can remember watching a pro game with (NBA stars) Jerry West and Oscar Robertson, but the players I really looked up to were my father's college team."

By the time Macy was about 15 years old, he and his father, Robert, were seriously considering going to a high school where they could work together. The father would coach his son. In the summer of 1972, just before Macy's sophomore season, they ended up at Peru, a city of approximately of 14,000. They had decided it was the best situation for them and also Macy's grandparents lived there.

So, for the next three years, Macy played for his dad's team at Peru High School. It was where Macy made a name for himself, becoming Indiana's Mr. Basketball in 1975 after his senior year.

Macy and his father have always been close. But they sometimes had words. And dad was very demanding; he wanted to do what was best for the youngster. Asked if his dad was tougher on him than his teammates, Macy replied, "Well, I don't know if he was tougher. I think he maybe just knew more of what I could do. So, he just pushed me to do those things. I was fortunate to be in that situation. If I had been playing for another coach, I wouldn't have been given the opportunity to do those things that I could do. So, that talent might have never come out. Because he was aware of how I could play and things I could do, he pushed me to try to be the best player I could be. In the long run, that helped me to be a better player."

As a prep All-American who once had a single-game high of 51 points and scored over 40 points 14 times, Macy was a highly-recruited player. Many major schools such as Kentucky, Purdue, UCLA and Cincinnati — they were Macy's top choices — wanted his services. Tennessee coach Ray Mears sought Macy, too. But Mears lost him because the Vols used fancy warmup drills. That turned Macy off and he didn't like the Vols. (Mears once had a reserve player by the name of Roger Peltz riding a unicycle around the floor in a circus-like atmosphere.)

His father and mother, Evelyn, helped Macy in the recruiting process, screening mail and telephone calls. If the recruiters wanted Macy on their side, they desperately tried to charm his father because he usually was the first person they came in contact with. And dad was Macy's coach, too. It was a big advantage so that the younger Macy did not have to deal with the recruiters very much.

When Macy announced his college choice, Purdue was the winner of the recruiting sweepstakes. Why the Boilermakers?

"Well, it's kind of a long story," remembered Macy. "I was real slow in deciding. I was kind of late. It more or less worked itself out to a point where other schools needed to make a decision. They felt like they couldn't wait any longer because if I didn't choose their school, then they'd be stuck without a guard or whoever they were looking for. So they, more or less, went through the process of eliminating themselves.

"Kentucky was interested in (guard) Truman

Claytor and at that time, I just wasn't ready and I wasn't going to jump into a major decision like that. I waited and they (Kentucky coaches) said they needed to go ahead and sign (Claytor) because I was taking a long time in deciding. So, that knocked Kentucky out. I also visited Cincinnati, whose program at that time was very strong. After visiting UCLA, it was so far from home and I was afraid I might get lost in the shuffle going out west that far. It just worked out where I went to Purdue."

Hometown fans played a factor in Macy's decision to stay in his home state. Purdue, located in West Lafayette, was about one-hour drive from Macy's hometown of Peru. "I think I was maybe influenced by the people of Indiana to stay in the state, being a Mr. Basketball in high school," he said. "You kind of feel a little bit of that pressure. Obviously, after one year I just wasn't happy there. It was a great school. It wasn't the academics I was displeased with, but more just the direction the athletic program was going with the coach (Fred Schaus) there. So, I transferred to Kentucky and fortunately things worked out."

Despite his unhappiness at Purdue, Macy had a relatively good season for a freshman. A 6-3 guard, he was the team's third-leading scorer with 13.8 points a game and poured in a single-game high of 38 points against Wisconsin.

At Kentucky, Macy had to sit out his first year because of transfer rules. It was a difficult time for him as he had played basketball all of his life. But, as he discovered later, the wait was well worth it.

On his first Kentucky team, Macy and the Wildcats won the national championship in 1978. He was a third-year sophomore playing with senior stars in 6-10 Rick Robey, 6-10 Mike Phillips, 6-4 Jack Givens and 6-5 James Lee. Macy said capturing the NCAA title in St. Louis was the highlight of his UK career. The expectations from the fans and media had been extremely high, creating extra pressure on the team. The Wildcats, who finished with a glossy 30-2 worksheet, had been the pre-season favorites, along with North Carolina, to win it all.

The 1978-79 season was a different story. Macy

was a junior and Kentucky did not have Robey, Phillips, Givens and Lee to terrorize the foes. It was a rebuilding year. Coach Joe B. Hall had to find three new starters for the young team, not to mention the loss of its "Sixth Man" in Lee. Nevertheless, Hall was facing one of his biggest challenges as a Wildcat mentor. Early in the season, the Wildcats struggled as they learned to play together. They began SEC action with only one victory in six conference games. Not accustomed to seeing their favorite team lose that often, the fans were getting very uneasy about their beloved Wildcats, even though they knew the squad was young.

The Wildcats, however, bounced back to finish the campaign with a respectable 19-12 record, including a 10-8 SEC mark. The high point of the season was the wildly exciting SEC Tournament in Birmingham, Ala. Kentucky, playing in an unusual role of underdog, stunned observers by winning three games in three consecutive nights before dropping to Tennessee 75-69 in overtime in the finals. And the news media covering the event voted Macy as the tournament's MVP. Because of Kentucky's surprising performance in the SEC Tournament, which was renewed for the first time since 1952, the National Invitation Tournament invited the Wildcats to its post-season event. Tired from the conference tournament the previous week, the Cats didn't go far as they lost to Clemson 68-67 in a first-round matchup at Rupp Arena.

"It was an exciting season," Macy told the author in an exclusive 1979 interview for the *Kentucky Kernel*. "We were young and we made a lot of mistakes. But at the same time, we learned from mistakes.

"I think the fans enjoyed watching us play. Even though we were small, we tried to make up with hustle. It was very different from the previous year.

"We didn't start out the conference race right. We were 1-5. As the year went along, we tried to get organized and we won some games down the stretch. That gave us the momentum for the tournament. We did keep the momentum and played good ball (in the tourney). The SEC tournament was the highlight (of the season)."

When Kentucky reached the cellar in the SEC in January of that season with its 1-5 record, Macy wasn't discouraged. "I wasn't depressed," he said. "I knew we could play better. The whole team was just a bunch of competitors. We would get behind, but we wouldn't give up. We never gave up. The fans had a lot to do with it."

Macy, who finished with a season average of over 15 points a game which was a team high, felt that his best overall performance of the season was probably against LSU in the semifinals of the SEC tournament. He hit 10 of 15 field goal tries and made all of his nine free throws for 29 points in UK's 80-67 upset of the Tigers. "I think it was maybe the LSU game because they were the top-rated team in the conference," explained Macy. "They had already beaten us twice. It was a very satisfying win for the team and me."

Members of Macy's family came to Lexington often to see him play. They were very supportive. "My mother came to every home game," Macy said. "My father came when his team wasn't playing. My sister once was expecting a baby at any time so she couldn't make it in the later part of the year. With all the excitement, she might've given birth in Rupp Arena!" Macy also has a brother.

When this 1979 *Kernel* interview with Macy began, there was a group of about 10 noisy high school girls — teenyboppers — standing outside the Joe B. Hall Wildcat Lodge, trying to get the autograph of their beloved star. And after Macy — whose kiss once sold for $600 at a charity auction — finished talking, a few of the diehard teenyboppers were still standing outside. They were waiting for their hero.

Months later, he represented the U.S. on the Pan American basketball squad after surviving a four-day tryout which attracted some 70 outstanding players from the nation. His Pam Am coach was none other than controversial Bobby Knight, who called him "the greatest guard in the nation." Macy was more than pleased to hear the compliment, especially since it came from one of the country's best coaches.

"It's very flattering when coach Knight says something like that," Macy recalled. "He's one of the greatest basketball minds there is and I enjoyed playing for him in the Pan Am experience.

"You hear a lot of stories about coach Knight so I wasn't sure about him at first. But for me, that was one of the most enjoyable times I've had in playing basketball, being on the Pan Am team and practicing the whole summer up in Indiana and working with a lot of great players. I have a lot of respect for coach Knight. That was a fun time."

Well, it certainly wasn't fun when Macy broke his jaw in the Pan Am Games, which were held in Puerto Rico. A Cuban player had purposely hit Macy on his jaw during a game and, the player subsequently was ejected.

"I got sucker punched," Macy said. "We'd played Cuba (earlier) and beat them about 40 points and we're playing against them in this game. The second half was just starting and we were already ahead by 20. I think they knew they were going to lose. I made a pass and went to cut away from the ball. The next thing I knew I was on my knees. I didn't even see the punch being thrown. It was just a flagrant foul and luckily the referee saw it and the player was expelled, but only for one game. There had been no altercations between myself and the player who threw the punch. In fact, I hadn't even guarded him in the first half.

"In the meantime, my mouth was wired shut for seven weeks. There wasn't a lot of justification for the blow. I didn't feel like (fighting back) on my part, but there was nothing I could do about it. (The injury) was very painful."

As a result, Macy had to depart Puerto Rico early, missing two games as the squad captured the gold medal. His parents, who had watched him in the Pan Am Games, accompanied him on a return trip to Lexington. While Macy was recovering with his jaw practically shut down, he lost over 30 pounds. Macy later was surprised when Knight contacted him, saying that he would like to come to Lexington to deliver a gold medal to the Wildcat star. Knight flew to the Bluegrass from Bloomington, Indiana. Macy appreciated Knight's gesture. "He came down personally and presented me with the medal," Macy said. "That meant a lot to me."

However, there was one other incident at the 1979 Pan Am Games that Knight will be remembered for, among his many controversies. The coach had been arrested for attacking a Puerto Rican policeman at a gym where the U.S. squad practiced. Many people who were at the scene, including Macy, said the episode was blown out of proportion, stating that it was the policeman — not Knight — who was more than willing to fight.

"We were finishing a practice session, and I think, more or less, the policeman was just trying to show that he was an authority or was in charge," Macy recalled. "It was like he was looking for trouble. It really never should have happened. I think it (the political tension) just kind of built up throughout the week."

Macy thought some of the citizens of Puerto Rico treated the American athletes well, but unfortunately some didn't. A lot of the problems were due to politics. "I think, at that time, it was just kind of a sentiment," he said. "The country was split (somewhat). There was some talk of (Puerto Rico) being taken in by the United States or the communist force. You had a little bit of both. I think that's kind of more political than in the feeling of the sport, which the Pan American Games are all about."

During Macy's last year in a Wildcat uniform, Kentucky fielded an excellent team with promising freshman star Sam Bowie, a 7-1 center. The Wildcats posted a remarkable 29-6 mark, including the SEC regular season championship.

Several hours after they shocked LSU 76-74 in Baton Rouge, La., on Macy's 22-foot jumper with one second remaining in overtime in the regular season finale, clinching the league crown, the Wildcats found themselves in a pep rally at Memorial Coliseum in Lexington. Kentucky faithful had gone bonkers over their favorite team. An excited crowd of over 8,000 spectators attended the Sunday night rally, honoring the Wildcat basketball team, and Lt. Gov. Martha Layne Collins proclaimed that the next day would be the "University of Kentucky Wildcat Day."

Interestingly, Macy, who was suffering from a bad chest cold, played one of the worst games of his UK career against LSU, as he could only connect four of 14 field goal attempts. Yet, he won the game for Kentucky.

After participating in the SEC tournament in

Birmingham where the Wildcats dropped a disappointing 80-78 setback to LSU in the championship game, they were surprisingly placed in the Mideast Regional by the NCAA tournament committee. That meant Kentucky did not have to travel out of state, with the tourney action first taking place at Bowling Green, Ky., and then Lexington. Kentucky won its first tournament game, defeating Florida State, for the right to play on its home floor the following weekend. Duke, nonetheless, spoiled Kentucky's dream of another trip to the Final Four as the Blue Devils narrowly won in a 55-54 thriller.

Kentucky, led by 6-8 junior Fred Cowan's game-high 26 points, had a chance to pull out in the closing seconds. After a timeout with nine ticks left, Macy, if the situation warranted, wanted to play the heroic role as he had done several times during his UK career. Closely guarded by Lexington native Vince Taylor of Duke, Macy attempted a possible winning basket. But Macy's shot didn't fall. It was Macy's last shot as a Wildcat.

About three years before legendary Adolph Rupp's death in 1977, Macy fondly remembers his first encounter with the Baron in Lexington.

"He'd retired from coaching then, but I was down here looking around the school during my senior year in high school," he said. "He was in one of the back halls of the (Memorial) Coliseum before one of the games. I was fortunate to just say hello and was introduced to him."

That was Macy's only meeting with Rupp.

Rupp would've been proud of him, perhaps saying, "By gawd, he's so cool and smart. And, how does he keep his hair in place?"

On coach Joe B. Hall, Macy described him as a firm individual who believed in running the roundball program like a military school. Macy supported Hall's approach. "Coach Hall was a very tough coach, a very disciplined coach," he said. "I think he taught me, not only about basketball, but also how to handle myself off the floor.

Through his discipline, I became a better player and person. In a work situation, one has to be disciplined to do certain things on the job and do things right and that's really what he was trying to do. Maybe not all his working was just for the basketball sense, but in preparing an individual for the real world when one is finished with basketball.

"So as a youngster, you may not understand that. At the time, you may think this guy's nuts and why are we doing this. You may question a lot, but then as you get older you realize that the coach had a purpose in mind when he was making us run 220 and do all those crazy things."

For Macy and his teammates, it wasn't easy to get to know Hall very well. The coach tried to keep his distance from the players.

"I think it was tough to actually feel close when you were playing for coach Hall," said Macy, who also did his student teaching at Lexington Tates Creek High during his UK senior year. "I mean you understand and you know him like a father, but at the same time, you don't get that close to him until you finish playing for him. I think he wants it a little bit that way. It (friendship) develops more afterwards. It's kind of hard to understand. There's a closeness but not a real closeness."

Somewhat shy, Macy has always been a quiet person. He doesn't show much emotion. Since he departed UK in 1980, he doesn't feel that he has changed much as a person and he now makes his home in Lexington. He is not married.

"I hope I haven't changed a whole lot since I left," he said. "I'm still pretty much the same person. I try to keep in touch with friends from school. I always enjoy coming back here to Lexington. For me, this is home now. Whether I've played so many years of professional basketball or I'd gone into some other profession and worked for seven or 10 years, I think I'd still be the same person.

"No matter how much money a person makes or whatever, that's not really the important thing. It's what kind of person they are on the inside. I've always been very close to my family and that's important to me. My friends are important to me, too."

12 GENTLE GIANT

"...there was the
tradition, the fan
support and
the exposure (TV)...
I decided to go to UK."

On a sweltering summer day in 1990 in Lexington, Sam Bowie was late for an interview for this book. He was supposed to meet the author at Nutter Training Center on the UK campus. For a couple of hours, he was nowhere to be seen.

It was highly unusual for Bowie to miss a meeting as the New Jersey Nets star is one of the most agreeable fellows around. He has the reputation of being very dependable. Eventually he showed up just to work out and saw the author who was preparing to leave.

"I'm sorry," said Bowie. "I forgot all about it. It just slipped my mind."

Bowie apologized several times, saying he felt bad about forgetting the appointment, which had been set up just a few days before.

Three months earlier Bowie had become a richer man despite the fact his NBA team was struggling on its way to a dismal 17-65 record — worst in the league. Playing well and healthy throughout the season for the first time since his rookie year of 1984-85, Bowie had signed a five-year pact worth $13.5 million with New

Jersey. In translation, it means he would be receiving an average of $2.7 million a year. It was more than twice what he had been making as his old contract expired at the end of 1989-90 season. At that time, he was drawing $1.2 million a year.

Bowie could have waited and opted for the free agency route after that season, possibly to get better offers. But he decided it was not the proper thing to do because he might be risking a career-ending injury. And no team would be willing to gamble on Bowie since he had already suffered numerous broken leg injuries in his college and pro career.

Despite his new sizeable contract, Bowie said money will not change him. "The first thing I did (after signing the pact) was to count my blessings and realize how fortunate I was," he said. "I've never been one who's motivated by money or materialistic things. I'll always be the same Sam Bowie regardless of how much money I ever get.

"I was raised in the Methodist church. When I came to school here at Kentucky, I went to a Baptist church and now I consider myself non-denominational. I just go to whatever church is available. I go there and give thanks for the lifestyle that I'm living."

Another key reason Bowie signed the contract early was because he wanted his family to have financial security. At that time his wife, Heidi, a high school sweetheart, was pregnant. About two months later, they became the proud parents of a nine-pound, 15-ounce baby girl named Samantha after her daddy. Bowie and his wife have been married for four years, and they have made Lexington their off-season home.

"My wife and I started dating my senior year in high school," said Bowie. "I went to Kentucky and she went to Penn State. We kept our long distance relationship."

His girlfriend, coming down from Pennsylvania, occasionally visited Bowie when he was a Wildcat star. "She had an opportunity to come down and watch me play a few games in Rupp Arena," he said. "She was amazed at the amount of fan support that the University of Kentucky has."

In 1979, when the author served as the sports editor of the *Kentucky Kernel*, student daily newspaper at UK, there was a great deal of interest in Bowie, who was one of the nation's most recruited prep stars. Coach Joe B. Hall was working hard at recruiting the player. A guy from the University of Virginia called the *Kernel* newsroom in February and wanted to know if Bowie had made a verbal commitment to attend UK. Contacted later at Memorial Coliseum, a spokesman from the UK sports information office said the rumor was unjustified.

Everybody was interested in the recruiting sweepstakes, especially in Bowie and 7-4 Ralph Sampson, who also was being wooed by Kentucky. Many fans figured if Bowie and/or Sampson signed with Kentucky, then the Wildcats would be on their way to another national championship.

A native of Lebanon, Pa., Bowie inked with Kentucky. But it wasn't an easy decision to make. He also liked Nevada-Las Vegas. Tark the Shark. The night-club atmosphere. Casinos. Showgirls.

"It came down to either going to UK or going to Nevada-Las Vegas," Bowie recalled. "(Coach) Jerry Tarkanian recruited me extremely hard. He was very anxious for me to sign to go to Nevada-Las Vegas.

"When I visited out there I enjoyed it. I liked the strip. It was my first time of really seeing that type of atmosphere with the lights glittering, the town that never shuts down, things like that.

"But then when I visited Kentucky, there was the tradition, the fan support and the exposure that I was going to get for being on national TV. It was just a situation that I couldn't turn down and I decided to go to UK."

Like day and night, Hall and Tarkanian were coaches of vastly different personalities.

"Tark the Shark was a more outgoing type of guy, looser and joked around a lot more," Bowie said. "(He's) a lot more liberal. Coach Hall is a straight forward type of guy, a disciplinarian, from the old school. (You would give) a 'yes sir,' 'no sir' type of response. They are literally two different type of individuals."

Bowie, meanwhile, was stunned when Sampson

changed his mind about going to UK and signed with Virginia of the Atlantic Coast Conference. Like Bowie, Sampson had been tabbed by scouts as another Wilt Chamberlain. Besides Virginia and Kentucky, his top two choices, Sampson seriously considered North Carolina and Virginia Tech. On June 1, 1979, he announced his selection of Virginia, which was located about 50 miles from his hometown in Harrisonburg, Va., ending one of the longest recruiting battles in college basketball history. The announcement was made at his high school gym before a large contingent of reporters and the bright TV lights. The press came to the affair from everywhere. From New York to Washington, D.C., to Los Angeles. It was a big deal and they came to hear a 17-year-old kid making an announcement.

"When I was playing in the all-star games coming out of high school, Ralph and I had talked about both of us going to UK," Bowie said. "He said that he was definitely going to UK and it was going to be exciting for me to be playing alongside of a guy like Ralph Sampson.

"But, at the last moment, (because of) some pressure from his mother to stay in the state, he decided to sign with Virginia. A lot of people really don't realize how close it was for the two of us to be playing at UK. Those would have been exciting years with Ralph. I was under the assumption that he was coming to UK. When I heard that he signed with the University of Virginia, I was shocked."

Bowie grew up in a lower middle-class family in Lebanon, a Pennsylvania town of 26,000 residents. And he followed NBA on TV with a lot of interest.

"When I was growing up, I used to watch NBA basketball, hoping that one day I'd be able to play in the professional ranks," he said. "At that time, Lew Alcindor (now Kareem Abdul-Jabbar), who played for the Milwaukee Bucks, was my childhood hero and I've always been amazed at the way he was able to adapt to whatever situation was put in front of him. Quite naturally, him being a center and me being a very tall kid and taller than my peers, he was the guy I idolized the most."

Basketball has always played a big part in his

family. Bowie's father was a semi-pro player and coached his son in the YMCA. His younger sister, Shelly, played college basketball at Penn State.

"My father Ben was 6-11 so that's where my height comes from," Bowie said. "He played for the Harlem Magicians, which were the team like the Globetrotters. He played back in the early 1960s. I grew up in a basketball environment. My sister played collegiate basketball. My mother was very athletic. She never played any collegiate sports but was always pretty much athletic-inclined and was very willing to make some sacrifices for her children. She was very busy running my sister and me back and forth to some type of sporting event. Our whole family pretty much revolved around the sports world.

"Back then, I came from a blue-collar type of family. A family that was making about $10,000 or $11,000 a year, trying to raise two kids. So, we weren't poverty stricken by any means, but we never were able to live high on the hog. I come from a disciplinarian family, a respectful family, one that raised the children to respect the elders and to be very courteous toward others."

Since Bowie was born in 1961, he never had the opportunity to watch his father perform for the Magicians. "I was about two or three years old when he finally quit playing with the Magicians," explained Bowie. "So, the only thing I recall is the newspaper articles and some old films. I don't remember him personally playing, but just from the scrapbooks."

His parents divorced when Bowie was in the seventh grade. Although his father and mother both continued to stay in the same hometown, it was a difficult period for Bowie and the family. "Although they divorced for the betterment of the kids, they still had a mutual respect towards each other," Bowie said. "They did not allow their divorce to affect the way the kids were raised and I really respect them for that matter. Coming from a divorced family, it's a bad situation. It's a situation that you wish would not have occurred, but I feel as though both of them did an excellent job in raising the two kids that they had."

In the summer of 1981, after his sophomore season in college, Bowie suffered one of the saddest moments of his life. He lost his father, whom he highly admired. "My father passed away when he was 45 years old," he said. "He had a cyst on his lung that burst and caused internal hemorrhaging. So, it was very unfortunate. It happened my sophomore year here at UK and it came by total surprise, but I always feel as though he's still upstairs looking down on me now. I just constantly have conversations with him."

Bowie's mother, Cathy, still lives in Lebanon and now works for the Hershey Foods Corporation, which produces chocolate candies, among other things. His sister is employed in Lexington after moving from her hometown in July of 1990. She has a degree in psychology.

Like most kids in college, Bowie had some good times as well as the bad ones at Kentucky. After two outstanding seasons — his freshman and sophomore years — which saw him garner many post-season honors (All-SEC twice and All-American), he suffered emotional and physical pain and was on crutches for two consecutive years as the result of his leg injuries. But that's not all. There was one incident which took place during the 1979 Christmas holidays when he was a freshman starting center. And, today, he admits that he is not proud of it.

Just a couple of days before the December 29 nationally-televised Kentucky-Notre Dame clash at Louisville, coach Hall announced at a press conference that he was suspending Bowie and freshman guard Dirk Minniefield for the Notre Dame game for breaking well-established team training rules. Hall refused to be specific on the violations.

Also, at about the same time, sophomore standout Dwight Anderson — who had been perhaps the country's top high school player two years earlier — decided to leave the squad for personal reasons. He was having academic problems, among other things.

Throughout the state, there were all kinds of rumors flying around concerning the somewhat confusing episode. Sportscaster Tom Hammond, now an NBC announcer who was then working for WLEX-TV in Lexington, reported on the air that Anderson had been caught using drugs in his Wildcat Lodge room. Also, Bowie and Minniefield were in Anderson's room at the time, but they were not involved with the drugs, according to the TV report. The media speculated that team rule violations included smoking marijuana.

However, 11 years later, Bowie said he and Minniefield were suspended because they were late returning from a campus party — perhaps on the same night after the Wildcats won the University of Kentucky Invitational Tournament on December 22. They defeated coach and Kentucky native Lee Rose and his Purdue Boilermakers 61-60 for the tourney championship.

Bowie said it was an embarrassing situation that he'll never forget. "There was one particular time when myself, Dirk Minniefield and Dwight Anderson missed the curfew and came in one night a little late," he recalled. "Coach Hall was in the lodge waiting on us. To say we were embarrassed and a little ashamed was an understatement. But, those were times that you never forget because the good times as well as the bad were all a lot of fun here at UK.

What was Bowie doing that night? "At that time, we probably were just going to a regular old fraternity party on campus," he said. "When you're at UK, you're always in the limelight and you're expected to be the All-American type boy. But there were some circumstances where we were no different from the average 18, 19-year-old kid who was missing curfew, not doing what he was supposed to do."

Even without the trio of Anderson, Bowie and Minniefield, the Wildcats — with only seven experienced players on hand — found a way to win as they surprised Notre Dame 86-80 behind senior Kyle Macy's game-high 21 points. Macy had six assists and made only one turnover in the entire 40 minutes against the Notre Dame press. Afterwards, Hall — who had to use walk-on Bo Lanter and little-used freshman Tom Heitz as his team was short-handed — said the victory ranks as one of the biggest of his coaching career.

And, although they might not have been the best-looking, Bowie and Minniefield, both well-dressed in their suits and ties, were the best cheerleaders that night. They loudly encouraged their teammates from the bench.

After sitting out the 1981-82 campaign at UK with a fractured leg that didn't heal properly, Bowie practiced but then realized in the summer of 1982– that he was having problems with his leg again. He was getting ready for the upcoming season, which was months away. But he visited the doctors and they consequently decided to put his leg in a cast. Yes, again. It was another disappointing setback for Bowie. And he underwent electrolysis treatment on his leg, hoping that it would heal on its own. However, the worst had yet to come.

As the season neared, another trip to the doctor's office revealed that his leg still had not healed. The news disturbed Bowie so severely that he said it was the most heartbreaking moment of his collegiate career. "They told me I was going to have to remain in the cast for an additional 10 weeks and that meant that I was going to miss another full year of competitive activity here," he recalled. "That was probably the most disappointing time of my being at UK." So, Bowie was out for another season. Later, he underwent bone-graft surgery on his leg.

Needless to say, those times were difficult. Visits to the doctors. Going through long, frustrating recovery periods. Uncertainty about his playing career in the future. It is something that no player wants to go through. Bowie, however, handled the situation like a mature adult. Coach Hall also gave emotional support to Bowie.

"I think I was blessed with a God-given ability to endure the so-called setbacks," Bowie said. "I've always been the type of guy who never wants to bring my problems to someone else and I try and deal with my problems within myself and not bear them on someone else. I feel as though my inner toughness, without boasting or bragging, was such that I was just the type of individual who could handle those situations.

"Coach Hall and I had great conversations, especially when I was injured and he was helping me get through those trying times. Coach Hall was a very tough coach. He was a guy who set a lot of rules, regulations and curfews, but I had a wonderful relationship with coach Hall. He was a disciplinarian. He believed that hard work paid big dividends and he never was the type of guy who thought short cuts were any way to success. I have nothing but respect for him."

At times, Hall can be very rough on the players, according to Bowie, who played on the 1980 U.S. Olympic squad against the NBA All-Stars (when the U.S. boycotted the Moscow Olympics). "When coach Hall got angry at a player, he never pulled any punches," said the player. "He told you what he felt and he did what he felt was right at that particular time. A lot of times it meant running up to the top of Rupp Arena and then coming back down and then going back up to the top of Rupp Arena. So, he had all kinds of ways to punish you. He would wake you up at 6:45 in the morning and make you do a lot of calisthenics and running exercises to discipline you. So, when he got angry, you knew you were in trouble."

Not playing in the Moscow Olympics was a heartbreaker for Bowie. But he understood the country's political situation when President Carter refused to let America's top athletes participate in the event overseas because the Russian soldiers had invaded Afghanistan. In a series of games against NBA all-star teams, facing centers like Artis Gilmore and Bob Lanier, Bowie was outstanding. He was the team's leading rebounder and second-leading scorer. Bowie said being a part of the Olympic team "was very rewarding. It (the boycott) was very disappointing because as a kid you always think about what it would be like to carry the American flag and represent your homeland. For us to be denied that opportunity, it was very disappointing. But when we were invited to the White House, they gave us an opportunity to meet the President and to receive a gold medal. It was a lot of fun."

Bowie and hundreds of U.S. Olympic athletes participated in Olympic-related festivities in Washington, D.C., honoring them for their efforts. He had his picture taken with President Carter, his wife Rosalynn, and their daughter Amy.

Like all UK seniors, Bowie was very emotional in his last regular season home game at Rupp Arena. That was in 1984 and Kentucky was playing LSU on national TV. From Pennsylvania, two of his closest relatives — his mother and sister — came to Lexington for the special moment, Senior's Day. Unfortunately, his father wasn't around to enjoy the ceremonies since he had passed away almost three years earlier. Pop would've been proud, saying, "That's my boy." His girlfriend, Heidi, didn't attend the game as she was at Penn State. When Bowie and his other senior teammates — Tom Heitz, Jim Master, Dicky Beal and Melvin Turpin — stood on the court in the pre-game ceremony as the crowd sang "My Old Kentucky Home," they became heavyhearted. Some tried to hold back their tears. Even the fans cried.

"It was very emotional," Bowie said. "They say that a grown man isn't supposed to cry but I couldn't help but let my tears flow when they played "My Old Kentucky Home" and my mother was there (to share the special moment). It was a tear jerker. That particular day will always be treasured in my heart. That's something that I will never forget.

"We came out and played probably one of the best games of the year and blew LSU out at our place. The fans had a lot to do with that."

For the record, Kentucky whipped LSU 90-68. In Bowie's last season at Kentucky, the Wildcats finished with a superb 29-5 record, including an SEC Tournament title in Nashville, Tenn., and an appearance in the NCAA Final Four. Bowie — who has 12 hours of graduate work after receiving a degree in communications — said Georgetown's Patrick Ewing and Houston's Hakeem Olajuwon were the toughest players he ever played against in college.

Looking for a big man to dominate its Pacific Division rivals, especially the Los Angeles Lakers, Portland selected Bowie as the NBA's No. 2 pick in the 1984 draft. The Houston Rockets had the top pick, drafting Hakeem

Olajuwon. But many Portland fans booed the selection of
Bowie and wanted the team to get North Carolina and U.S.
Olympic star Michael Jordan instead. With the league's
No. 3 overall pick, the Chicago Bulls drafted Jordan.
Turpin, Bowie's teammate at UK, was selected as the
league's No. 6 choice.

As it turned out, Bowie had a good rookie season.
He led the team in rebounds and averaged 10 points a
game with a high of 26. He made NBA's All-Rookie team
with Jordan, Olajuwon, Charles Barkley of Philadelphia,
and Sam Perkins of Dallas. Also, Bowie was one of the
league's top shot-blockers, ranking third with 2.67 blocked
shots. With a 42-40 mark, Portland finished second in the
Pacific Division, 20 games behind the Lakers. In the
playoffs, the Trail Blazers were eliminated in five games
by the eventual champion Lakers in the Western Conference
semifinals.

"My first year in the pros with Portland was a very
good year," Bowie said. "I stayed healthy. I played in 76
out of 82 regular season games. I had a very, very
productive rookie year and was very excited about the fact
that I had finally made it to the pros. I was establishing
myself as a legitimate player."

Not surprisingly, traveling was the toughest part
in Bowie's rookie life in the NBA but he adapted. "Traveling
from one city to the next, trying to adjust from playing a 30-
game season in college to playing a hundred games in the
regular season and the pre-season in the pros (is the
hardest)," Bowie explained. He said it's very easy to lose
track of all the games. He doesn't remember a lot of games
he's played. "You just kind of get on the plane and go
wherever that plane's going."

Then, along came Bowie's series of leg injuries in
the next four seasons. During that span, he played only 63
out of a possible 328 regular season games. "In the pros,
I had fractured my left leg once and my right leg twice,"
said Bowie.

After recovering from his first leg injury suffered in
his second NBA season, Bowie briefly played in the 1986-
87 season. In the fifth game of that season, Bowie again
hurt his leg. "The toughest moment (of his pro career) is
when I refractured my leg the second time," he said. "It
was 1986 and we were playing the Dallas Mavericks. It

was very disappointing because I had just fractured my leg the year before and had done a lot of rehabilitating. I thought my problems were over with and to refracture, it was just devastating." Bowie completed the five-game season with an average of 16 points with a high of 31.

He sat out the 1987-88 season and played only 20 games in the 1988-89 campaign. During the summer of 1989, while in Kentucky, he received a jolt when he heard on the car radio that he was being traded to the New Jersey Nets. Bowie was happy at Portland and there had been no indication of trade talks.

"I was shocked that I got traded," he said. "I never knew that my name was involved in any trade talks but in the NBA you never know what is going to happen. But I had five great years out there and met a lot of nice people in Portland, Oregon. I have no negative thoughts about Portland.

"I heard it on the local radio. I had played in a Children's Charity Golf Classic (in Lexington). I finished playing golf, got in my car and was driving home and heard on the radio that I was traded to New Jersey. That's the first I had heard about it."

Bowie, who calls former Laker star Kareem Abdul-Jabbar the most interesting person he has ever met in the NBA, says there is no comparison between the news media from Kentucky and New York. "Like night and day," he said. "The media in New York have a lot of poison pens and there's a lot of negative articles that are written. Here at UK, they were very supportive. They were always backing you and trying to make you feel good about the effort that you were giving. A lot of times that's not the case in New York.

"There have been some comments and some articles written (about Bowie) that I didn't care for, but not to the extent that it got me where I was verbally upset with the media. I've always gotten along with them."

When UK mentor Rick Pitino was coaching the New York Knicks for two years, Bowie didn't know him personally. "All I knew about Rick Pitino was that he was a motivator and that he was a winner, but I never had the chance to meet him personally," he said. "His record speaks for itself. Everywhere he's been, he's been a winner."

Going into the 1991-92 campaign, after seven NBA years, Bowie felt his biggest moment in the pro ranks has yet to arrive. And he can hardly wait. "The most thrilling moment as an NBA player?" Bowie said, repeating the question. "I feel as though that is yet to come and I'm looking forward to that day happening. That may be a personal accomplishment or a team accomplishment, but I can honestly say that time hasn't come yet."

After the interview ended, Bowie again apologized for forgetting the appointment. He said he felt bad.
Call him a Gentle Giant.

13 DEAD CHICKEN

"I really didn't have
that steel attitude
that it takes to play for
Joe Hall."

Since his playing career at UK ended in 1985, Bret Bearup has found himself in a couple of controversies. Although they are never pleasant, he doesn't seem to mind revealing his true feelings about those situations. He chose to be open and honest.

"Bret's never shied away from controversy," said ex-Wildcat assistant coach Joe Dean, Jr. "He's a very interesting young man."

In October of 1985, Bearup got into hot water when the *Lexington Herald-Leader*, in a series of articles about corruption in Kentucky's basketball program and college athletics, quoted him and other former Wildcat players about cash payments from boosters, selling tickets and other benefits in violation of the NCAA rules. Eventually, the NCAA could only reprimand UK for the school's lack of cooperation in the investigation and the Wildcats were off the hook. But the unfavorable publicity resulting from the affair had damaged their image, especially on the national level.

Unlike some other players who later claimed that they were misquoted, Bearup refused additional comment, letting his quotes in the newspaper stand. Several weeks later, even though Bearup didn't really say that much to the newspaper, Kentucky's then first-year coach Eddie

Sutton was nevertheless upset with Bearup, banning him from the Wildcat program. The former Wildcat standout had told the newspaper that he sometimes sold tickets for his teammate, Troy McKinley, usually at $50 each, but he returned the money to McKinley.

Now an attorney with Greenebaum, Doll & McDonald in Louisville, Bearup said, "I did not deny what I said. A lot of people did. That's their business. That's what they chose to do. I chose not to do that."

As a result of his refusal to change the story, Bearup was ignored by Sutton and his coaching staff. He became and is bitter because of the way they treated him. "I quickly became persona non grata around the basketball office despite the fact that I was Academic All-SEC, despite the fact that I was on the Dean's List, despite the fact I was going on to represent the program in a very positive manner in the field of law," he said. "I was going on to a graduate school which happens very rarely to the major college basketball program like the University of Kentucky. They said that I was disloyal. I told them that wasn't what loyalty was all about. Blind loyalty. Loyalty without principle is fanaticism.

"I was told by coach Sutton that he didn't want me around the players. He didn't want me around the (Wildcat) Lodge. He didn't want me around the locker room. I had played with all these guys, except for (freshman) Irving Thomas, the year before. These were my friends; these were the guys that I lived with. He cut my feet right out from under me."

And Bearup attempted to make friends with Sutton but the coach refused. "I tried to make my peace with him," he said. "I wrote him a few letters and went to see him. And nothing worked."

On the *Herald-Leader* articles which resulted in a Pulitzer Prize for the newspaper, Bearup further commented, "There were 31 players quoted in that article and almost every player quoted in that article later denied what they said. They said they were misquoted, in the aftermath. It probably would have been better for me (to deny), and I did say hardly anything in the newspaper, but what I did say I wasn't going to go back and lie about.

"Number one, I knew they had it on tape and some of these guys came out afterward and said, 'Well, let them play the tape.' They were idiots because I know that they (the newspaper) had a lot on tape that they didn't use because they couldn't get it confirmed by more than one source. I also know that the *Herald-Leader* would never ever have printed that story unless they were shielded from liability to the greatest extent possible. Unless they had a good, solid tape or from more than one source, they weren't going to use it. For people to think otherwise is idiotic. I mean you have to face the facts. We can't all get on a big demagogic train and curse and revile the *Herald-Leader* for their perfidy. That's their job."

Then in early 1990, in another case, Bearup contacted Lawrence Funderburke, one of college basketball's most controversial figures, offering to help the confused youngster who was attending tiny and historic St. Catharine College in Springfield, Ky. The 6-9, 210-pound player had quit coach Bobby Knight's team at Indiana after playing six games in the fall semester of 1989, averaging nearly 12 points and seven rebounds as a freshman. Although Kentucky had previously recruited him hard when he was a high school star in Columbus, Ohio, Funderburke became a player whom UK did not want to touch. The player had been previously mentioned in several allegations of recruiting rules violations by Kentucky, resulting in NCAA penalties against the school.

Bearup, however, felt Funderburke needed help and suggested that the player was certainly not a villain. Funderburke had just received bad advice in his basketball career. Bearup explained the player deserved another chance. In January of 1991, Funderburke transferred to Ohio State.

Bearup's mother, Judy, cost her son thousands of dollars when she placed his baseball, basketball and football cards in the family's garage sale in Long Island, N.Y. Bearup didn't know it until it was too late as he was several hundred miles away in Lexington, a freshman at UK. After finding out that he had lost his cards, he was terribly crushed. He had kept them in shoe boxes.

"I grew up being a baseball card collector, being a football card collector, basketball, you name it," Bearup said. "I was fanatic about it. I knew all of the statistics of everybody in all of the major sports. I grew up that way and just continued to be that way even after I became pretty good in basketball and was named to a lot of high school All-American teams and began to be recruited by the biggest powers in college basketball.

"I don't have them (now) because my mom sold them. They'd be worth thousands and tens of thousands of dollars today. I still get on her about that sometimes."

Bearup said he doesn't collect cards anymore. But he sure enjoyed them when he was a little boy.

Because of his father's management-related job with the DuPont Corporation, the Bearup family, which included three brothers, moved around a lot from east to west throughout the nation. They lived in Arizona (Phoenix), Montana, Idaho, New York and Washington, D.C., among several places.

His parents met when they were students at Idaho State University in Pocatello, Idaho. Dad played on a basketball scholarship for the school and later coached at a nearby high school in American Falls, Idaho.

Traveling wasn't easy for Bret when he was a young kid growing up in the 1960s and '70s. "It was difficult in the sense that for a long time I had to make new friends every year," he said. "I think that contributed to the personality that I enjoy today. I am very outgoing and I make friends very easily. I don't have any hang ups about meeting new people. I'm not really shy. I have to contribute that from moving around a lot when I was a kid. It really, really helps me in the practice of law."

During his younger days at Harborfields High School in Greenlawn, N.Y., the 6-9 Bearup was one of the country's most sought-after players. Practically, every major school wanted his services. Not only was he a superstar, making several prestigious All-American teams, he excelled in the classroom. He posted a 3.4 grade-point average and made the top five percent nationally on the

National Merit Test. In other words, Bearup was truly a complete All-American, not just as a player.

And, in the fall semester of his high school senior year (1979-80), Bearup decided he wanted to attend Kentucky after making official visits to various universities. Besides UK, he visited North Carolina, Ohio State, Duke and North Carolina State. He canceled a November visit to the UCLA campus in Los Angeles so he could attend Kentucky's homecoming football game in Lexington.

About 19 months earlier in 1978, Bearup first became interested in the Wildcats when he watched the national championship game between Kentucky and Duke in St. Louis. However, at that time, he was rooting for Duke, which dropped a 94-88 decision as Jack Givens sparked UK with his career-high 41 points.

"Growing up as a fan, I was familiar with Kentucky and its tradition, but I thought Duke was an exciting team on the rise," he said. "I really had expected someday to be recruited by somebody like Duke because of the academic standards. I had always done well (in the classroom). I didn't know whether I'd be good enough (player) to be recruited by somebody like Kentucky.

"When they did and when I visited Kentucky, it was where I wanted to go to from the start. I came down and I saw the facilities. I met the players. I met coach (Joe B.) Hall. I saw the absolute reverence that the state has for the game of basketball. That sold me, right there. The other visits I took were just a mere formality. I visited Duke, North Carolina, Ohio State, etc., but none of these teams came close."

The day after Kentucky opened its 1979-80 season against Duke in the Hall of Fame Classic in Springfield, Mass., with a disappointing 82-76 setback in overtime, Bearup made a public announcement which pleased Hall and his coaching staff. He was coming to Kentucky. At the time, it was believed to be the earliest commitment ever made by a prep star going to UK. He would be joining three other prized recruits at Kentucky the following season. Tabbed by some as the nation's best recruiting crop, the Wildcats had inked 6-11 Melvin Turpin, 6-5 Jim Master and 5-11 Dicky Beal in addition to Bearup.

Celebrating his 18th birthday, Bearup attended the Kentucky-Duke game with his family. And, like any

Kentucky fan, he was proud to cheer the Wildcats. He felt like he was a part of the program. Although Kentucky lost the nationally-televised game, it marked the sensational debut of Wildcat freshman Sam Bowie, who poured in 22 points and grabbed 17 rebounds, both game-highs, outplaying Duke All-American Mike Gminski. Because of Bowie, Bearup and the Wildcat faithful didn't really cry over the loss. Instead, they were excited and looking forward to UK's promising future.

And Bearup started to sign his name "Bear Cat." Actually, he had already been doing it for about a month or so.

"I'd always go someplace and play basketball and I'd always have to leave a note on the fridge telling my mom where I'd gone and I started signing my name the 'Bear Cat,' " Bearup explained.

If he hadn't gone to the Bluegrass, he would've probably ended up being a Tar Heel. North Carolina was Bearup's second choice.

"I loved the tradition there, (coach) Dean Smith and his players," Bearup said of the Chapel Hill school. "I enjoyed my visit. I met guys like Mike O'Koren, Al Wood and Jimmy Black."

One of the nation's top basketball minds, Smith liked Bearup and wanted his awesome talent at North Carolina. The Tar Heel mentor visited the Bearup family at their New York home. Although Bearup respected Smith's knowledge of the game, he was somewhat disappointed in coach's personal approach.

"I think he deserved his reputation as a brilliant game strategist, but he seemed to be a little more aloof than I figured that he would be," Bearup said. "I just don't know why that is. Most of his players seemed to love him long after they graduated, which is something I found to be extremely rare.

"He was personable enough. He wasn't a Jimmy Valvano (ex-North Carolina State mentor) by any means. He was far more reserved than Valvano. The thing I loved about Dean Smith was his practices were so choreographed right down to the last second. He put time on the clock and the players would practice a certain drill until that five minutes or that 10 minutes round was over. It didn't matter how well they did, they went on to the next thing.

In fact, practices were snappy, they were quick, the players got out of there in two (hours). There were no long three-and four-hour practices. I remember those when I was at UK. They were torture."

As a very personable teenager, Bearup liked to joke around. But, many times these things did not sit well with the Wildcat coaching staff, especially Hall. Bret loved to do silly stuff. Or even act crazy. He just wanted to have some fun. He and a few of his teammates even went to see Monty Python's humorous-type movie, "The Life of Bryan," which he had already seen several times.

"Bret was a prankster," said Joe Dean, Jr. "He liked to pull pranks and cut up. He was always involved in mischief and things. I think one time he went a little too far and coach Hall got after him."

Bearup said, "I was probably a little later maturing than most (of the other players) when I came down to Kentucky. It was probably one of the reasons coach Hall and I didn't see eye to eye all the time.

"I remember in my freshman year I got a dead chicken from a local horse farm. The dog had just killed it. I snatched the chicken from the dog and drove back into Wildcat Lodge and put it under (teammate) Jim Master's bed. He and Dicky Beal had the same room. That night we left for the Notre Dame game. We didn't come back for two days. When we came back, they opened the door...oh, did it stink to high heaven in there! They didn't know what in the world it was and, meanwhile, one by one I had told the rest of my teammates and they had gone by and looked under the bed (to see if it was true).

"The thing about it was that the chicken kept making the rounds. I think what Master did was he taped the chicken's feet to a clothes hanger and hung the dead chicken up in my closet. When I discovered that I had the dead chicken, I went around to the outside of Wildcat Lodge and I got a ladder and hung it outside at the top of their window ledge. I knew Dicky Beal used to get up in the morning and open the windows and get fresh air into the room. I know the next morning when he opened the blind, there was that dead chicken staring him right in the face!"

Was Hall ever embarrassed about Bearup's silly pranks? "I don't know," Bearup said. "Coach Hall was hard to read. I'm not sure that he was embarrassed so much that he was trying to ride hard on us and make us grow up. I can't tell you how many times he told me I needed to grow up. He was right. If I had come into UK when I was 22 years old instead of when I was 18, I'd been a first-string All-American in college, too.

"I came in at 18 and I was still young and immature and intimidated by the whole thing (UK's basketball tradition). I really didn't have that steel attitude that it takes to play for Joe Hall. I didn't have that. I didn't develop it until after I graduated or grew up some more."

At Kentucky, Bearup was a disappointment after he had impressed Hall with his All-American moves in prep ranks. The coaches and fans had developed big expectations of him. But he failed to meet them. Although he started all of UK's 31 games during his senior year, he completed his Wildcat career with low scoring and rebounding averages. Bearup didn't see a lot of action early in his UK tenure and he admits that he didn't live up to his potential.

But that doesn't mean Bearup didn't have exciting moments as a Wildcat, such as the 64-59 victory over Indiana in Knoxville.

"I came off the bench against Indiana in 1983 in the NCAA and put in eight quick points to bring us from behind and put us into the lead," he said, "and blocked a couple of big jump shots and grabbed a couple of rebounds. I contributed greatly to a game that we had to win. That was against an Indiana team which was supposed to beat us. That was the game before the 'Dream Game' (when Kentucky lost to Louisville by 12 points in overtime in the first meeting between both schools since 1959)."

Off the hardwood floor, Bearup admits he did miss some curfews imposed by Hall. "You've got to be kidding. Of course, I did," he said, laughing. "I really did. Not badly. I mean I would miss a curfew by a matter of minutes but I would never stay out all night in violation of the curfew."

It sounds like he sure beat your system, coach Hall. Are you listening?

Bearup received both of his academic degrees at

Kentucky — business administration in 1985 and law in 1989. He was admitted to the Kentucky Bar in 1990.

While Bearup was at UK, his younger brother, Shon, signed a basketball scholarship with Cumberland College in Williamsburg, Ky., prompting the Bearup family to move to Kentucky. And they settled for London, a rapidly-growing town located on I-75, right on the edge of Kentucky's famous mountains.

"My dad thought that it would just be very convenient to move the family down there so he could watch both Shon and me and be there while we were in college," he said. "Then, my little brother, Todd, could go off and play high school basketball right there (at Laurel County High) in Kentucky. So, we'd all be at the same place, playing basketball. It was basically a move of convenience."

A few years later, Todd was playing for coach Rick Pitino at Kentucky as a sophomore walk-on member of the 1990-91 squad with the help of Bret. A 6-5 swingman, Todd had transferred to Kentucky from Utah State. After his freshman season at Utah State, Todd served on a two-year Mormon mission in South Korea.

"He (Pitino) didn't have very many scholarships to give (because of NCAA sanctions) and the scholarships he had needed to go to big men," Bearup said. "When he had the chance to get a walk-on player (Todd), a player for free, he was ecstatic. I told the people at the basketball office down there that I would help, along with my dad, pay for my brother's education. I'm going to repay the University of Kentucky for what it did for me by giving them, by paying for them a Division I player that they don't have to give a scholarship to. That's what I'm doing to repay my university."

Todd has since quit basketball at UK in August of 1991 and transferred to Brigham Young University in Utah where he has several relatives. But he will not be playing basketball at BYU as he is preparing a career in law or international business. Todd was a member of SEC's All-Academic team for the 1990-91 campaign with a 4.0 GPA.

Upon his graduation from UK, Bearup did some traveling, playing pro basketball in Europe for about a year. Unlike some of his American teammates, he enjoyed his European stay, playing for teams based in Italy and Switzerland. He also tried to understand the Europeans' attitude and their way of living.

"I particularly enjoyed the different cultures in Europe," he said. "I know a lot of Americans on the teams over there counted down the days until they got back in the United States. Obviously, the food is different. The customs of the people are different. Their outlook on the entire world is different. I would sit for hours in a café and talk to the natives about these things, about how they work, what their political views were. The Europeans think that we don't care very much about the rest of the world. They are offended that we don't speak more than one language. They are offended that we couldn't name all of the countries in Europe. They're offended that we couldn't name the capitals of the big countries. I can't tell you how often I had debated that the Soviet Union was still the big bad guy. I enjoyed it.

"I enjoyed taking the weekend flights over to Paris where I would get up in the morning and go to the Louvre, the museum (one of the world's largest, featuring famous paintings and sculptures). I would go in there and see young art students with their notebooks taking notes about different styles and different painters. At least that's what I thought they were doing. They looked scholarly and so forth.

"So, I went back outside and bought a notepad and a pencil. I came back in there and walked around. I sat down in front of the Mona Lisa. I started writing "Mona Lisa" at the top of my page. Well, she has a little smile, there's nuts in the background. Pretty strange. Then I'd turn the page and go down to the Venus de Milo. Missing an arm. I don't know what these people were writing down. The guys that I played with just didn't have the least interest in going to those places."

Some of Bearup's English-speaking teammates in Europe included former North Carolina standout guard Jimmy Braddock; ex-Virginia 6-8 forward Craig Robinson;

and Mike Brown, a 6-9, 260-pound center from George Washington who later was playing for the NBA's Utah Jazz.

And Bearup eventually went back to Lexington to study law. His basketball career was over.

When the May 29, 1989 edition of *Sports Illustrated* arrived at newsstands with the negative cover story attacking Kentucky's basketball program which just had been hit by the NCAA with penalties, Bearup was obviously very upset. Mad enough that he contacted the person who wrote the article. He didn't like the tone of the story.

"I got on the phone to Curry Kirkpatrick of *Sports Illustrated* the day after the 'Kentucky's Shame' headline came out (on the magazine cover)," commented Bearup, who had just graduated from law school. "(I didn't like) the way he couched what had happened, the terms in which he described it. He talks about illegal (payments, etc.). He talks about corruption. Giving a kid $50 is not illegal. If you get a parking ticket, that's illegal. It's against the (NCAA) rules. That's all it is. It's like cheating on your diet. I mean, 'Give me a break.' It's against the rules, it's not against the law. You can't go to jail, you don't pay fines.

"I know a lot of players from both Europe and over here in the United States. Very few of them, I think, are corrupt. When they were kids, they needed some money. Somebody gave them some money. Who cares? The system's got to change. The decorum punishment is not going to change it. I have news for you, it's not going to change unless you change the system. You've got to change the rules. You can't change the people. People don't change."

Bearup basically agrees that every big school, including Kentucky, commits NCAA violations. "There's no question in my mind that it is an occurrence to a certain degree at every major college program," he said. "Here's the way I look at it. Is it wrong to pay players or is it just against the rules? I think it's just against the rules. There's nothing wrong with it."

It was at a 1986 beauty pageant in Paducah, Ky., where Bearup met his future wife. Her name was contestant Beth Ann Clark of Mayfield, Ky., a student from UK. She was entering the Miss Kentucky-USA pageant and one of the contest judges was none other than Bearup. His friend and a former teammate, 6-11 Robert Lock, who was still playing for Kentucky, also traveled with Bearup to check out the pageant as an interested spectator. Later, coach Sutton and his assistants chastised Lock for his close friendship with Bearup, whom they didn't like.

On his future wife at the pageant, Bearup recalled, "I met all the girls, interviewed them and scored them on interviews. I remember when she sat down in front me, I thought 'Oh, man, this is one of the most gorgeous girls I've ever seen in my life.' She did well in the interview and I gave her a high score there. Then she did well in the other portions of the pageant and she ended up winning the pageant. After she won the pageant, I asked her out that very night." As the Kentucky representative, Clark later participated in the Miss USA pageant.

And, about four months before Bearup's marriage in December of 1989, Clark captured another beauty title, beating out 61 other contestants from the United States, Mexico, Puerto Rico and Canada. She was named the Miss Swimwear Illustrated 1989 by the celebrity judges in San Francisco, Calif. As a result, she won a week-long trip to a Caribbean island where the handsome couple later went on their honeymoon. She appeared on the cover of the magazine's March 1990 edition. On her winning the swimsuit pageant, Clark admitted that she was stunned when the officials announced her name. Also, *Inside Sports* magazine featured her as one of the models in its annual swimsuit issue in 1990.

Her future husband did not see her win the swimsuit title in California. "I didn't go with her," said Bearup. "I was out fishing in Montana at that particular time. I was enjoying it too much. I didn't really expect that she would win. I was amazed."

Bearup said he has no problem of her entering swimsuit contests or working as a part-time model. "I encouraged her to do what she wants to do," he said. "If entering those contests makes her happy, that's fine with me. I know she works out like a demon before those contests. It keeps her in great shape and that's fine. She loves to do that kind of stuff. She does well at it."

Bearup's wife does a lot of traveling throughout the state of Kentucky working as a sales representative for a supply company, based in Dallas, Texas.

Bearup is a Mormon. Although he had several relatives in the West who were Mormons, he did not take their religion beliefs seriously when he was a teenager.

"I didn't grow up Mormon," Bearup said. "The summer before my senior year (at UK), I started reading about it and becoming somewhat interested because I had gone out and visited some relatives out there and noticed their lifestyle, how they live their life and how happy they seem to be. They attributed it to their religion.

"So, instead of just brushing it off like most people usually do, and like I used to do, I looked at the religion and investigated it and decided that was the religion I would like to be affiliated with. My dad was a Mormon. My little brother, Todd, converted about the same time I did and he went on a mission to Seoul, South Korea."

14 Mr. String Music's Boy

"I think the majority of people in college athletics are honest and decent people who are trying to run good programs."

In 1977 Joe Dean, Jr. was searching for a coaching job and sending out letters to many major universities. He was 23 years old and had just spent his first year as a graduate assistant coach under mentor Kermit Davis at Mississippi State, his alma mater.

Like any young person fresh out of college, Dean was a typical man looking for experience and an opportunity to move up in the coaching profession. During his job search, he sent one of his letters to coach Joe B. Hall at Kentucky. As a three-year letterman at Mississippi State where he saw action mainly as a key reserve player, he was already familiar with the Wildcats. And Hall already knew about Dean. After all, they had faced each other several times. Hall's Wildcats had the upper hand, winning five of six games against the Bulldogs from 1974 to '76. Impressed with Dean's youthful enthusiasm, Hall hired the youngster.

"I was just finishing up my master's degree (in physical education) and wrote several schools letters with a resume, expressing interest to try to get on the college staff," Dean said in his office at Central Florida University in Orlando where he is the school's head basketball coach. "One of the letters went to Joe Hall. It was at a time when his part-time assistant was moving on and he was looking for someone to fill that position. He wanted a young person who was energetic and eager to get out on the road and help Leonard Hamilton, who was the chief recruiter then. Coach Hall liked the fact that he knew who I was. We had played against each other and he felt like I was the type of person he was interested in. He called me so I flew up and interviewed with him and I got the job. It was obviously a great break in my young career."

Indeed, it turned out to be a great career move. The Kentucky job gave Dean an inside look at one of the nation's top roundball programs. And it also gave him instant recognition even though he was just a low-ranking assistant on Hall's staff. After spending six years at Kentucky, he moved to Birmingham Southern College, an NAIA school in Alabama, where he was named the head coach in 1983. In his six years at Birmingham Southern, he compiled an overall record of 137-45 as each of his teams won at least 20 games.

Then the University of Central Florida, which has over 20,000 students, came calling in 1989 and Dean was offered the job as the school's head basketball coach. He accepted it as he signed a four-year pact with a reported annual base salary of $50,000. Like Kentucky, Central Florida is a member of NCAA's Division I in basketball. And the school is located in one of the country's largest TV markets, ranking among the top 25.

In his first year at Central Florida, Dean posted a record of 7-21 and the squad played its home games in a tiny campus gym which seated less than 2,500. But he saw his Running Knights improve in the following season of 1990-91 as they posted double figures in the victory column. And the school now has a sparkling new 5,100-seat arena.

Needless to say, Dean's future is bright. Although he is delighted to be coaching at the Orlando school, he admits that he would love to return to the SEC wars someday as a head coach.

"I think that's probably a dream that I've always had — to coach in the SEC," Dean said. "If it doesn't happen, it's not going to be the end of the world. I'm very, very happy here at Central Florida. We're in the building process of our program but I think over the next five years it's going to be a very good program here and be in the spirit. As the guy who's kind of leading the charge to build, it is very exciting and very challenging and I enjoy it immensely. I think if the good Lord sees fit to have me in an SEC school in the future that's something I would certainly enjoy. But, it's not something I'm going to count on or expect to happen. We're just going to have to see and play it by ear."

How about Dean at LSU when coach Dale Brown retires? Dean's dad, Joe Dean, Sr., is LSU's athletic director. It would be a very interesting father-son combination. But the younger Dean said he doesn't care which SEC school he would go to if the job opportunity ever comes up.

"Not really," Dean said. "I've always enjoyed that conference because I grew up in Baton Rouge and played in the league and coached in the league. So, I really have seen the league from three different perspectives as a young boy growing up as a fan, as a player and as a coach. I feel like the SEC is kind of my league. So, if I ever had an opportunity to coach in the league, I would be honored to have that chance."

In the late 1980s, Dean, still young at the age of 31 or so, was considered by a couple of SEC schools for the head coaching post. In 1986 when Mississippi State coach Bob Boyd stepped down from his position, the school had several candidates in mind. Dean was one of them.

"When the job opened five years ago or so, I talked with them," Dean recalled. "The timing for me was bad. I was in the second year of a five-year contract with Birmingham Southern. So, it just didn't feel comfortable trying to get out of the contract.

"The program at Mississippi State was really down at that time and I just didn't feel real comfortable with it. I didn't feel like I was ready for it. The contract at Birmingham was the main thing that kept me from really going after the job. We had a good talk and discussed everything."

Three years later, Auburn officials talked with Dean when popular coach Sonny Smith quit his Tiger job and became the head coach at Virginia Commonwealth. "I interviewed at Auburn," Dean said. "The Auburn job was open. There were about eight or nine people considered."

Several years ago, while Dean was gaining some valuable experience at Kentucky, Hall encouraged the assistant to begin looking around for head coaching positions after the 1980-81 season, even though Hall was quite pleased with Dean's work. Dean, however, stayed with the Wildcat program for two more years before departing Lexington.

"After the end of my fourth year at Kentucky, I sat down with coach Hall and talked to him about my future in coaching," Dean said. "I wanted to be a head coach and he encouraged me to start looking and I began to do that a little bit. I actually interviewed for a couple of jobs at the end of my fifth year there and then at the end of my sixth year I interviewed for several positions and got the Birmingham Southern job. I was young and eager to coach. So, when the opportunity came in 1983, I jumped at it."

The legendary Pete Maravich is the NCAA's all-time leading scorer with 3,667 points, averaging 44.2 points a game. "Pistol Pete" was a big LSU star, playing from 1967 to '70, before starring in the NBA for 10 years. And when Dean was a teenager growing up in Louisiana, Maravich was his biggest hero.

"When Pistol Pete came into Baton Rouge in 1967, I was a very enthusiastic basketball player, trying to develop to be a college player," Dean commented. "Pete came in with all of his tricks, abilities and talents, and really captured the imagination of a lot of kids, not only in Baton Rouge, but all over the country. So, I started to emulate him a lot and picked up a lot of his drills that he did to become a good player and really admired him very, very much.

"I met him on several different occasions. I was always, certainly, in awe of him. He was a phenomenal college basketball player and it was quite a thrill."

Some 20 years later, the entire nation was stunned when Maravich suddenly died at the age of 40. In January of 1988, he suffered a fatal heart attack while playing pickup basketball in California.

"I was shocked and very sad," Dean said. "He was

a person, I felt, who gave so much to the game of basketball and affected so many people and had a tremendous effect on my life as a basketball player. He was only 40 years old but he was a guy who had gone through a lot of personal problems. He went through a lot of different tough times in his life and he eventually found Christ and became a Christian. I think that was what gave him the peace that he was searching for prior to his death."

Today, many people know the Central Florida mentor as Joe Dean's son. Or the son of LSU's athletic director. Or the son of Mr. String Music. His father was once a TV star. Well, not quite, but he was a long-time basketball commentator on SEC basketball telecasts. He liked to say "string music" on the air. It was his favorite saying when the ball swished through the net.

The younger Dean enjoys a close relationship with his father. "My dad and I are very close," said Joe Dean, Jr. "We have a very close knit family. We run a basketball camp together in the summer (in Summit, Mississippi). So we spend two weeks together in the summer and we stay in touch quite a bit. Dad started the camp when I was 10 years old."

Before becoming the athletic director at LSU in April of 1987, the elder Dean was associated with the Converse athletic footwear company for 28 years. But he kept his office in Baton Rouge to be with his family.

"My dad spent a lot of quality time with his (three) children and he primarily was a sales representative for Converse, working throughout the Southeast," said Dean, Jr. "He covered six states for Converse, selling Converse products. He became a regional manager and a national director and then eventually became a vice president and a part owner of the company."

A native of Brazil, Ind., Dean, Sr. was a two-time All-SEC basketball performer at LSU in the early 1950s before serving in the U.S. Army for two years. It was at LSU where he met his future wife, the former Doris Hall.

When LSU hired Dean, Sr. for the AD job, he was very excited as he had strongly campaigned for the school's top post in the athletic department, according to his son.

"I think it's something that he had always dreamed about through the years," said Dean, Jr. "As a businessman with Converse and a former athlete and the guy that had done TV games, he felt he had the qualifications to be an athletic director, having lived in Baton Rouge all his life and being an LSU graduate. I think it's something he always looked at and thought that he might be good at if the opportunity presented itself. I think it's been a good situation for him. He seems to be comfortable with it now and he seems to be fitting in real well. He's got the program rolling on solid ground. I think he's very happy and I think the school's very happy with him."

In the lengthy press conference which announced the hiring of Dean, Sr. at LSU, the younger Dean wasn't in attendance since he was coaching at Birmingham Southern at the time. But his father told reporters, "We called him when we got the word (about the job). He wanted to come. He coaches and he said, 'Dad, I only have one request. I want you to fire Dale Brown and hire me.' "

Of course, Dean, Jr. was joking. But there is no mistake that he would to love to have Brown's job someday.

While Dean, Sr. was a successful sportscaster, he had a share of embarrassing moments on the air. One such event took place in a first-round game between Florida and Auburn at the 1981 SEC Tournament in Birmingham. Mentor Norm Sloan of Florida created a stir among the regional TV audience when he used foul language at his players during a timeout.

Said Dean, Jr. of his father's embarrassing moment, "They put the microphone in Norm Sloan's huddle. He (Sloan) didn't realize the microphone was there and he said some cuss words over the air. It was embarrassing for the announcers to try to cover that up and try to explain it. I remember that was a real tough time for him."

A red-faced Sloan was visibly angry and had told the players, "G___d___it! You all are giving up too many f_____layups." His team, however, later won the matchup, defeating Auburn 50-48 in overtime.

Moments after Sloan's outbursts hit the airwaves, Dean apologized on TV. He explained that Sloan didn't know about the live pickup. Sloan stated that he "regretted" the remark.

In a 1984 interview, Dean, Sr. recalled his most

embarrassing moment as a TV announcer, saying, "I was interviewing people at halftime during an NCAA tournament and they ran a guy out to me to interview and I didn't know his name. I didn't know who he was so I had to say to him, 'I hate this, but I don't know your name. You've got to tell me who you are.' "

While a basketball and football standout at Baton Rouge High School, Dean, Jr. was recruited by several universities, including two SEC schools. He wanted to play basketball in college. And he eventually ended up on the campus of Mississippi State University where he had no previous ties. No family connections or whatsoever.

"I was recruited by several (schools)," he said. "I really chose between Louisiana Tech, Alabama and Mississippi State. My dad really encouraged me to go away. I guess I grew up dreaming about playing at LSU because I had grown up there but he felt like it would be in my best interest to go away from home and reap the benefits of being out on my own and establishing my own identity. As I look back, it was the greatest thing that ever happened to me because I was able to establish an identity for myself at a different school and not be Joe Dean, Jr. all the time. So, that was a very positive (move). I was very immature. It helped me grow up and become a man and learn how to deal with life as it comes."

At Mississippi State, Dean never became a star for the Bulldogs, playing as a reserve guard although he did start a few games. He had some good moments. He once scored a collegiate career-high of 17 points in a game against Ole Miss. In his senior year, he was named to the 1976 Academic All-SEC second team. And as a junior, he helped the Bulldogs defeat his hometown school, LSU, and its third-year coach Dale Brown by a score of 93-84 in Baton Rouge where he played in front of his family and friends. According to Dean, that was the highlight of his college playing days.

"My junior year, we went to LSU to play and coach Davis put me in the game the last 10 minutes," Dean said. "Of course, my family and friends were there and it was a real close ballgame and I scored 10 points the last 10 minutes of the game to help us beat LSU. I made some free throws in the last minute or so to ice the game and that was quite a thrill."

At Kentucky, Dean, Jr. went through all kinds of experiences. They were mostly good. Like winning the 1978 national championship as an assistant. That was his most thrilling time at UK.

However, he did have some trying moments such as when Kyle Macy missed a last-second shot to win as Kentucky dropped a narrow 55-54 heartbreaker to Duke in the Mideast Regional of the NCAA tournament. Also, his last game as a Wildcat assistant was a terrible disappointment. In the 1983 NCAA tournament in Knoxville, Tenn., Kentucky lost to Louisville 80-68 in overtime in the so-called "Dream Game."

Away from the hardwood floor, one scary moment took place in 1978 when he and his wife, Ellen, flew in a small airplane which crashed near an airport in Tennessee, killing the pilot. The weather was bad. They were on a recruiting trip to Bristol, Tenn., to visit prep All-American Derrick Hord, who eventually came to Kentucky.

"Well, I had a lot of incredible experiences," Dean said. "My wife and I were involved in a plane crash when we were going to recruit Derrick Hord. That was certainly a very traumatic experience. We lost a friend, Dr. Harry Bailey. He was the pilot of the plane. That was a very, very difficult time for us."

About a year later, Dean went through another bizarre recruiting experience. The UK assistant, along with Joe B. Hall and Leonard Hamilton, were recruiting a highly-regarded prep star by the name of Bret Bearup in the New York area.

After spending some time with the Bearup family, the coaching staff, especially Hall who is an avid fisherman, decided to go deep sea fishing out in the Atlantic Ocean with a couple of local high school coaches. Dean and Hamilton didn't care too much for the idea. Although the ocean was rough, they nevertheless went out for a few hours.

Dean said, "All three of us got real sick. Leonard

almost turned white. It was just choppy water and it was real rough. (We were) way out in the sea trying to catch some big fish and we spent the whole time hanging over the sides of the boat."

Two months later, Bearup announced that he would attend Kentucky. Dean was especially elated as he had developed a close friendship with Bearup when the Wildcat aide was recruiting the youngster for UK.

"Bret and I got to be very close," Dean said. "(I) got to be very close to his family. I really think a lot of him. He's a fine young man. He was easy to recruit. He fell in love with the Big Blue early on and I just had to kind of hang in there with him and keep encouraging him and certainly I did that.

"Bret was a very talented high school player. We were very, very excited about Bret. He could run, jump, shoot, rebound and pass the ball. He had all the makings of a great player. So, the opportunity to get him to come to Kentucky was a thrill for our staff."

Bearup's signing with Kentucky was extra special for Dean as he was truly the first high school All-American that Dean had successfully recruited for Kentucky.

After spending six years with his boss, Dean says the public often did not see the "real" Joe B. Hall. Sometimes, Hall came across as sort of a cold person.

"I think that coach Hall, in some respect, was very misunderstood," he explained. "He was very demanding on the players but he had to be. The players were placed on pedestals, the players were pampered, the players were idolized and had all the recognition that they could ever hope to have just because they played at Kentucky. So, coach Hall had to bring them down a little bit and he did that by being a very demanding on how hard they worked. They always played very, very hard. That's a credit to him as a coach.

"Yet, off the floor, he was very compassionate. He cared a great deal about the players, he cared about the people in his program. He was very approachable as a head coach. If a player in the program said that he could not feel comfortable approaching coach Hall, I think it was the player's problem, not coach Hall's problem because he was easy to sit down and talk with. He had the players over to his house a lot. His wife cooked for them all the time. She was great with the players. I don't ever remember a player not feeling comfortable with coach Hall on a personal basis. At least, he could walk in and sit with coach Hall and talk about anything he wanted to. They may have preferred to bounce it off of Leonard first or myself or Dick Parsons or whoever, but in the end result they could walk in and sit down with coach Hall and he was a very compassionate, understanding man."

As the Central Florida coach, Dean was asked if he would like to play Kentucky some day. He just laughed, knowing that if he did his squad would probably get whipped on the floor. "I have no desire to play Kentucky," he said.

"If they asked to play, we would take advantage of that. We're looking to play teams on our level but we always take advantage of opportunities to play a prestigious school. Those are opportunities for you to put your school on the map, if you can upset those teams."

As for corruption in college athletics, Dean agrees there are some coaches and administrators who deliberately break the NCAA rules. But he believes many horror stories about recruiting violations have been blown out of proportion by the news media.

"I think things of that nature are always exaggerated," Dean said. "You never can believe everything that you hear but yet there are problems. I don't think that we, in college athletics, can sweep those problems under a rug. There is corruption in every walk of life — banking, law, medicine, politics. You know it's going to be there. Certainly, college athletics has its share of corruption, too. I do think the majority of people in college athletics are honest and decent people who are trying to run good programs. The recruiting process is very difficult. It's the most unpleasant area that I deal with because the kids are just being bombarded (with offers) and at some schools, it's just not a real healthy situation.

"I don't know the answer to it, really. I think (the

recent rules) to reduce the periods of time you can recruit, to reduce the number of visits you can have with prospects and the number of visits they can make are very positive rules. I don't think it's going to hurt anybody to recruit. The academics involved now are getting tougher and tougher and that's certainly the major issue — trying to find quality athletes who can go to college and get a degree. That's the major balancing act today. It's the No. 1 problem that we deal with.

"The biggest problem is: Where do you draw the line to try and help an athlete get a college degree and do college work? A young man has talent in one particular area. It's like a student who is a world class singer or a very talented musician. We make provisions for those people to try to encourage them to fulfill their promise in those areas. Athletics is no different. An athlete deserves an opportunity to fulfill the promise that he has as an athlete. I really believe that a student is better off having gone to college, even if it's just for two or three years than if he never went.

"I think the educational process helps that youngster but academicians would say that you only think that because you want them to play basketball for you. That's true to a certain extent but I do have the best interests of the kids at heart and I've seen where these kids grow up. I've seen their backgrounds and I know they have not been afforded the same opportunity that I had as a kid. So, I'm willing to go a step further to help them try to make something out of their lives and I can do that as a college coach.

"The biggest thing is getting them in school and getting the tutorial help they need and trying to motivate them to get through. Once they get through, they've made it and now they have a chance to have a very nice life. Let's face it — we are in education. We are about trying to help young people even though, from a selfish standpoint, we want these players to help us win games. We are also committed to trying to help them as human beings, too. That's my mission. That's my commitment and I believe that's most coaches' mission in college."

Asked if he ever ran into a situation where a prospect asked for a free car or nice clothes, Dean replied, "I've had prospects talk about small things but never anything of great magnitude. I've never had a kid say he wanted a car."

What about a free pair of basketball shoes? Do they ask for them? "Yeah, a t-shirt, things of that nature," Dean said. "But most of the time it's after you've already signed them. They say, 'Coach, I'd like to have a t-shirt to show off the school colors in my hometown.' We can't give it to them. It's kind of sad because our university here recruits valedictorians from all over the state and they'll send them t-shirts, hats, buttons, bumper stickers. Anything they can do to the valedictorians but to a great athlete, you can't give him anything.

"It's not fair at all. I don't think a t-shirt is going to make a difference about whether or not a kid decides to come to your school or not, but I understand the rules. And I understand they try to tighten everything up to try to avoid problems but some of the rules, quite frankly, are ridiculous.

"I think they need to throw the (rule) book out the window and start all over and simplify things."

For instance, let's say that Dean had a player from Los Angeles whose father had just died. Could the coach or the school pay for the player's transportation expenses so the youngster could be with his family during the time of sorrow? "No, technically, you cannot," Dean said. "There are just so many (silly) rules like that. A kid comes to take summer courses and then he needs money to eat on and you can't give him money. He's got to wait until he gets paid for a summer job or wait until his Pell Grant money comes in. If his parents don't have money to give him, what do you do, if he walks up to you and says, 'I don't have any money to eat on?' There are certain times when it's very, very difficult not to help. Your heart bleeds for these kids. Yet, you're bound by NCAA rules not to do anything to help them and it just makes it tough."

15 REX AND HIS GRANNY

"I didn't think it was
to be as much of a
goldfish bowl as
it was."

It was a night that ex-Wildcat star Rex Chapman
will never forget.

For a very special occasion on a 1989 September
evening, Chapman and his immediate relatives — including
his folksy grandmother, Mayme Little Hamby of Lexington
— traveled to London, Ky. It was a homecoming of sorts
as many of his family members had lived there for a long
time.

They came to Sue Bennett College, a small Methodist
school, where Chapman's grandfather had played and
coached basketball in the 1940s and early '50s. The college
was honoring his grandfather, the late Calvert "Red"
Little, in a fund-raising dinner for the purpose of
establishing an endowed scholarship fund in Little's name
and raising additional funds for the school's athletic
program. Approximately 125 people, including many of
his grandfather's former teammates and players, attended
the $100-a-plate affair at which Chapman was the guest of
honor.

Chapman learned more about his grandfather whom
he never knew, as Little's ex-teammates and players told
stories and jokes. They shared old newspaper articles and
photographs of Little and his teams. Chapman had never
met his grandfather who was killed in Rockcastle County

during a tragic car accident in 1963 at the age of 40. After playing in tennis matches in Lexington, Little was driving home in a heavy rainfall and his car slid across the road, hitting a tractor-trailer. A prominent attorney and businessman in London, Little was pronounced dead on arrival at the Mt. Vernon Hospital.

At the dinner, Chapman's grandmother naturally was very emotional but tickled that Rex was able to continue "our basketball tradition. Rex is able to learn about his grandfather through Red's former teammates and those young men he coached."

An accomplished musician, Rex's Granny ended the festival with her rousing piano music, playing a special selection "New York New York" for Kenny Walker, then of the New York Knicks, a surprise guest who came along with the Chapman family. Like Chapman, Walker starred at UK. But the two never played together as Wildcat teammates. Coming off his two All-American seasons in college, Walker was a highly-regarded NBA rookie in 1986 when Chapman arrived on the UK scene as a celebrity freshman.

Besides Chapman's parents — Wayne and Laura Chapman of Owensboro — his younger sister Jenny and his uncles also attended the affair. The family and the audience had a good time. It was a moment they all cherish. Red, the grandfather, would've been proud.

During the fall semester of his senior year at Owensboro Apollo High School, Rex Chapman announced one of the most important decisions of his life. Where was he going to play in college? Louisville fans wanted to know. Kentucky fans wanted to know. Everybody wanted to know. One of the nation's most heavily-recruited players, Chapman informed the reporters and interested observers at a press conference held at Owensboro's Executive Inn that he would attend UK.

Kentucky coach Eddie Sutton was ecstatic. Sutton called Chapman one of the top two or three players in the country. And Rex's Granny was thrilled, too. His signing with the Wildcats meant that she would get to see him a lot in Lexington.

"I think I would have died if he had gone anywhere else," recalled Mrs. Hamby, who was once a music teacher in Laurel County. "He really did want to go to Louisville. Laura and Wayne thought the UK situation was best for him, but in hindsight we don't know if it was or not. He certainly got the exposure he needed. He developed and he was able to make it with the pros."

After two somewhat stormy seasons at Kentucky, Chapman began his professional career early in 1988, playing for one of the NBA's two expansion teams, the Charlotte Hornets. He was the Hornets' top selection in the 1988 draft and the league's eighth pick overall.

"Had he had a better situation (at UK), I think he would have graduated," explained Rex's Granny. "He was just unhappy." Granny now follows his NBA career closely as she subscribes to *Hornets Tipoff*, a monthly publication covering the Charlotte Hornets.

Perhaps Chapman was somewhat overwhelmed by his great "White Hope" popularity at Kentucky. He was under heavy microscopic watch from Kentucky fans and the news media. Although he handled the situation well, it seems that he had all kinds of problems — some good and some bad. He was "King Rex." Even the city of Lexington was sometimes referred to as "Rexington" in coffee shop conversations. He didn't have any privacy when he went out with friends. In a situation made worse because of the Bluegrass state's conservative views, many people didn't really like the fact that he dated a black coed from his hometown. Sutton, his coach, had publicly complained about his shot selection on the floor. The NCAA was investigating the school's basketball program.

Despite the nagging problems, Chapman, however, did have an outstanding but brief career at Kentucky. He made the All-SEC squad as a freshman and a sophomore. He was the SEC's Freshman-of-the-Year. He played on the silver medal-winning Pan American team in 1987. He captured MVP honors at the 1988 SEC Tournament in Baton Rouge, La., where he helped the Wildcats win the title. The team's MVP in his sophomore season, he led the squad in the classroom with a GPA of 3.75 his last semester at UK.

And don't forget that wintry day when he guided the Wildcats to a stunning 85-51 victory over defending national champion Louisville in a nationally-televised matchup at Freedom Hall. The 6-5 freshman pumped in a game-high 26 points, including five three-pointers. His performance resulted in a lot of national press, including a cover story by noted writer Curry Kirkpatrick in *Sports Illustrated*. Chapman shared the magazine's cover with controversial college football star Brian Bosworth, who had failed his NCAA drug test, using steroids. Actually, the Boz had a bigger share of the cover as Rex was pictured in a small square box at the top calling him the "Kentucky Hero." Chapman's popularity mushroomed and he was the toast of every Kentucky town.

When Chapman was feeling sick or wanted to get away from the spotlight, he'd drive over from Wildcat Lodge to visit Granny in the northern part of the city. Just to relax. She would fix home-cooked meals for him and, sometimes, his teammates.

"He said one time, 'I just don't understand why they want my autograph,' and he would have to come out here," commented Granny at her home. "He would go to a drive-in restaurant and have to bring his food out. He couldn't go to a restaurant; people would want his autograph. He had no privacy but he got it here at my house. I was so glad that I could be here for him. It meant a lot to all of us. I'm glad that he came to UK.

"Mostly, we didn't talk sports. We talked mostly about the family. He liked to cut up and he is a big tease. The last year he roomed with Reggie (Hanson), I fed Reggie all that year. The year before, he was with Winston (Bennett) and I fed Winston that year and did their laundry. Whoever he wanted to bring out, he could bring out. They didn't talk as much as they ate and I loved it. It wasn't so much the bad food (on campus), but they knew they could get what they wanted here — mashed potatoes, wieners with cheese, cakes and cookies, things like that. You know, granny foods.

"Reggie is one of the finest boys. He's sweet and kind and laughs from ear to ear. I met his mother (Katie). I sat with her during a lot of the ballgames. She's just like Reggie. Just a big smile and thinks well of people."

Speaking of Chapman, his father Wayne couldn't pinpoint a particular proud moment at Kentucky, but he is very gratified by the way his son had conducted himself in college.

"I was proud of the way he handled himself," said the father. "There were a lot of great moments, but I was probably prouder of the way he handled himself off the floor than anything else. He was thrown into a lot. A lot was expected (of him). He fulfilled many people's dreams. Maybe he was unduly given credit sometimes but I know he was often unduly blamed for things and he handled it very, very maturely"

Wayne knows the Wildcat fans can be very demanding. Yet he realizes it is primarily because of the school's rich tradition in basketball. He said Rex wasn't overwhelmed. "I think the entire state is overwhelmed by the University of Kentucky," said the elder Chapman. "One of the things they have done, that is very profitable, is they have marketed the team very well. Maybe too well because the players are exposed to too much and they're scrutinized too much. If they want to have their coaches' shows and things, I think a lot of emphasis should be on talking about the program itself. Leave the individual players out of it as much as possible because it's very difficult for young kids to understand some of the things that go on.

"It's very difficult for a young person not to be able to go out and buy Christmas presents because people won't leave him alone, and not be able to go to the movies, not be able to go to the grocery store because fans are the way they are. On the other hand, if it weren't for the fans, we wouldn't be playing this game, we wouldn't be in coaching and there wouldn't be a lot of fun. But they have to keep things in perspective. I think at times the University of Kentucky has a way of getting things out of perspective."

Rex's Granny fondly remembers her happiest moment when she saw her grandson play for the first time. No, Chapman wasn't wearing a Wildcat uniform at that time, but he had already signed with Kentucky about three months earlier. He was playing for his high school team against Lexington Henry Clay in a specially-arranged game at UK's Memorial Coliseum.

The matchup, which had been set up only a few

days earlier, attracted a near sellout crowd of 11,000 fans, who came to see King Rex play against Sean Sutton — son of the UK coach — and his Henry Clay teammates. The spectators went bonkers over Chapman's superb 37-point performance as Apollo upset the fourth-ranked Blue Devils 68-67 on his 22-foot bomb with seven seconds remaining.

"It was a sellout and I sat with a friend of mine," said Mrs. Hamby, "and I had my Rex's granny shirt on. My friends had given me that. When he came out on the floor we both cried. It reminded me of Red (her late husband), just to see his grandson on the floor....that had to be the happiest moment. That was his first game here in Lexington, aside from (state) tournaments. The crowd was just wild."

By then, she had some idea of what Chapman's career at Kentucky would be like, with all the fanfare and hoopla surrounding her grandson.

"I had a little taste then of what it was going to be like," said Granny. "I didn't think it was to be as much of a goldfish bowl as it was. I had people who would want my autograph because I was Rex's grandmother. That's carrying it a little bit too far. It's ridiculous. He said to me one time, 'Have you read that sports column on Big Blue mentality?' He said there is a lot of truth to that — our team, right or wrong. They're (fans) not objective at all. He was cognizant of the fact that there are a lot of people who are rabid. When you are just a young kid, it's tough. He went through some bad times."

As far as Chapman and his close relatives are concerned, the night of Feb. 24, 1988 has to be ranked as one of most scary times they've encountered. Even the Wildcat faithful were alarmed.

That's when Chapman suffered a back injury in a regionally-televised game with LSU at Rupp Arena. While attempting a driving layup, he hurt his back late in the first half as he clashed with LSU's Lyle Mouton in the air, falling flat on his back on the floor. After Chapman and the doctors decided it was just a bad bruise, he told the coach he wanted to play. He started the second half in pain before Sutton took him out for good. Later he was taken to a hospital where x-rays revealed a small cracked bone in the lower back.

First, it was feared that he would have to sit out a couple of weeks, but he missed only one game — a national TV date with Syracuse at Rupp Arena. It was such a big deal that one of the state's largest newspapers, *Lexington Herald-Leader*, ran a front-page story two days later about Chapman's accident with drawings of the lower back, detailing his injury.

"The worst moments were when I watched TV and saw him injured," said Granny of her most heartbreaking moment of her grandson's UK career. "The cameras just kept focusing and he looked like he was dead. I just nearly died. I think that was the most terrifying time. It certainly was with his parents."

Chapman's father happened to be at the game, one of the few times he saw his son play at Rupp Arena. Wayne couldn't come to many UK games because of scheduling conflicts with his coaching job at Kentucky Wesleyan. "Yeah, it was scary," remarked his father. "But, you know, players fall all the time in this game and they're going to fall more often the higher they fly and the faster they go. He was very fortunate that he wasn't injured any more seriously than he was. I knew he was in capable hands. They had good trainers and good doctors. They took care of him. He might have come back from it a little too soon but that was a decision he made along with the doctors. He's fine and didn't show any after effects of it.

"They thought he'd be out a week to a month and maybe miss the playoffs but he ended up missing one game. So, a lot of people don't understand that he played in a lot of pain the rest of that season."

Although there had been some talk that Chapman would turn pro early, Wildcat fans, nevertheless, were surprised in May of 1988 when he announced that he was leaving UK, creating an uproar between sympathetic and selfish supporters. Some didn't blame Chapman for taking the money. Some criticized him for leaving UK in a difficult spot for the following season as the Wildcats had already lost key seniors Winston Bennett, Rob Lock, Ed

Davender, Richard Madison and Cedric Jenkins.

In one way, Rex's Granny was one of the "selfish" supporters because she would not get to see him much anymore. And she wanted him to complete his education, too. "The only bad time was when he quit and went to the pros," said Mrs. Hamby. "I was sad about that. Again, I was sadder for myself because we knew we wouldn't see him and I wanted him to finish school."

She is not sure if Chapman will ever return to school. "I don't know. He talks about it. But it's so far in the future and I know how it was for me. I was always going to go back and I didn't. It's awfully hard to get into that groove again."

However, she believes he is more content with his professional career after three years on the NBA circuit. "He kind of put that (UK fanfare) into a compartment all by itself because he loves playing basketball," said Granny. "I think he is actually happier now, more satisfied and relaxed. He is not in the public eye and that's the biggest thing."

Not surprisingly, a lot of roundball experts and coaches had mixed reactions about Chapman's decision to turn pro early. Vanderbilt coach C. M. Newton, now the athletic director at Kentucky, expressed some reservations. TV analysts Dick Vitale and Al McGuire both agreed, feeling that the youngster should have stayed at UK.

Some have speculated that Chapman, who was later named by *Basketball Times* as one of "the five most intriguing people in basketball in 1988," wished to leave because of his coaches. Or some say because he was unhappy. Or because of the NCAA investigation. Or because of a possible career-ending injury would cost him millions of dollars. Or whatever. But Chapman's father said Rex left UK for one reason.

"That was to play professional basketball," he said. "You've got to understand that you can't make that decision if you don't have the ability and he had the ability to play pro ball. He made a rational decision based on facts and nothing else. You don't make decisions of that magnitude based on personalities, based on happiness or unhappiness. There are a lot of things in this world that make us all happy and unhappy. But you live with it. That's part of life. You don't change jobs because you don't get along with somebody. He made the decision based on rational facts and the facts were that he was capable of playing pro ball. And he was wanted in professional basketball. So, that was the decision he made."

After a slow start in his NBA rookie season, Chapman showed promise as he finished strong for the Hornets, averaging nearly 17 points a game for the campaign. Although Charlotte had the second worst record (20-62) in the league, it led the NBA in attendance, drawing an average of over 23,000 spectators. The Hornets were a big box-office success story, becoming the first expansion franchise ever to lead a major pro sport in attendance in their first year. (That feat, however, only lasted one year as the Minnesota Timberwolves, another expansion team, took the honors in 1990, drawing an average crowd of over 26,000.)

And in the next two seasons, Chapman continued to improve as he gained maturity. No longer a youngster who left UK at the age of 20, he has become a solid NBA veteran.

Granny, who is now in her mid-sixties, has loved sports all her life. She and her late husband even had a swimming pool and tennis courts at their London home years ago. But she did not actually become a UK basketball fan until the mid-1970s when she met coach Joe B. Hall and star player Jimmy Dan Conner.

"When my husband and I married in 1973 — Mr. Hamby and I — he had a place on Kentucky Lake (in western Kentucky)," she recalled. "Joe Hall visited us there. Jimmy Dan and some of his buddies would come down and visit us there. My husband had a nephew who is a good friend of Jimmy Dan's. I really became a Wildcat fan then and we went to a lot of ball games when Jimmy Dan played.

"But, up until then, I was so much of a Western (Kentucky) fan that I really couldn't give UK much."

For good reasons. She had known coach Ed Diddle at Western Kentucky for a long time. And her son-in-law, Wayne Chapman, played for WKU. "I saw Wayne play at Western one or two times," said Mrs. Hamby. "They

(Wayne and her daughter, Laura) married while he was still a student."

She also saw Wayne play for the Kentucky Colonels in the ABA. "I was living in Louisville for a short time and we went to all the ball games," said Granny. "Rex was a little baby. We took him to the games.

"I had the zipper fixed on an old warmup jacket of his that I kept. When they came up (to Lexington) last weekend, he said, 'It's so cold' and I told him I had one of his old warmup jackets. He asked if it was a Pacers. I said no, this is a Kentucky Colonels. He said 'I can't believe you have this.'"

Even though her grandson is no longer at Kentucky, Granny still follows the Wildcats. At times, she is very opinionated. She talked about former UK guard Sean Sutton and coach Rick Pitino. There were discussions in the spring of 1990 that Sutton might return to UK as a walk-on.

"I was interested in seeing that Sean Sutton might be back," she said. "He was the pathetic figure in all the (NCAA) mess. He was caught by loyalty to his father. I never thought it was smart for a father to try to coach a son. It might work, though. It seems like Allan Houston (of Tennessee where his father is the coach) is doing a good job. Their situation is OK, but I just don't think you can be too objective. If he (coach Sutton) played Sean at all, they (the fans) said he ought to be playing Richie Farmer. And, no matter what you do, as far as the fans are concerned, Richie should play. It was a no-win situation and I think Sean will be better if he comes here under Pitino. He can probably help the team."

Of course, Sean never did return to UK as the new coaches told him no.

On Pitino, Granny said, "I've met him at some parties where I've played (piano). I think if the players get along and they like him, and the fans certainly like him, I can't see anything but good things happening. He seems to be motivated."

16 HARD TIMES

"They ended up as
the losingest team in
the school's basketball
history with a
13 – 19 record."

About a year after then-UK president Dr. David Roselle had forced Eddie Sutton to resign from his high-profile position as the Wildcats' head coach, Sutton found another job.

On April 11, 1990, Oklahoma State, satisfied after doing some heavy investigation of Sutton's problems in the past, named him its new head coach. So, that meant Sutton was returning to his alma mater where he played and served as graduate assistant coach under Henry Iba, a legendary figure in college basketball. It was a homecoming of sorts. He graduated from Oklahoma State (then called Oklahoma A&M) in 1958 and obtained his master's degree from the school in 1959.

Sutton's wife, Patsy, is also a graduate of OSU and two of their three sons, Sean and Scott, later joined the elder Sutton at OSU at different times. After sitting out the 1989-90 campaign as the result of his father's departure from UK, Sean had sought to remain at Kentucky but coach Rick Pitino and his staff had decided that they couldn't use him as a walk-on. UK received statewide criticism of the way Sean was treated and informed of the decision. Pitino said it was a case of a big misunderstanding.

Speaking of Oklahoma State, Sutton was excited at another chance to coach after his stormy bouts at Kentucky with the NCAA probe and his alcohol-related problems. It is likely the new job will be his last coaching post.

But before Oklahoma State gave Sutton a five-year pact with an annual base salary of $85,000, the school officials did some serious checking on his background. After all, the Cowboys had been hit with a three-year probation on their football team by the NCAA in January of 1989. Concerned with the school's image, the officials didn't want to risk any more trouble with the NCAA. They wanted to make sure that Sutton was capable of running a clean program even though the former UK mentor had been cleared by the NCAA of any direct wrongdoings at Kentucky. They had questions about his past drinking problems.

While Sutton was at Kentucky, the fans and news media frequently joked or told stories about his alcohol problems. Since he was a public figure, the problems intensified and it made things more difficult for him and his family to handle. However, to their credit, they did well under the circumstances, at least publicly.

Later, at the press conference when he was hired at Oklahoma State, Sutton admitted that some of the rumors about the bottle were probably true and said he has dealt with the problem.

"I did a lot of probing on Eddie Sutton because I had some anxieties," Oklahoma State chancellor Dr. John Campbell told publisher Larry Donald of the *Basketball Times*. "I even had my secretary go out and buy a copy of the book (*Raw Recruits*) because I wanted to learn everything I could. I'm very sincere when I tell you I don't want to be the president who presided over Oklahoma State University with athletics getting sudden death (penalty if more violations were found).

"I had a legal pad with three-and-one half pages full of questions. Tough questions. Personal questions. I was very concerned about the alcohol problem, so it was almost embarrassing how tough these questions were.

"But I was very impressed because he (Sutton) addressed every one. By the end of our discussions my concerns were put to rest."

So, Sutton became a Cowboy.

One person glad to see Sutton getting the Cowboy job is Oscar Combs of *The Cats' Pause*, who had refused to support Sutton publicly in the coach's last year at Kentucky. He sent a congratulatory telegram to Sutton on the day after he was hired at the Stillwater, Okla., school. Combs, who once had a close relative with alcoholic problems, was sympathetic to Sutton's personal woes.

"The man is a wonderful human being," he said. "I wish I could be as kind and gentle I knew about his problems (alcoholism) for a long time while he was here and it hurt me to see a great man being brought down by the disease. I think this is one of the things so many people don't understand. They looked at him and they frowned on him. It really is a disease. People who don't understand are ignorant.

"I really feel he made some poor decisions here (at Kentucky) but they were the result of his battling this disease. Otherwise he would have never made them. So I attribute all of his shortcomings to that problem and the fact that he could not see through it and get help.

"As a little kid, I had a very close relative who went through this and lost his entire family because of it. I knew what it did to him and I knew Eddie had so much to offer to people. There's nothing Eddie Sutton wouldn't do for a person. He'd take his coat off his back and give it to them. You could write a story about him and rip him from shred to shred and the next day he would call and say 'Let's go and have lunch.' He was that kind of person and it hurt me to see him brought down.

"I am so happy (about Sutton's new opportunity) and really hope and faithfully believe that he is licking that thing and he has another chance to come back. He has a lot to prove, but doesn't have anything to prove on the court. He is a great coach and everybody knows it. All he has to do is prove to himself that he can win a battle much bigger than basketball."

Said former Sutton aide Dwane Casey, "That (alcoholism) was a concern. He got it straightened out and I'm glad of that. I'm sure that had a lot of motivating factor with Dr. Roselle in his decision not to support the coaching staff with the rumors and things that were being said about his problem at that time. I just happened to be in the middle of the situation then. I'm glad to see that coach Sutton made a recovery and that he made a commitment publicly.

"I don't know the statistics on alcoholism across the United States but it is very high. He happened to be in the situation where the scrutiny and the visibility of his position was very high. If you were a CEO at a corporation, you might not go into the office for a month or so. But at Kentucky you can't do that, so that caused a lot of problems."

The day after coach Rollie Massimino's Villanova team shocked the college basketball world, upsetting Patrick Ewing and his Georgetown teammates for the 1985 NCAA championship in Lexington, Sutton "crawled all the way" from Arkansas to the UK campus to get the coveted Wildcat post. Sutton charmed his way through the selection process, impressing UK officials — president Dr. Otis Singletary and athletic director Cliff Hagan, among others. He came to the Bluegrass after 11 successful seasons at Arkansas.

It marked the beginning of Sutton's four-year bittersweet tenure at Kentucky. Despite Sutton's "perm" hairstyle which many Wildcat fans didn't care for, he was the most popular man in the state of Kentucky during his first year at the UK helm. He guided the Wildcats and All-American Kenny Walker to a glamorous 32-4 record, using a three-guard starting lineup. Kentucky won both the SEC regular season and tournament titles, and reached the Final Eight of the NCAA tournament. And, for his efforts, he was named the National Coach of the Year by the Associated Press and the National Association of Basketball Coaches. It was a dream season for Sutton. He couldn't ask for a better honeymoon as far as any new coach was concerned.

But Sutton encountered some minor problems off the court nearly three months after he became the Wildcat mentor. Besides his controversial switch from Converse (which former UK coaches Adolph Rupp and Joe B. Hall had done business with for many years) to Nike sneakers, Sutton was a no-show at a TV studio for the taping of a public service spot. His absence irritated officials at Kentucky Educational Television (KET) network and the Kentucky Commission on the Deaf and Hearing Impaired. It was a brief charity work that he had agreed to do.

With the exception of some 35,000 readers in south-central Kentucky, not too many people in the state knew about this incident. Sutton's no-show was reported in The *Commonwealth-Journal*, a Somerset (Ky.) daily, where the author was SEC columnist. Here are the excerpts from the author's column:

If you are looking for a celebrity to participate in a public service TV spot, University of Kentucky head basketball coach Eddie Sutton would not be a good choice, at least for the time being.

That's because Sutton was a no-show, missing two appointments within a four-day period at the Kentucky Educational Television (KET) studio in Lexington for taping of a 30-second spot about the deaf and hearing impaired. The officials from KET and the Kentucky Commission on the Deaf and Hearing Impaired (a state governmental agency) expressed unhappiness over Sutton's no-show.

Sutton was to appear in the TV spot with a deaf boy who was to hold a basketball while the coach spoke. The spot, which would be open-captained, would also be distributed to Louisville and Lexington commercial stations for showing — that is, whenever the taping is completed.

It was agreed earlier that Sutton was to arrive at KET (located near the UK campus) for a 3 p.m. appointment last Friday. Everyone involved in the project was ready, including KET producer Tom Ward, Commission Executive Director Bill Rogers, and Lamarc Williamson, the deaf youngster from Lexington who was accompanied by his mother.

But there was one problem. No coach Sutton.

The UK Basketball Office called at 3 p.m. sharp, explaining that the coach was tied up, and the taping was rescheduled for (last) Monday at 3 p.m.

Then on Monday, the same people showed up at KET only to find out that Sutton would not be able to come. Sutton's office earlier (in the day) called KET to cancel the appointment.

Sutton could not be located at his Memorial Coliseum office or his basketball camp on the UK campus later that day. But UK Basketball Office manager Marta McMackin — who has been with the Wildcat basketball program for over eight years — said she was aware of the situation and apologized for the trouble.

McMackin said Sutton and his family were looking for a house in the Lexington area. She added that the coach has not settled in yet. She also said that Sutton was thinking about doing the taping tonight at 6 p.m. However, KET said no.

After missing two appointments, McMackin was asked by this columnist if Sutton is actually interested in the TV spot. She said, "Yes, he still wants to do it."

Well, KET is now even considering doing an on-location TV spot (at Sutton's office or basketball camp), according to Ward. Officials hope the taping can be rescheduled very soon, hopefully this week.

Therefore, the current situation is in limbo.

The deaf youngster sure was a disappointed little boy. He walked slowly out of the KET building, holding his mother's hand. Who knows what childish dream of playing basketball for UK and meeting coach Sutton had just gone down the drain.

In case you're wondering, Sutton and KET never got together for that charity project.

After his first year at UK, Sutton continued to find coaching success on the hardwood floor for the next couple of seasons as the Wildcats posted records of 18-11 and 27-6 (even though NCAA later deleted Kentucky's two victories and one loss from the 1988 NCAA tourney, making its record 25-5, as part of the sanctions placed on UK). In his second season, Sutton had to direct the young team without star Winston Bennett who sustained a pre-season knee injury, sidelining him for the year. With the help of rising freshman star Rex Chapman, the Cats were able to salvage the season. Some of their memorable games that season included a big 34-point victory over Louisville at Freedom Hall, a win over center David Robinson's Navy squad, and an exciting one-point victory over 12th-ranked Oklahoma on Senior's Day. All of these games were on national television.

In the 1987-88 campaign, Sutton had veteran players to work with in seniors Rob Lock, Ed Davender and Bennett. He also had Chapman and promising newcomers in Eric Manuel and LeRon Ellis. Ranking No. 6 in the final poll, the Wildcats finished the season on a disappointing note with NCAA tourney setback to Villanova in Birmingham, Ala. It was a team that many observers thought should have gone to the NCAA Final Four.

Then came the nightmare. Sutton's basketball empire began to fall apart. The whole mess started in April of 1988 when a Los Angeles newspaper reported that a package had popped open in the transit, allegedly containing $1,000 and a video tape. The parties to the package involved Emery Air Freight, UK assistant coach Dwane Casey and the family of Wildcat recruit Chris Mills. And the rest is history, resulting in a severe three-year penalty placed on Kentucky by the NCAA in May of 1989 after a lengthy, troublesome investigation also uncovered other rules violations committed by the school.

According to a ballot by the U.S. Basketball Writers Association, the Kentucky scandal ranked fourth among the Top 10 stories of the 1980 decade.

While the investigation was continuing in his roundball program during the 1988-89 season — which would be Sutton's last at UK, his distracted Wildcats struggled throughout the year. They ended up as the losingest team in the school's basketball history with a 13-19 record. And Sutton hinted to reporters that he might write a book about his horrible experience at Kentucky, possibly scaring some people who have close ties with the UK program.

Several days after his 53rd birthday, Sutton announced his resignation on national TV during the halftime of an NCAA tournament game. It was about a couple of months before the NCAA verdict was revealed.

One of the nation's winningest coaches in NCAA Division I, posting a 20-year career record of 430-164, Sutton finished his four-year stint at Kentucky with a 88-39 Wildcat mark. But his coaching reputation had been tarnished. Things would never the same for Sutton and his family. He had become a fallen hero.

While Kentucky's program was in the midst of

heavy scrutiny by the NCAA, there was a lot of talk about "bad" Wildcats at the 1988 SEC media affair, a pre-season event which was held in November in Atlanta. Reporters were constantly asking questions about Kentucky. And, interestingly, LSU coach Dale Brown publicly supported Sutton, something that some other SEC coaches would not do.

Brown later called Sutton, wanting to give some encouragement to the embattled Kentucky coach. And Sutton told Brown that he appreciated remarks the LSU coach had made at SEC's Media Days. A few years earlier, Brown had gone through the NCAA investigation and understood what Sutton was feeling.

In a recently-published book, *Don't Count Me Out*, which takes a detailed look on Brown's personal life and his coaching style along with his Tigers, it contains an interesting telephone conversation between Brown and Sutton. (The following passage is reprinted with permission from *Don't Count Me Out* by Bruce Hunter, Bonus Books, Inc., 160 E. Illinois, Chicago, IL 60611.)

"I really appreciate your attitude, Dale, " Sutton said. "It's been a difficult time, as you can imagine. Some reporters came back and told me that you were straight forward and never once jabbed me. I've heard other coaches have. I appreciate your fairness. You've always been my friend. Now I know just how much of a friend you are."

"Eddie, you know what the media wanted to talk about," Brown said. "It wasn't about our teams. They were trying to get everyone to talk about Kentucky. I told them very simply that I feel for what you're going through and I think it's wrong the way the NCAA treats people. It's absolutely wrong. I also found out something I didn't know existed. I found out that most of those writers that I thought would die for the Blue and White have changed their colors now that they've got a little story. It was totally brutal."

Brown was surprised at Sutton's openness and remorseful attitude regarding the investigation. He could tell there had been a dramatic change in his friend of more that 20 years.

But Brown wasn't ready for what he was about to hear. "I know I've made mistakes in my profession," Sutton told him. "I want to clean my life up. And I just realized that this isn't worth it. I know wrong that has been done, and we're not going to refute that. And I know wrong that has not been done, and they're making more of a story out of that.

"I'm just changing. All the things that I thought were glorious and beautiful, I've come to a rude awakening that they're not. I feel now that I've got to step back and look at this whole thing again. I really need you as a friend."

Sutton extended a dinner invitation whenever Brown came to Lexington. Then Sutton thanked him again.

Almost at a loss for words, Brown finally responded, "Eddie, I really appreciate what you've said to me. Maybe all of us coaches can really help each other. I really think we can. I am going to say a prayer for you. OK, bye Eddie, and thank you."

Brown couldn't contain his happiness about Sutton's attitude. He rushed out of the office to find someone with whom to share this secret. He looked in (assistant Johnny) Jones' office, but Johnny was gone. Then he went a few more steps down the hall and found assistant coach) Ron Abernathy in his office.

"Ron, God has touched Eddie Sutton," he said, drawing a puzzled look from his assistant. "I just got off the phone with Eddie, and you wouldn't believe some of the things he said. That's the first time he has ever talked like that. It made me feel good, man. That's the best thing that's ever happened to him. He is really searching things out. I know he is trying to find God. He is just a different person. I think I can really help him."

Sutton and Brown have known each other since the late 1960s when they coached against each other in a junior college game in the west. For three years from 1967 to '70, Sutton guided Southern Idaho Junior College, a school which had never fielded a basketball team before he took over. He posted a 83-14 mark before moving to Creighton University in 1970 as the head coach.

"I coached against Dale Brown when he was a freshman coach at Utah State and I was coaching at a junior college in Idaho," Sutton told the author in a 1986 interview. "So, I have known him for a long time, probably known him longer than any of the coaches in the conference."

Sutton was not the only person who left Kentucky as the result of the NCAA mess. All of his assistant coaches, including Dwane Casey, departed as well. NCAA later banned Casey — who was charged with putting $1,000 in a package containing his return address to a recruit's father — from coaching for five years as part of sanctions placed on Kentucky. Casey maintained his innocence and sued Emery Air Freight for $6.9 million for defamation of character, among other things. He eventually won an undisclosed substantial amount in an out-of-court settlement with Emery.

A relieved Casey and his attorney, Joe Bill Campbell, admit that getting a large piece of monetary pie will make the former Wildcat financially comfortable for a long time. But Casey said he is still bothered by the fact it took him a couple of years to prove his innocence.

In the late 1970s when he was a reserve guard for coach Joe B. Hall at Kentucky, the author got to know Casey. He was well-liked by the public. He was very cordial and cooperative. I didn't know of anyone who disliked him.

I always will respect him because of one small incident. It all started during my first year at UK when I was working for the school's daily newspaper, *The Kentucky Kernel*, as a young, insignificant reporter. At that time, I wasn't known by many in the UK sports camp.

I had scheduled an interview with Casey to take place on a Saturday afternoon after a UK football home game. We were to meet at Holmes Hall (a dormitory where basketball players formerly stayed before Wildcat Lodge was constructed). But Casey didn't show up for the interview and I wasn't too happy. I thought, "Oh, well, he didn't care."

I went back to my dorm room. About an hour later, the telephone rang. My roommate answered the phone and relayed the message. It was Casey on the other end, saying he was terribly sorry and apologizing for missing the appointment. He explained that he had car trouble.

However, the most impressive characteristic about Casey was that he had to make an effort to call me. He didn't know where I lived and didn't have my number. He had to find it himself. It showed that he was reliable and trustworthy.

That is a very good example of what has made Casey the man he is. So, I have always admired Casey. He always had time to talk, whether he was at the library, my dorm or practice. We became mutual acquaintances, but were never close.

Casey's former boss, coach Sutton, once said that he couldn't find anyone to say anything bad about Casey during the interview screening process before he was hired to replace Leonard Hamilton, who had moved on to become the head coach at Oklahoma State.

In addition to the departure of Casey and others, ex-Wildcat All-American Cliff Hagan earlier had resigned from his athletic director post at Kentucky in November 1988 during the NCAA investigation. Previously, Hagan had complained that he was being unfairly labeled a scapegoat by some UK administrators. He had been the school's athletic director since 1975.

Hagan said that he deeply regretted leaving his post under very difficult circumstances in the sports program but felt like his resignation was the proper thing to do for him and his family. But some UK supporters believed that Hagan received a raw deal. They argued that the school's handling of Hagan's departure was something less than appropriate as he had been associated with UK since his college days with the exception of his outstanding pro career.

President Dr. Roselle, who later left Kentucky for a similar post at the University of Delaware, and his administrators thought it was time to houseclean the athletic department. Partly to please the NCAA bigwigs, they began with the No. 1 sports administrator in Hagan. In the course of the reorganization shakeup, the sports program was placed under more direct control by the president's office. Joseph T. Burch, a long-time UK official, was named to replace Hagan on an interim basis until April 1989 when C.M. Newton left his Vanderbilt coaching job to assume Kentucky's AD post.

During the 1990 Final Four in Denver, upon learning

that Hamilton had quit the Cowboy job at Oklahoma State to take the Miami (Fla.) post, Sutton became so excited that he had to run to the phone. He wanted to inform his wife about that job opening at his old school.

"We were standing around the lobby at the Final Four and an assistant coach, I don't remember who, came up and asked if I knew that my alma mater and my former assistant coach weren't married any longer," he told the *Basketball Times*. "I can tell you I sprinted to the telephone and called my wife to tell her about it."

On his Kentucky days, Sutton said, "I don't have any bitter feeling toward Kentucky. A lot of people there have been very supportive. The same way at Arkansas. I regret the statement about crawling all the way to Lexington, but I hope people in Arkansas understood it wasn't meant to be a shot at the people, but only at a couple of guys.

"I'm thrilled to be back."

And Combs, whose weekly magazine continuously ran articles and columns about the NCAA investigation on UK much like a daily newspaper during Sutton's last season at Kentucky, had this to say. "Near the end of his career last year (at Kentucky), there were a lot of times when we didn't get together but he never gave me a hard word in his life and I never gave him one and I love Eddie Sutton to this day. "I know that he is a good and decent person."

17 THE FALL GUY

"I wasn't even
in town when
the package
was mailed."

In the 1960s and the early 1970s, during the flower days of Kennedy, Johnson and Nixon, when Dwane Casey was a boy in his hometown of Morganfield in western Kentucky, he had his share of heroes. He followed the guys who played for the St. Louis Cardinals' baseball team and the University of Evansville Purple Aces' basketball squad. They were close to his home in Union County.

"Baseball-wise, Bob Gibson was my big-time idol," recalled a mild-mannered Casey in a 1991 interview. "I followed the baseball team that had Mike Shannon, Lou Brock and Orlando Cepeda. Red Schoendienst was the manager of the Cards. We got all of the St. Louis games (on radio and TV)."

As a youngster Casey had never met Gibson, the flame-throwing pitcher who is now a Hall of Famer. But he finally got to meet his hero at a dinner a few years ago. "I met Bob Gibson but he had already retired," he said. "I met him at a 'Say No To Drugs' banquet in Washington, D.C. It was a group of people who were invited to a drug conference. At last I got his autograph.

"Roberto Clemente was also a great inspiration to me at that time because he was a heck of a baseball player. I remember he used to twitch his head when he was going to bat. Of course, I loved Willie Mays. Growing up, I was probably more of a baseball fan than a basketball fan."

In the basketball world, Casey's hero was 6-4 All-American Don Buse of the University of Evansville who played in the early 1970s. Buse later played for the Indiana Pacers. "You probably don't remember him," Casey said of Buse, "but when I was growing up he played for the Aces. They were the only college team that we saw on television on a consistent basis. (Evansville) coach Arad McCutchan was one of the top coaches in the country."

Elizabeth Miller, 79, is a very special person in Casey's life. She is his devoted grandmother.

"She's probably the most influential person in my family and in my life," he said. "She did such a great job of raising me, taking care of me, clothing me and feeding me. When times were hard, it would seem like she would come through with money or new clothes for school. She was and still is the most important person in my life.

"My mom had me (in Indianapolis in 1957) about a year before my mom and dad got married. So, she was a single parent at the time and we moved to Morganfield where my grandparents and my mom are originally from. She started working there in Morganfield and my grandmother was trying to help her out. Then all at once, she got a better job at Fort Benjamin Harrison in Indianapolis. At the time that was a pretty good job for black people. She had to go and take it. Instead of being a single parent in Indianapolis, she let my grandmother keep me while she was working in Indiana. She would come in on weekends and visit me. But I got so attached to my grandparents that once my parents got married, I went ahead and stayed in Morganfield and went to my parents during the summer.

"We were low middle class. We weren't real poor. At that time we had a big Motorola. We were one of the first families in our neighborhood to have a black-and-white television set. That was a real feat.

"I know that this sounds like a hard luck story but I can remember we had an outhouse and had to go out there to use the bathroom. I remember when we got an inside toilet. And I still can remember when I was in junior high school, we got our first gas stove. Before that we had coal heat. We had to go out, chop the wood and bring coal in. We were really uptown when we got that (stove) back in the middle sixties."

According to Casey, the second most influential person in his life was former Kentucky Gov. Earle Clements, whom his grandmother used to work for. "I used to go over there with her as a child and hang around his house. He probably had as much influence on me coming to Kentucky (in 1975) as anybody because he was good friends with the people in Lexington, with (president) Dr. Singletary."

In the 1970s, Union County High School, under the leadership of basketball coach Ernon Simpson, sent three players to UK — Larry Johnson, Casey and Fred Cowan. Johnson was the first one. The 6-3 floor general was a defense specialist who played under the shadows of Jack Givens, Rick Robey and Mike Phillips. During his senior year at UK, Johnson was chosen to the 1977 All-SEC third team by the Associated Press.

And Johnson was Casey's hometown buddy. They were two years apart. The duo ran around together a lot during their college days. Johnson was one of the biggest reasons why Casey decided to cast his lot with the Wildcats.

"One of my best friends at that time was Larry Johnson," Casey said. "He was already here playing. I used to come up and spend the summer with Larry in his apartment and play with the guys like Jimmy Dan (Conner), Kevin Grevey and Bob Guyette. I really fell in love with the University of Kentucky. Not until that time did I become a Kentucky fan."

While a four-sport star at Union County High, the 6-2 Casey was being recruited by many colleges, including several SEC schools. An all-stater, he averaged nearly 24 points and eight rebounds as a senior. Casey also captained both basketball and baseball teams.

"Tennessee recruited me real hard. Stu Aberdeen, who used to be assistant coach there, recruited me for Tennessee," Casey commented. "Vanderbilt recruited me real hard. Roy Skinner was the head coach and Wayne Dobbs was the assistant coach at the time. The University of Georgia was another school that recruited me real hard and that was before coach (Hugh) Durham came."

Evansville, Western Kentucky, Murray State, Eastern Kentucky and Southern Illinois also expressed strong interest in Casey. "Southern Illinois recruited me very hard to play baseball, and the University of Evansville wanted me to come and play baseball and basketball," Casey said.

Speaking of Johnson, he now lives in Atlanta, Ga., where he works for the Panasonic Corporation after playing 11 years of pro basketball in Japan. Years ago, before going to Japan, Johnson had been a state employee in the Department of Human Resources. It appeared that his basketball career was over as he had been released in the NBA after a brief stint with the old Buffalo Braves (now the Los Angeles Clippers) during the 1977-78 campaign. But Casey changed all that.

Kentucky's basketball connection with Japan practically began in the summer of 1978, a few months after the Wildcats had won the national championship. UK went on a seven-game exhibition tour in Japan, playing against the Japanese National Team at various sites. Japan was getting ready for the 1980 Olympics.

The Japanese officials were so impressed with Kentucky that they sent two coaches to observe the Wildcat program in 1979 and '80. One of the coaches was Mototaka Kohama who followed the program when Casey was a graduate assistant under Hall.

"I introduced Coach Kohama to Larry Johnson. He was the reason Larry went there (to Japan)," Casey noted. "Coach Kohama was the national team coach at that time and spent a year at the University of Kentucky. He (Johnson) had a long career (in Japan). His team won, I think, three or four championships, so he's a legend in Japan. They love him very much."

Johnson is not the only Wildcat who went to Japan. Fred Cowan, now retired from basketball, played for the Toshiba Corporation, an electronics firm, in the Far East for nine years. The 6-8 Cowan and Casey were very close buddies when both were at UK.

"Freddie Cowan was probably the closest friend I had on the team," said Casey. "He still is one of my best friends. Freddie is back in Madisonville in the screen printing business.

"But I had a lot of good buddies to go to if I was hungry and needed some cookies out of somebody's room or whatever. In my freshman year Reggie Warford and I were close. He was a senior and I was a little freshman so he kind of took me under his wings."

And Casey, for the first time, is following Johnson and Cowan's footsteps to Japan on a full-time basis. (He had previously worked at coaching clinics in Japan in the 1980s.) In the summer of 1991, he signed a three-year pact with Sekisui Chemical Co. to coach its basketball team after serving as a part-time consultant for one year. It marked Casey's first coaching post since he was banned for five years by the NCAA in 1989. Before returning to Kentucky in 1986, he had worked as an assistant coach at Western Kentucky for five years under coach Clem Haskins.

"The company that I work for is well-known in Japan but you don't see the name very much here in the U.S.," said Casey who speaks "enough" Japanese to get by in normal conversation and to be polite. "It's a chemical company and it's the equivalent to our Dow Chemical and DuPont Chemical companies. They create chemicals to make tires, paint, etc. It's a very large corporation and they have offices here in the United States. They put a lot of money into the team because this is a form of advertising for their company. It creates a lot of pride and distinction about their company if they can win a championship with their basketball team.

"(The players) are hired by the companies not to do book work, but to play basketball. The guys have to go to the office from 9-12 and then after that they are free for practice. So, their actual job for the corporation until they retire from playing is to play basketball.

"We have quite a few American players who are playing in the league. Clarence Martin, who played for me at Western Kentucky, is playing over there now for the Sony Corporation. (Ex-UK player) Cedric Jenkins was playing there as well as Ted Young who played at Vanderbilt and David Dunn who played at Georgia.

"There are three different divisions in the league —

the first division, the second division and the third division. There are like 12 teams in each division and all of them are sponsored by Fortune 500 corporations such as Panasonic, Isuzu, Toyota, Sanyo, etc. The season goes from September to December. So, I'll be back here in time to enjoy the NCAA season."

Back in his college days at UK, Casey never did play much. He only started four games and had a Wildcat career average of 1.3 points, but his work ethic earned him respect from the coaches and fans. In his sophomore year, he gunned in what would be his Wildcat career-high 13 points, including nine of 10 free throws, in UK's 90-63 victory over Kansas in only Kentucky's third game at the brand-new Rupp Arena. And it was also the Dedication Night for Rupp Arena where the school officials and fans honored Adolph Rupp.

Another memorable game for Casey took place in the 1978 NCAA Tournament. Playing against Florida State in Knoxville, Kentucky was losing and coach Joe B. Hall had to do something. Trailing 39-32 at the half, Hall decided to start three little-used reserves — Casey, Cowan and LaVon Williams — in the second half. Although the trio didn't score much (they had six for the entire contest), they put Kentucky back in the contest with their inspiring aggressive defense. And the rest is history. Kentucky won 85-76 on its way to the national title.

Casey's role was not to score, but to be a playmaker and play good defense. He was a dedicated leader. In his senior year Casey served as co-captain with senior guard Truman Claytor.

But Casey will never forget one incident. It happened on a two-game road trip in February of 1978, shortly after Kentucky had just suffered its second loss of its championship season with a 95-94 overtime setback to LSU in Baton Rouge.

"Oh, man, the most embarrassing moment that I ever had was in my junior year," Casey said. "We had just gotten beat by LSU. Freddie (Cowan), LaVon (Williams) and I were up in the motel room watching Redd Foxx — Sanford and Son. It was morning and we were getting ready to go to shooting practice down at Ole Miss. All at once we heard the bus motor rev up and we had lost track of time. So, we jumped up and looked out the window (from the second floor) and everybody was down there on the bus except us. We were already dressed for practice.

"Coach Hall was on a rampage. He was in one of those moods that if you did anything wrong, it was going to be over. So we sprinted down to the front of the Holiday Inn and I reached out to get the door of the bus and I almost got my hand caught in the door. But the coach told the driver to shut the door. We had to hitchhike all the way to the gym which about 10 miles away, but we ended up beating the bus there to the shooting practice. The players never let me forget that."

And, for the record, Kentucky later defeated Mississippi 64-52.

Casey also has other stories about Hall. "I'll never forget one day when (teammate) Marion Haskins was snoring in the training or film room at Memorial Coliseum," he recalled. "Everybody was pretty tired. It was early on a Saturday morning. We had just played somebody the night before — I forgot who it was. All at once we would hear some snoring. I mean he was just blowing z's left and right. He was just dozing. And coach Hall suddenly turned off the projector but couldn't see anyone in the room. He reached over and turned the light on, and when he did, Marion was just wide awake. That was one of the funniest moments because Hall never knew who was asleep in the film session that morning."

Another episode. Moments before Kentucky's 1978 NCAA championship encounter with Duke in St. Louis, Hall was trying to find a way to keep his squad from feeling too much pressure. He wanted his team to relax. "He was trying to do (some funny acts) to get us loose from a coaching standpoint," Casey said. "So he took his tie off, messed his hair up, put one leg down in the big barrel trash can and unbuttoned his shirt. He was funny, but at that time we were so scared he couldn't have done anything to make us relax."

Another incident happened in Nashville in 1977 or '78. Hall was in a horrible mood. He didn't like what he saw in Kentucky's victory over Vanderbilt. "You would look at coach Hall and think that he wasn't very animated,"

Casey commented. "We had just gotten through beating Vanderbilt, but we played very badly. We had numerous turnovers. We should have beaten them by at least double figures. We ended up beating them about four points. So after it was over with, coach Hall was going through one of his rages and accidentally knocked over some ice water on Walt McCombs who was our trainer. The coach was just handing him the water.

"Coach Hall, still in a rage, goes over to one of these huge water coolers. He took the lid off of it and just poured the whole thing on himself. And it was below zero weather outside and he started shaking and shivering and we died laughing. We couldn't hold it back any longer. His hair was drenched and the nice black suit he had on was all wet. That was just one of the antics he did."

In his first two years at UK, Casey felt intimidated by Hall. "I was only in the basketball office probably a grand total of three times," he said. "I went into his office only when I had to until my junior or senior year when I got really comfortable. In my freshman and sophomore years, I didn't know whether to speak to him or walk past him or whatever, but that's just how much in awe I was of him. He was the head coach at the University of Kentucky and I was becoming a big Kentucky fan.

"Now, I wish I could go back and play with the confidence I have in myself as a person. As a player, I would probably be 10 times better now than I was back at that time."

For one year, Dwight Anderson was one of Casey's teammates at UK. In the 1978-79 campaign, Anderson was a freshman sensation from Ohio, while Casey was a senior. They were more than teammates. They are related to each other.

"Dwight Anderson was my cousin," Casey said. "Our grandmothers were sisters, so we're distant cousins. He was one of the greatest athletes I've come across. It just so happened he was from Dayton and I knew that my grandmother had a sister who lived in Dayton. So, I asked him if he knew Ann Lee Walker."

Anderson replied, "Yes, I do. She's my grandmother."

Casey said, "Well, that's my grandmother's sister."

And the duo didn't know they were related until they met at UK. They were stunned.

"It's a small world," Casey smiled.

After leaving his Kentucky post as a graduate assistant in 1980, Casey headed for Bowling Green to become a full-time assistant coach at Western Kentucky. He stayed with the Hilltoppers for five years.

And once he got to meet his alma mater as an opponent in a 1986 NCAA tournament game. It was an awkward situation for Casey because he had such strong feelings for the Wildcats. He loved UK.

"It was very mixed," Casey said of his feelings about the matchup in which Eddie Sutton's Wildcats won 71-64 in Charlotte, N.C. "My paycheck said red (WKU's school color). I was for Western. I wanted to beat Kentucky in the worst way, but I had mixed feelings. I also knew they had a chance to win the national championship and we had a young team. The whole weekend I kept seeing old friends and all the old boosters from Kentucky and they were wishing me luck, but not too much luck. So that was a very difficult time because I had mixed emotions. Once the basketball was thrown up, we definitely wanted to beat Kentucky. It was a little bit different because at that time coach Hall had already retired and I didn't know coach Sutton that well. So your feelings of beating your former coach and your alma mater weren't there as it would have been if coach Hall was still the coach. It was also the last game before I got ready to come to Kentucky as an assistant coach. At the time I didn't know that was going to be the situation."

Earlier in 1982, Casey had left WKU after two years because he wasn't making enough money. He returned to Lexington, taking a job with WKYT-TV as a sales representative which eventually lasted only about six months. "At that time the salaries at Western were very low and we had fought and fought the athletics board for a raise," Casey said. "I was telling Clem I was barely making ends meet for the time I was putting in. Clem was very sympathetic with me and he tried to get us raises.

"Then I got this job offer. I ran into (WKYT executive) Ralph Gabbard and he said if I ever wanted to work in television to let him know. The pay was almost double to what I was making at Western. The pay was so ridiculous for an assistant coach that it was like $17,000 or 16,500. I went back to Western (later) because they got their pay scale up. It almost doubled. I went back as an assistant."

Recruiting stories. Casey has several of them while at Western Kentucky. One was about the recruitment of prep star Patrick Ewing, a 7-footer from Cambridge, Mass., who was the only high schooler invited to the 1980 Olympic Trials. Another involved a jealous boyfriend of the mother of a recruit from the state of Georgia.

On the Ewing case, Casey said, "Coach Haskins and I were called in to meet with Pat Ewing. He invited 10 schools to meet with him and seven people on a (so-called screening) committee — he had his headmaster (at Rindge & Latin High School), the mayor, a guidance counselor, a lawyer and the coaching staff. Clem and I had just taken the job at Western Kentucky. So we were sitting in the Holiday Inn in Boston before meeting Pat, and Clem and I looked at each other. Then we just fell back on the bed and died laughing because we knew we were out of our league. The other schools that were in there talking to Pat were Georgetown, North Carolina, St. John's, Villanova and here we are little old Western Kentucky.

"But we had done a great job of making contact with (Ewing's coach) Mike Jarvis who is now head coach at George Washington (of the Atlantic 10 Conference). We did a good job of recruiting Pat and we had to go for it. We had nothing to lose. We were lucky enough to be one of the 10 schools to get in and meet with him. We were talking about how we had wasted good recruiting money to come up here and try to recruit Pat Ewing, but it was well worth the trip because it was a great experience going through that type of recruiting situation and to have our name associated with Patrick Ewing was really a treat."

A couple of years later, in another recruiting episode, Western Kentucky sought the services of a 6-7 youngster in Georgia by the name of Dwayne Rainey. A 260-pound hulk, Rainey eventually signed with the Georgia Bulldogs but he transferred to Middle Tennessee State after his freshman season. And Casey tells one of his favorite traveling stories.

"We went into this home and it was a single-parent home," Casey recalled. "The mother was single and was a very attractive lady but heavy set. She had a boyfriend there who was very small about 5-5 or 5-6 and Ms. Rainey was about 5-9 or so. Ms. Rainey was really in awe of coach Haskins. She thought he was the best-looking guy who recruited players. Clem's very clean-cut and always very nattily-attired.

"So we were sitting in the living room and coach Haskins goes and sits on the couch beside Ms. Rainey. Here comes her boyfriend and he goes and sits down on the couch between them. Coach Haskins had his arm on the back of the couch. All at once he takes his arm out and there was a 'bad' look given by the boyfriend. Just like he was going to do something if coach had looked at Ms. Rainey. She had her eye fixed on coach Haskins because he was a nice-looking guy. But her boyfriend was going to have nothing of it. He was very possessive so he wasn't going to let coach Haskins get close to his girlfriend. Coach Haskins had no interest at all that way. We were just trying to recruit her 6-7 son. That was something we laughed about all the way from their home to Atlanta."

Haskins and Casey both left WKU in 1986. They parted — Haskins to Minnesota and Casey to Kentucky. But before Casey took the Wildcat job to replace Leonard Hamilton, he was one of the leading candidates to take Haskins' job at WKU. "I was in the final two or three for the head coaching job and they hired Murray Arnold," Casey said. "At the time I was only 27 and probably was too young to be a head coach. But I was going to give it a try because I had recruited all the players who were there at the time. I knew the program. I knew the people in the community so I felt like I was ready for the job but they hired Murray Arnold. (Haskins) tried to convince me to go with him to the University of Minnesota as an assistant coach but I came on to UK as an assistant under coach Sutton."

Speaking of coach Sutton, Casey had never personally met him before he came to Lexington for the job interview. But Casey felt like he knew coach Sutton because "we were running the same type of defense, etc. I really wanted it (the position) bad because when you play somewhere, really, it's your dream come true to go back and coach there," explained Casey. "It's a lot easier to play at Kentucky than to coach because you have so many other things to worry about except just playing basketball and going to school. Coach Hamilton tried to get me to come to Oklahoma State with him when he went there. So, I had a lot of opportunities. I could have stayed at Western. I could have gone to Minnesota. The opportunity to come back to Kentucky was second to none because as I said it was my dream come true being able to come back to my alma mater."

On the Kentucky scandal in the Eddie Sutton era, Casey is not angry about the whole ordeal. He is hurt. He is the man who was accused of putting $1,000 in an envelope sent to the father of a UK recruit, which led to the short-lived downfall of Kentucky's basketball program. In other words, he was the fall guy.

"I have never done anything wrong," Casey said. "I was in a bad situation at the wrong time. Our lawsuit (against Emery Air Freight) showed that I had nothing to do with putting money in the package. It showed the fact that was the only violation. They (NCAA) investigated me as hard as anyone could and still only came out with one allegation. That was the Emery situation. Then we go to federal court and it clearly shows that I had nothing to do with putting money in the package. I didn't seal the package. I wasn't even in town when the package went in the mail. I was in Louisville, Kentucky.

"I've got letters from the Emery company and the security company stating the fact that throughout the whole investigation there was no evidence — not even circumstantial evidence — that proved I had anything to do with putting money in that package. We haven't even appealed (Casey's five-year coaching ban) to the NCAA with those letters yet.

"Then the NCAA's guidelines of standard proof is totally different than a court of law. Basically if they think you did something then you're guilty if they feel like you are. And you have really no recourse. You can appeal but they have a hundred percent conviction rate. No one has ever won an appeal against the NCAA.

"When the university took the stand that they did — (interim athletic director) Joe Burch and judge (James) Park said they were caught in the middle in my situation. They didn't say that I did and they didn't say that I didn't. To me, they might as well have said that I did it because of where they stood in that gray area.

"It was a situation that happened. It hurt more than it made me angry. You have faith in an institution and you have faith in certain people. When you know that you didn't do anything wrong, it hurts you that they wouldn't stand up and fight for you or wouldn't have enough faith in you because I had given my whole life to the University of Kentucky.

"If I was wrong, if I was clearly guilty, yeah throw me to the wolves. But if there was a shred of hope — and I had a lot of shreds to show that I wasn't guilty, then stand behind me and fight. That's why I was hurt. I'm not angry, not bitter. Dr. Roselle's gone now. He wasn't there very much longer after I left. Life goes on.

"I still go to the (UK) basketball games and cheer for them. The institution and Kentucky, and what it stands for, didn't run out on me, only certain people did. That's the thing that bothers me. But I'm a Rick Pitino fan. Some of the people that were there in that situation are no longer there so that's why I'm a big Kentucky fan."

Casey's attorney throughout the NCAA mess was Joe Bill Campbell of Bowling Green. Casey knew him from his earlier days at Western Kentucky.

"Joe Bill was the chairman of the Board of Regents at Western Kentucky and he was more or less my boss when I was at Western," Casey said, "and we developed a friendship there. We still stayed in contact (after Casey moved to Lexington) and I knew his reputation as being a successful lawyer and some of the big lawsuits he had won in Bowling Green.

"I had one meeting with the university. They told me right off the bat they thought I was guilty and indicated that I needed to get a lawyer which I never dreamed of since I knew I didn't do anything wrong. I never thought it would happen that way. They were ready to give up to the NCAA right away from the tone of the conversation that day. Their minds were made up at that time. So I called him (Campbell) that Saturday night. I left a message on his recorder to have him call back.

"Joe Bill Campbell was a great source of hope for me as a friend, as a lawyer. We turned out to be best friends in the situation because he was seemingly the only person who stood behind me during the entire investigation. I'm really grateful to him. He believed in me when everybody else started looking at me cross-eyed. I'm sure they (Emery) settled because they knew that we were on the winning side."

During the ordeal, the news media obviously had a ball. It gave them something to write about. Some of them loved to crucify the Wildcats. Perhaps they, especially the national columnists, were jealous of Kentucky's past success. Just like they hated the old New York Yankees. There were stories splashed across the newspapers, magazines and TV sets all over the country from *Sports Illustrated, The Sporting News, Basketball Times, USA Today, Basketball Weekly,* ESPN to CNN.

And Casey has an opinion about them. He refused to criticize the press too harshly. "I sympathized with the news media because it became such a competitive situation," he noted. "I saved my tapes from the news media almost every day of the investigation. I had six or seven calls daily. I mean that's the pressure. They just wanted to know what's going on. They were all after me wanting to get the scoop when really nothing was going on. That's why a lot of times they would put rumors in the paper, which to me if there's something true, go ahead and put it in the newspaper. But they got to the point where they started putting rumors in the paper. People began to give their editorial opinions about college athletics and about the Kentucky situation. I'm sure it was very successful in selling the newspapers. It had people watching the news so they made the best of it.

"It's not the people. It's just temperament of the

media, their zeal and zest of going after a story when nothing was there for a long period of time during the investigation. You would read in the paper about some of the allegations. Yet, you never read where some of the allegations were thrown out or proven untrue. The only thing people remember are the initial stories. It seemed like there were so many allegations. When you read it, you would think in the beginning there were hundreds of allegations. That's what people across the country thought. They thought there was a lot of money changing hands. The only allegation involving money was the Emery situation which we disproved in a court of law.

"In the end you had the allegations and other rival coaches were saying stuff like that. I'll give you an example. One investigator came in and said, 'We want to see Eric Manuel's brand new car.' First of all, Eric Manuel didn't even have a driver's license, but one of the rival coaches said that Eric Manuel had received a brand new car for coming to the University of Kentucky which was totally untrue. He didn't even know how to drive. Those are the type of things you'll hear out there. They (rival coaches) probably didn't have a shot of signing him but they had to justify to their alumni and news media why they didn't get a certain player. The easiest thing to do is to say, 'Well, he went to Kentucky because he got a brand new car.'"

Casey, 34, tries to be a good Christian person. He wants to set a good example for the kids in the community by being a good role model. "I'm a religious person, but not overly religious," Casey pointed out. "I'm not as strong a Christian as I should be. I'm Baptist. I should be stronger in my faith than what I am, but I'm a God-fearing person. I pray regularly. So, hopefully God will forgive me for my sins and what I've done wrong in life. But most of us come short in how we should be as Christians. Prayer and faith help us to become stronger people and stronger Christians."

Asked if he still has dreams of coaching at UK again in the future, Casey replied, "No, those dreams evaporated when I got that call from the Los Angeles newspaper that day (in 1988 about the Emery package). I have no illusions. I'm sure there is no way I could ever work at the University of Kentucky. There are other schools in Kentucky where I feel I could be an asset, schools like Western Kentucky and Eastern Kentucky. Time heals a lot of wounds."

But what if UK comes calling in 20 years from now, offering Casey another opportunity to coach the Wildcats?

"It would be hard to come back because you know when a dog bites you once you don't come back two or three times and get bit again," he said. "But again, it was the people who really ran and put their head in the sand — they are not here. Athletics is a very competitive world. There are so many rumors and if you don't stand up and fight for yourself, you'll get swept under the rug. You'll get taken away if you don't stand up for what's right. That's what I like about coach Pitino and coach Newton.

"If you're wrong, then you expect to lose your job. But when you're right and you know you're right, and the people that you work for take the easy way out you have to question that. But they've got good people there now. (UK president Dr. Charles) Wethington is a fighter. He's going to fight for the Kentucky basketball program. So will coaches Newton and Pitino, they'll fight for what's right."

18 ITALIAN MAGICIAN

"...the program's
savior..."

Kentuckians treat boyish-looking coach Rick Pitino as if he was some Hollywood movie star. In accepting his role, he realizes the exposure — although sometimes irritating — comes with the territory of being the head coach at a very public place like Kentucky. Yet, he enjoys the spotlight. During his first two years at probation-ridden Kentucky, Pitino, labeled as the program's savior, has already appeared as the "coverboy" of several national sports publications, including *The Sporting News*. And it wouldn't be surprising to see him enter the television broadcasting field some day when he quits coaching. With his good looks and personality, the TV job is his if he wants it.

"I think that one thing you can't do in life is look ahead and want for something else," said Pitino, who received good reviews for his brief TV studio role as a basketball analyst on ESPN during the 1991 post-season tournament action (his Wildcats were ineligible due to NCAA sanctions). "If you want for something else, you are tired of what you are doing. I am not tired of coaching. I love coaching. I love dealing with young people. I want to enjoy what I am doing now. I just want to concentrate on what I am doing now.

"I have done quite a bit of TV work. I had my own

TV show in New York, commenting on the NBA playoffs, and had a lot of coaches shows. I hosted a show for the (NCAA) Final Four out in Denver (in 1990). I have been on the David Letterman show and some talk shows."

Pitino says he admires outspoken Dick Vitale, the colorful TV analyst, for saying what he thinks and for creating enthusiasm in the game of basketball. "There are two ways of looking at Vitale," he commented. "You can admire him for what he has accomplished as an ex-coach or you can be jealous of him and say he speaks too much. I kind of admire him for what he has accomplished."

Pitino, asked if he ever gets upset over Vitale's comments, replied, "No, because you can't throw stones when you make mistakes yourself. There are comments I wish I had not made, but anytime you make comments you are going to say things that don't always come out right. You have to respect him not for the bad comments but all the good ones he made."

Both Pitino and Vitale are Italians. They first met in the 1970s when Vitale, then the head coach at the University of Detroit, spoke at a prestigious basketball camp where Pitino was working.

In Pitino's second year at Kentucky, Vitale covered the UK-Indiana game at Bloomington for ESPN. The matchup between Pitino and coach Bobby Knight of Indiana intrigued Vitale so much that he said it matched the nation's best young coach against the nation's best veteran coach.

June 1, 1989 marked a new beginning — actually a rebirth — of Kentucky Wildcat basketball. It was the historic day that UK lured Pitino away from the bright lights of New York City. The successful Italian had been the head coach of NBA's New York Knicks for two years. Pitino, who was hired to coach the scar-marred Wildcats and to restore Kentuckians' pride in UK's roundball program, became the youngest mentor in the SEC at the age of 36.

Just several days earlier, the NCAA almost hammered Kentucky with a death penalty for breaking several NCAA rules. Instead, the Wildcats were hit with a severe three-year penalty which included one year of no live television and two years of no post-season tournament play.

Pitino's highly-publicized arrival in Lexington gave the Wildcat faithful high hopes that the school's basketball program could soon return to its age-old status as a national contender. He was the man the fans had sought to take over the Wildcat helm, vacated by the departure of Eddie Sutton. Kentucky athletic director C. M. Newton indicated that if Pitino or someone of similar stature had not accepted his offer, he would have coached the team himself until a suitable replacement could be found.

Pitino primarily came to the Bluegrass for three reasons. One, he loved the challenge of rebuilding a program. Second, he wanted to return to coaching in the college ranks. Third, he wanted an ideal place to raise his family. And not to mention that Kentucky has a long tradition-rich history of successful basketball.

"I came to Kentucky because it was right for my family and I am happy about that," Pitino said.

However, Pitino's attractive wife, Joanne, wasn't too crazy about moving to Lexington. Not that she didn't like Kentucky's second-largest city, she just hated to uproot her family again as they had previously moved several times because of her husband's rising coaching career. "She was unhappy about moving, whether it be Florida, Hawaii or wherever because we had moved too much," explained Pitino, who now has four sons. As a family, they made the decision to move to Kentucky. "I was not overly happy and excited with the lifestyle I was leading," Pitino admitted. "I wanted to make a change at this point." Also, Pitino did not enjoy a good working relationship with his boss while at New York. He had some philosophical differences with then-Knicks general manager Al Bianchi.

Pitino didn't come cheap, as he was doing well financially in New York. In addition to outside income, Pitino's salary with the Knicks was reported to be in the $425,000 range. His seven-year pact with UK calls for an annual base salary which began at $105,000 with periodic raises. (By comparison, coach Rupp's last coaching salary was $29,000.) Pitino's outside income coming from various sources such as commercial endorsements and TV/radio shows would push his total income to nearly $1 million. During his first year at Kentucky, Pitino's total income was estimated to be around $800,000. Pitino, however, later said the move to Lexington from New York had cost him a lot financially.

"You make good money in coaching. When you are in the professional limelight, you deserve the money but you give it away to charities and people expect that," said the coach from his refurbished Memorial Coliseum office. "This was a bad move for me economically and I don't care about that because I enjoy basketball so much but I lost my life savings on my move from New York. It was not a good financial move to come here. People say you will make it back. We'll never make it back. Every time you move you have to purchase a home and put new things into the home but that is OK with me because I enjoy the place (UK) basketball-wise and that is the only important thing."

Weeks before Kentucky's 1989-90 season opener with Ohio at Rupp Arena, the doomsayers predicted the Wildcats would be very lucky to win perhaps eight games out of a 28-game schedule. The Wildcats only had eight scholarship players on the squad and none of them were taller than 6-7. Key players such as Chris Mills, LeRon Ellis and Sean Sutton had left the campus. Short of experienced players, the Wildcats only had two proven players in 6-5 senior Derrick Miller and 6-8 junior Reggie Hanson.

Unlike the past, interest in the program had dropped considerably. But still there was plenty of faithful support for the Wildcats and their new mentor. Kentuckians prepared for a long winter.

As the season progressed, the Wildcat players and the fans alike started to catch Pitino's fever — his running game, his three-point offensive bombs, his pressing defense, his work ethic, his optimism, his blazing personality. The Wildcats stunned observers as they won five of their first seven games with hustle and heart. Everybody was shaking their heads in wonderment. A *Sports Illustrated*'s article about Kentucky's new beginning with Pitino was appropriately titled, "The Bluegrass Isn't So Blue." The

Wildcats were on the road to recovery. Pitino had just given the program a shot in the arm. Interest in Wildcat basketball grew. Everybody was having fun.

Meanwhile, at Pitino's suggestion, his post-game radio show with legendary announcer Cawood Ledford was moved to the courtside of the Rupp Arena floor so the spectators could hear and see him in the show. Expecting only a small group of faithful supporters to stay around after the Mississippi State game on Dec. 4, Pitino was stunned when 5,000 showed up for the radio show. Attendance for the show grew and the radio program ended up attracting a season-average of more than 13,000, which by the way would have ranked 24th nationally in GAME attendance in 1989-90. Moments after UK's last home game of the season with Auburn, Pitino conducted the team's post-season awards ceremony on the radio show with an appreciative crowd of over 20,000 looking on. Describing the event, Pitino jokingly remarked that it was the world's largest awards banquet.

Although there were some rough times, Kentucky nevertheless finished the season on a high note with a remarkable 14-14. And the Wildcats even surprised LSU coach Dale Brown and his ninth-ranked Tigers with an exciting 100-95 victory before a then-record Rupp Arena crowd. In SEC action, Kentucky placed fourth with a 10-8 record.

Pitino said he wasn't all that amazed his first Kentucky edition, popularly known as Pitino's Bombinos, was able to finish with a break-even record. "I wasn't surprised," he said. "I thought we would win and I was very pleased with the effort that was put out so it was a pleasant surprise if anything."

After the NCAA hit Kentucky with sanctions, the school had difficulty in finding a proven coach who was acceptable to UK officials. But they found and grabbed Pitino away from the big city lights, surprising many observers. "To say that I was ecstatic when we hired Rick Pitino was an understatement," said former UK player Bret Bearup. "We couldn't have hired anybody better. I mean people talked about (NBA coach) Pat Riley, this and that. Pat Riley wouldn't have come in and had the impact that Pitino has. (Georgetown coach) John Thompson and (North Carolina coach) Dean Smith wouldn't have. Nobody would have. It's Rick Pitino. It's him. His style of basketball is fun. It's entertaining. It's fun to talk about. It's fun to watch. He brought magic back to where it should be."

For his miraculous efforts, Pitino received a couple of individual honors in 1990 as he was named the national Coach-of-the-Year by the *Basketball Times* and SEC Coach-of-the-Year by the UPI. Two Wildcat players also won regional awards as Hanson and Miller received All-SEC recognition. Not to be forgotten were the team's other key contributors such as sophomores Deron Feldhaus, John Pelphrey, Sean Woods and Richie Farmer as well as freshman Jeff Brassow. There were others who did not see a lot of action, but they sweated it out in grueling practices. That group included Johnathon Davis, Junior Braddy, Tony Cooper, Skip McGaw and Michael Parks.

This young, three-point shooting team will always be remembered. Playing against incredible odds, the Wildcats were amazing. Even the critics had to agree. And the following season — 1990-91 — saw a much-improved Wildcat squad on the court. Far better than anyone, including Pitino, had anticipated. Finishing with a 22-6 mark and a No. 9 national ranking against a tough schedule, Kentucky once again had become a powerhouse like in its old, glorious days. Although they were ineligible for the SEC regular season championship, the Wildcats, indeed, were the No. 1 team in the SEC as they posted the league's best record with 14-4. Needless to say, it was a fun season.

"A championship is won and lost on the basketball court, and no matter what anyone thinks or what anyone says, we won this (SEC) championship," said Pitino moments after the Wildcats whipped Auburn 114-93 in a regular season finale before a record-breaking Rupp Arena crowd of 24,310. "We had one of the toughest schedules in the nation and when you come in and play as hard as this team plays, you deserve a championship season."

For the first time since Kentucky's 1977-78 NCAA championship squad, UK had five players who finished the season averaging double figures. Hanson and Pelphrey paced the Wildcat attack with 14.4 points each.

Pitino and his three Wildcats captured individual SEC honors. While Pitino was named Associated Press

SEC Coach-of-the-Year, Hanson, Pelphrey and freshman Jamal Mashburn were chosen to All-SEC AP second and third teams. In addition, *The Sporting News* selected Pitino as its 1991 national Coach-of-the-Year.

On senior Hanson, Pitino said, "I think I will miss him more than anyone I've ever coached." To show appreciation of what Hanson has meant to Pitino and the Wildcat program while recovering from Kentucky's ugly scandal, the coach created the "Reggie Hanson Sacrifice Award," to be given annually to a player who makes great personal sacrifice for the sake of the team. The first winner of the new Hanson award went to Feldhaus in 1991. Hanson, a product of Pulaski County High in Somerset, Ky., completed his UK career with 1,167 points, placing him 27th on the all-time Wildcat scoring chart, behind No. 26 Bill Spivey's 1,213 points.

During his initial season at Kentucky, Pitino said he didn't seek advice from ex-coach Joe B. Hall about the program. Although they met each other several times in social surroundings, they only once had a serious discussion. It regarded the Joe B. Hall Wildcat Lodge which primarily houses the basketball players. When Pitino was hired, he had expressed some reservations about the so-called basketball dormitory which he said "is not a very pretty place. It's run down because of all the things they had to do (in accordance with the NCAA rules several years ago)." He wanted the players to live like regular students. And he even talked about converting the lodge into a weight room.

On his infrequent meetings with Hall about the situation, Pitino explained, "I kind of wanted to develop my own feel of the program rather than have any preconceived notions of what it was all about. I wanted to establish feelings of my own. Joe felt it (the lodge) was a positive influence. David Roselle, the president, felt it was a negative. In fact, it was a positive. Because now under the jurisdiction of (UK) housing, it is considered a dormitory rather than an athletic lodge. So, now other students live in there. They are monitored by housing. They are under the same guidelines as other dormitories on campus."

Pitino first became aware of the stature of the Wildcat program in the late 1970s when he worked at a basketball camp for Hall on the UK campus. At that time he was the young head coach at Boston University.

"About 12 years ago, I did a clinic for Joe B. Hall and I got to tour a little bit and understand what Kentucky basketball was all about," recalled Pitino, who later guided Providence College to the Final Four in 1987. "I think in the other places that I lived there were other avenues of interest. There were professional teams. In New York, there were the Giants, the Jets, the Yankees, the Mets, the Rangers and the Devils. In Providence, (R.I.), there were the Red Sox, the Celtics and some New York fans as well so there were other interests. Here it is more focused on Kentucky basketball. I think there is not as much diversity here, so it makes the concentration level for one program that much better."

So while he was coaching elsewhere, Pitino had to share the media spotlight with other coaches and teams from various sports. But that's not the case in Kentucky where Pitino dominates the news. In the eyes of Kentuckians, he's the top-dog. "I don't mind sharing," said Pitino of his New York days. "I really don't pay too much attention to the fanfare. I try to just focus in on what we are trying to do and the program so really the spotlight is not that important. After a while, it becomes secondary."

However, with Pitino virtually being the sole spotlight in the state, it at first created some hardships for his wife and their sons. They had to adjust to the glare of enormous public attention. "It was more so (of an adjustment) for my family than it was for me," said the coach. "I had a pretty easy adjustment because I am around my job so much. I didn't notice it as much as my wife and family, but now everyone is used to it and they have adjusted. Like anything else, you try to make the good as big as the sky and the bad as small as a pea."

One noticeable difference Pitino has found in Lexington is that the Kentucky sportswriters aren't as tough as the ones he faced in New York City. "It is like asking the difference between Atilla the Hun and Mary Poppins," he said. "It is quite different. You are more of a target and there is not as much reverence paid to a New York coach. There you are an open target for anything at anytime. I think the people (in Kentucky) focus more on the team than the individual. There is nothing in life more difficult than the New York media. I am not saying that Kentucky is easy. It is just that there is only one major newspaper here (in Lexington). In New York you have three or four tabloids and seven other newspapers that cover you, so any time you have that competition the truth can be stretched a little bit."

Although Pitino now lives in Lexington, he will always be a New Yorker.

Born on Sept. 18, 1952 in Manhattan, Pitino grew up in Queens. He was the baby of a very close-knit, middle-class family with two older brothers. His parents worked extremely hard to support the family. His father, who passed away a few years ago while Pitino was coaching the Knicks, was a truck driver most of his life and he owned a trucking business. Then he became the manager of an industrial building in Manhattan. His mother is a retired nurse.

"Both of my parents grew up in Manhattan," Pitino said, "and both worked over 30 years. They traveled together leaving at 5:30 in the morning and getting home about 6:30 at night so they put in long days. Both were blue-collar workers. We had everything we needed to have. We didn't have much money, but we never starved or wanted for food or clothing. It was a very good family. Anytime you are from an Italian household, you are very, very close (to your parents)."

Later, when Pitino was a teenager, the family moved to Long Island in Oyster Bay. He attended St. Dominic's High School where he played basketball. He was the captain of the roundball squad and broke several scoring records.

It was during his high school days in the summer between his sophomore and junior year that he met his future wife, Joanne Minardi. "I met her while I was playing basketball in the backyard with a group of friends," Pitino said. "We decided to get a bite to eat so we walked to a deli about a mile away and we were throwing a ball with lacrosse sticks. Somebody threw me the ball and it went on her front lawn. She was combing her hair on the steps because she had just come back from the beach. I said hello. I asked my friends who she was. We were having a party that night and I said, 'Why don't you invite her to the party?' and that is how we met."

Pitino said it was not easy to change his New York lifestyle when he moved to the Bluegrass. He still misses the New York life, especially his immediate relatives. "It is difficult just because you miss your family," he said. "One brother still lives in New York. My mother lives in New York. My wife's family still lives in New York and some of my closest friends live in New York.

"I love the New York sense of humor. New York people are very witty and a lot of fun. They joke around quite a bit. But I think I have enjoyed it as much here with the exception of maybe the all-night diners — a great restaurant that's open 24 hours. I think I miss that aspect.

"People are people wherever you go. Maybe they talk differently in Kentucky. There is good and bad in every place you live and the only thing that is difficult is not acclimating yourself to a new environment. The difficult thing is that you miss your family.

"The pace is much different here (in Kentucky). The lifestyle is much different. You don't stay up as late. There is not as much stress here with traffic. I would like to think I have enjoyed every place I have lived and you adapt to the different lifestyles rather than say one is better than the other. You just adjust and say when in Rome do as the Romans and that is what I do here in Kentucky."

Pitino, in fact, has added an Italian New York touch to the Bluegrass. Early in the 1990-91 season, he and some 25 investors opened a well-publicized restaurant in downtown Lexington. Called Bravo Pitino, it is modeled after his favorite Italian establishment in New York.

Pitino has a good sense of humor. He frequently jokes with sportswriters at press conferences. He puts on a good show, something that would make Ronald Reagan proud. Describing his outside income, Pitino once jokingly said, "I'm going to be making about $11 million a year." At another press conference, on rumors that his wife wasn't happy in Lexington, Pitino quipped that Joanne had run off with a so-called wealthy New Yorker by the name of Donald Trump.

During an intense Kentucky-LSU game in 1990 in Baton Rouge, an angry shouting match between Pitino and LSU mentor Dale Brown nearly erupted into a full-fledged boxing match with their noses only inches apart. Sportswriters later quizzed Pitino if he and Brown had made up. Pitino responded by saying, "I think he's a great guy. He recruited me as a high school player and offered me things....just kidding."

On a serious note, Pitino said he respects "Dale Brown because he has great love and affection for his players and that is what counts. He treats his players so well and I like him."

Asked where he got his humor from, Pitino replied, "I think when you pick out things about different cultures and different places, I think New York, because there is so much stress in New York that you have to laugh. You have to smile and joke around to get through the day and week and all this stress. If you don't laugh about going one mile in 45 minutes, then it is going to be very difficult to take and that is how you get through it. I think it (humor) comes from friends more than anything else."

After high school, Pitino moved on to the University of Massachusetts in Amherst where he was a point guard in the early 1970s. While a senior, he served as the team captain in the 1973-74 campaign. Then he began his coaching career in Honolulu, Hawaii where he was a graduate assistant at the University of Hawaii. As many observers would find out, Pitino was *"Born to Coach,"* a book he would co-author years later while in the NBA.

The year 1987 had both happy and sad times for Pitino. A season he will never forget.

Making their first NCAA tournament appearance since 1978, his Providence College Friars shocked the nation when they went to the Final Four in New Orleans. By employing the press and three-point shooting, they engineered a couple of big upsets over Alabama and Georgetown in the Southeast Regionals. They were the nation's darlings, playing the role of a Cinderella. Pitino's former boss at Syracuse, Jim Boeheim, knocked the Friars out of the national championship picture as the Orangemen won 77-63 in the semifinals. Providence finished with a 25-9 worksheet and Pitino earned a couple of awards in winning the John Wooden National Coach-of-the-Year and the *Sporting News* Coach-of-the-Year honors.

Pitino later said that was the happiest moment of his life.

During the Final Four hoopla, the sportswriters, as well as TV guys, found Pitino's life intriguing. Hundreds of newspaper articles and columns about Pitino were written, many of them on the front page. They were human interest material. His one-night honeymoon. His tragic loss of a baby son. Pitino was good copy.

The coach prefers not to talk about the down moments of his life, especially the death of his infant. "From a sad point of view, those are personal things," he explained.

But it is no question that perhaps the worst moment of his life came after Providence had just finished playing in the Big East Conference tournament in New York. En route to Providence on the team bus on a Sunday afternoon, Pitino and his petite wife learned that their six-month-old son, Daniel Paul, had passed away. A highway patrolman — with his cruiser's flashing lights on — had stopped the northbound bus on I-95 to inform the Pitinos of the disturbing news. Their babysitter had attempted to contact them but the squad had already departed. (Daniel Paul had suffered a variety of disorders, including a congenital heart ailment, with his mother making daily one-hour trips to a Boston hospital from their Rhode Island home for several months.)

An hour or two later, CBS-TV announced the NCAA tournament bids and Providence received its first NCAA invitation in almost a decade. Normally, this would have called for a big Sunday night party, watching the tournament pairings on television. But there would be no pizza party for the Pitinos.

A few months later, Pitino left Providence for the NBA, despite the fact he had inked a new five-year contract with the Friars. He was named head coach of the struggling New York Knicks, an organization he had previously worked for as an assistant under coach Hubie Brown in 1983-85. It was a move that Pitino later wished he hadn't made.

"The only move that I have ever regretted was in leaving Providence the way I did because I left for the wrong reason," Pitino admitted. "I loved being that coach and it has made me a better coach today, but I left for the wrong reason and that is why I am bothered by it. I left because my ego got in the way. I just felt my ego could not turn down a big job — especially when you were a boy growing up in New York and you were just 10 blocks from Madison Square Garden — and I left Providence because of my ego and not because of what was right for my family."

Asked if the Providence College officials have forgiven him for leaving them, Pitino said, "I think some people appreciate the fact that Providence went from dead last place to the Final Four in two years and other people feel like they are jilted lovers or it is a divorce. They love you but they divorce you."

Pitino and his wife were married in the summer of 1976 just after he had completed a two-year coaching stint as an assistant at Hawaii. Staying at a New York City hotel, their honeymoon plans abruptly changed on their wedding night. The couple had planned to leave for San Francisco the next day on the way to Hawaii for their honeymoon. But Syracuse's Boeheim somehow contacted Pitino that night and offered him a job to become an assistant coach for the Orangemen. It took some persuading and an increase in salary on Boeheim's part before Pitino finally accepted. And Pitino was off recruiting the next day and the honeymoon had to be postponed. Of course, Joanne wasn't very happy about the timing of her husband's new job. But she reluctantly understood the situation. Boeheim said in 1987 that he didn't think Pitino's wife will ever forgive him for what he did on their wedding night in offering Pitino a job.

On his wife, who does not grant many interviews, Pitino said, "She is a very social person but she does not like the limelight — sticking out like a coach would. She likes being one of the people, but not the key person. She doesn't feel that is her place."

Like Joanne, Pitino is a social person. "I am a people person," said the coach. "For instance, I would not like living in a rural area on a farm away from people. I enjoy being around a lot of people and having neighbors. I don't mind crowds. If I had a choice of having solitude or being around people, I would choose being around people."

As far as their religion is concerned, the Pitinos are both Catholics. Her late uncle Martin, who was a priest, married them.

A new member was added to the Pitino family in June of 1990 when Joanne gave birth to Ryan Martin Pitino in a New York City hospital. The baby boy weighed 6 pounds and 9 ounces. He joins his three older brothers — Michael, Christopher and Richard. Joanne spent the last several weeks of her pregnancy in New York — not in the Bluegrass — because her physician's office was located there and she had encountered some problems in a previous birth.

However, she was surprised when she learned she was pregnant with Ryan Martin. The Pitinos didn't expect to have any more children. Pitino says that her pregnancy had created some false rumors about her unhappiness in Lexington and their separation.

"The biggest problem was that she had been told she couldn't have any more children and here she moves to Lexington and she is pregnant at age 38 in a temporary home," said the coach. "We were building a home and she just took on a lot at one time. The chances of her getting pregnant were very slim and the doctors were nervous. She had to go to New York to have the baby, but she didn't want to go. She was told to do so. She was only allowed on her feet for one hour per day. She went to New York for three months and for eight weeks she was in a hospital bed just trying not to lose this baby while doctors monitored her. People here (in Kentucky) didn't realize the problems encountered and that she was in the hospital for eight weeks.

"When she had the baby she needed to be around her doctors because they were expecting something to go wrong, so she went through one of the toughest pregnancies you could ever go through. After she delivered the baby, she needed a lot of help because the circumstances weren't normal, due to the loss of our last child. So, when I told people that, they just started rumors about her leaving me and not coming back.

"One thing I can say is that I have been a very rich person not in money but in the type of marriage we have had and in our family. People don't realize this here but that is something we can't do anything about.

"We kid around about it (her leaving for Donald Trump) because it is so far from the truth. We wouldn't really care about it too much except for the fact that we are going to make Kentucky our home for a long time. It bothers me that people make up things about me. That is the problem with living in a small town.

"We just thanked God that the baby was healthy."

Pitino knows there are a lot of rival coaches who are jealous of Kentucky's rich tradition in basketball. But he philosophically understands that it is an undesirable part of living.

"Jealously is a word that a lot of people have," he said. "Anytime a person can't have something he either admires that person or he is jealous of that person. There is very little indifference in people, so jealously is a word that is sad. It is a shame that people are jealous.

"But anytime you are at Kentucky, people are going to be jealous because we have the best fans, the best facilities, the best tradition—so it is normal. Other people admire it and try to copy it and those are the people you try to help. You can't worry about the jealous people. That is a part of life."

Pitino's favorite SEC place other than Lexington is Nashville, the capital of country music. Vanderbilt has the league's largest city in Nashville with approximately 500,000 citizens. Although Pitino enjoys the city atmosphere, Music City is nevertheless a surprising choice because he doesn't care for country music.

"It is not that I don't like country music, it is just that I don't listen to lot of it," Pitino explained. "I very rarely listen to music. I would listen to a talk show, but if I was going to listen to music, it would not be country. It would be Frank Sinatra, Tony Bennett. I would listen to some Motown music but not country western. It is not my cup of tea."

Pitino an Olympic head coach in the future?

Even if he was eligible for the post, Pitino is definitely not interested. Only a mentor with NBA ties is considered for the prestigious job.

"That is one of the things that I have never concerned myself with because unfortunately I don't agree with the way we do it today," Pitino said. "I think an Olympic coach should devote all his time to the team. He should not be a college coach and not a pro coach. It should be maybe a coach who is retired and would devote all his time to the Olympics because if I become an Olympic coach I know I am going to throw my heart and mind into it every day and I would take away from the Kentucky program or wherever I am and I don't think that is right. I think they should take an Olympic coach and make it a paying job so someone can concentrate all his efforts on that.

"I think you should concentrate all your efforts to the University of Kentucky. So I have never really concentrated on that (Olympics). My goals are to win the championship for the University of Kentucky and that is the way it is."